LITERARY LONDON

For My Dad

WALKING
LITERARY LONDON

STEPHEN BROWNING

WHITE OWL

AN IMPRINT OF PEN & SWORD BOOKS LTD.
YORKSHIRE – PHILADELPHIA

First published in Great Britain in 2023 by
White Owl
An imprint of
Pen & Sword Books Ltd
Yorkshire - Philadelphia

ISBN 978 1 39909 687 4

Typeset in Times New Roman 10/12
by SJmagic DESIGN SERVICES, India.

Printed and bound in the UK by CPI Group (UK) Ltd., Croydon. CR0 4YY

Pen & Sword Books Ltd incorporates the imprints of Pen & Sword Books Archaeology, Atlas, Aviation, Battleground, Discovery, Family History, History, Maritime, Military, Naval, Politics, Railways, Select, Transport, True Crime, Fiction, Frontline Books, Leo Cooper, Praetorian Press, Seaforth Publishing, Wharncliffe and White Owl.

For a complete list of Pen & Sword titles please contact

PEN & SWORD BOOKS LIMITED
47 Church Street, Barnsley, South Yorkshire, S70 2AS, England
E-mail: enquiries@pen-and-sword.co.uk
Website: www.pen-and-sword.co.uk

or

PEN AND SWORD BOOKS
1950 Lawrence Rd, Havertown, PA 19083, USA
E-mail: Uspen-and-sword@casematepublishers.com
Website: www.penandswordbooks.com

CONTENTS

ACKNOWLEDGEMENTS

Thanks to the British Library for permission to use photographs taken by the author on their premises. Thanks also to City of London Corporation for permission to take photographs in Bunhill Fields Burial Ground. Thank you to the National Archives at Kew and the British Library for help with research. I am grateful to Graham Smith for copy editing. At Pen and Sword, thanks to Janet Brookes for all her help during the production process. All photographs are by the author.

www.stephenbrowningbooks.co.uk

INTRODUCTION

Why, Sir, you find no man, at all intellectual, who is willing to leave London. No, Sir, when a man is tired of London, he is tired of life; for there is in London all that life can afford.

Samuel Johnson

London possesses a literary heritage which is unique and in large part unrivalled in any city in the world.

In these pages London presents itself through its authors and literature, that is, the lives and words of William Shakespeare, Andrea Levy, G.A. Henty, Geoffrey Chaucer, P.L. Travers, Samuel Pepys, Charles Dickens, Una Marson, Joe Orton, John Keats, Percy Bysshe Shelley, Phillis Wheatley, Abdulrazak Gurnah, Katherine Mansfield and Samuel Selvon to name just a very few. And all of these writers, to a greater or lesser extent and in differing ways, have a continuing impact on London and the world beyond the city walls.

In this book, literary London is presented in a series of walks, each of which is original and unique, the result of 20 years' exploration of this wonderful city by the author. A series of maps has been specially commissioned.

This study is to some degree selective and subjective, as any attempt to be comprehensive would produce a tome too heavy to pick up. Yet in these pages you will find the details of hundreds of writers and their works; wherever you walk in the great city of London – even if solely in imagination from an armchair – the experience is going to be extraordinary.

Notes

Throughout the text, fictional characters are referred to using *italic* type.

In any given section, the first mention of a writer is in **bold** type.

WALK 1

Baker Street, Regent's Park, into Wimpole Street and on to Oxford Street, Regent Street, Piccadilly Circus and Leicester Square

In This Walk: The lives and works of the following people and *fictional characters* are highlighted: *Sherlock Holmes*, Sir Arthur Conan Doyle, Edgar Allen Poe, Ian Fleming, Ken Follett, H.G. Wells, Arnold Bennett, Virginia Woolf, Theodore Roosevelt, Bram Stoker, Oscar Wilde, Rudyard Kipling, Hall Caine, Anthony Hope, James Stephen Phillips, Bernard Shaw, Grant Allen, Sir J.M. Barrie, H.A. Jones, Marie Corelli, Stanley Weyman, Winston Churchill, Dorothy L. Sayers, Elizabeth Bowen, Wilkie Collins, Edmund Gosse, Alfred Noyes, Edward Lear, George Bernard Shaw, William Makepeace Thackeray, Stevie Smith, Kingsley Amis, Martin Amis, Claire Tomalin, Alan Bennett, Ian McEwan, Peter Cook, Dudley Moore, Jonathan Miller, Sylvia Plath, Ted Hughes, William Macready, Elizabeth Barrett Browning, Robert Browning, Lord Byron, Richard Brinsley Sheridan, Sidney Franklin, James Boswell, Edward Gibbon, Thomas Hardy, Thomas Gray, William Blake, E.M. Forster, Edmund de Waal, Doris Lessing, Laurence Sterne, Ignatius Sancho, George Frideric Handel, George Meredith, George Eliot, Lord Alfred Douglas, John Buchan, *Lord Verisopht, Mulberry Hawk*, Sir Max Beerbohm, Frank Harris, Charles Dickens, William Hogarth, Sir Joshua Reynolds, Harold Pinter.

Distance: *See pages 10–11; about 9 kilometres (5.6 miles)*

Time to allow: A complete morning, afternoon or evening – longer if you plan to visit the Sherlock Holmes Museum, take a picnic in Regent's Park, go to the zoo or see a Shakespeare play in the park's open-air theatre. Theatres, cafés, pubs and cinemas abound at the end of the walk, in Piccadilly and Leicester Square.

This walk splits readily into two: the first part covering Baker Street and the Regent's Park area, and the second, from Devonshire Place to Leicester Square.

Walking conditions: Fairly easy and flat but visitors need to be mindful of heavy traffic generally throughout the route. There are some unique photo opportunities, especially of Baker Street, Regent's Park and Wimpole Street and at the end, around Piccadilly. There is public seating at the beginning in Regent's Park, about halfway along in Hanover Square, and at the end in Leicester Square.

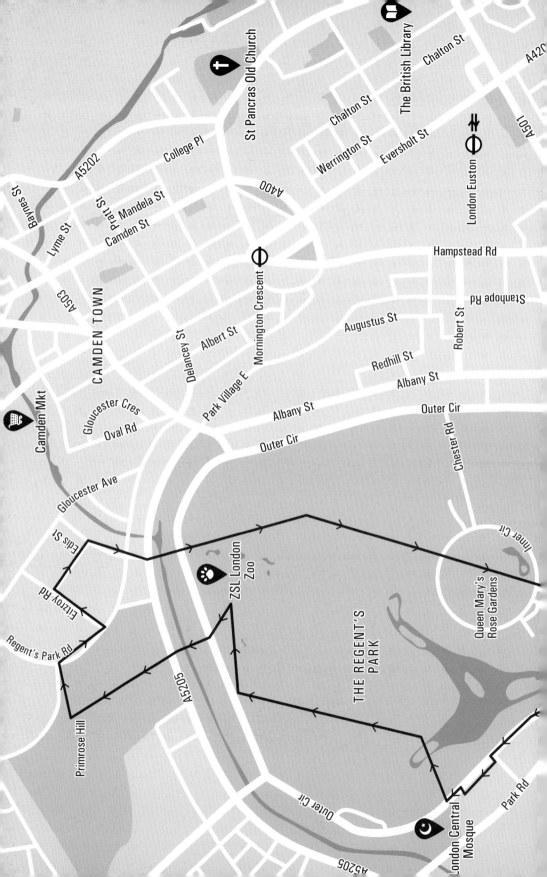

Route

Baker Street tube station
Marylebone Road
Baker Street
Regent's Park and area to the north
Upper Wimpole Street
Wimpole Street
Oxford Street
Regent Street
Piccadilly Circus
Leicester Square

This walk begins in Sherlock Holmes country, at Baker Street tube Station. The first story by **Arthur Conan Doyle** – as he was then, only being knighted in 1902 – was in 1887.[1] Twenty years later, the impecunious young doctor waiting in vain for any patients to turn up in his expensively rented surgery near Harley Street, and writing *Holmes* stories to fill in the time, had become wealthy and world-renowned as the creator of the inimitable *Sherlock Holmes*, the world's greatest, indeed only according to *Holmes* himself, Consulting Detective.

Baker Street tube station is in Zone 1 and served by five lines – Metropolitan, Circle, Hammersmith and City, Bakerloo and Jubilee – and is one of the world's first underground stations, opened in 1863. It is worth a linger on the platforms to see the custom-made tiling celebrating *Sherlock Holmes*. This is a major tourist area – Madame Tussauds is a short distance away – and is served by numerous bus routes; a useful one to know is the 139 which travels via Waterloo, Trafalgar Square, Piccadilly Circus and Oxford Circus to Baker Street and beyond.[2]

Holmes and other notable detectives

On Marylebone Road, outside the station, is a statue of *Sherlock Holmes* by John Doubleday. **G.K. Chesterton** originally had the idea for a statue in 1927. There are other statues to Holmes – one at Meiringen, also by John Doubleday – at Karuizawa, Japan, at Edinburgh and one of both *Holmes* and *Watson* near the British Embassy in Moscow. One of the most successful television series of all time on Russian television has been the superb *The Adventures of Sherlock Holmes and Dr Watson*, which began in 1979 and starred Vasily Livanov as *Holmes* and Vitaly Solomin as *Watson*.

This two-metre high bronze was unveiled in 1999 – you will see it gives *Holmes* a deerstalker and pipe which were originally made famous by the illustrations of Sidney Paget in *Strand Magazine*.[3] Conan Doyle saw him as a man with a thin razor-like face and what he called 'a great hawks-bill of a nose' with two small eyes set close together. He said that when he gave the commission to Sidney Paget, the talented artist, who was to tragically suffer a premature death, decided to model Holmes on his handsome younger brother, Walter, and thus was produced a less lean, more handsome but not so powerful a man.

There is a message for visitors, written by the best-selling author, **Anthony Horowitz**, which is accessed by scanning a QR code.[4]

Before *Holmes*, there were two other notable detectives in the literary firmament, although none grasped the imagination at the time or since to the extent of *Holmes*: **Edgar Allan Poe**'s *C. Auguste Dupin*, who made his first appearance in print in 1841 and **Émile Gaboriau**'s *Monsieur Lecoq*, a detective employed by the French Sûreté ; they are both discussed by *Holmes* and *Watson* at the beginning of *A Study in Scarlet*. Another French author, **Henry Cauvain** published a novel in 1871 about a detective with some characteristics not unlike those of *Holmes* – depressed sometimes, anti-social and opium-smoking. He is called *Maximilien Heller*.

Above and right: *The statue of* Sherlock Holmes *by John Doubleday is outside the tube station, just before the junction of Marylebone Road and Baker Street. There is another one by the same artist at Meiringen, Switzerland.*

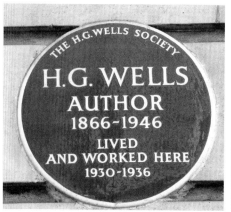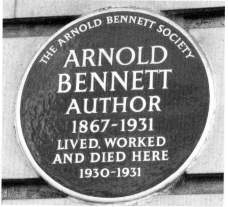

Baker Street derives its name from William Baker, who laid it out in the eighteenth century. It originally housed Madame Tussauds but this subsequently moved to Marylebone Road, a short walk from where you are standing.[5] The street contains one of the ever-changing and secret homes (it was actually at number 64) of the Special Operations Executive (SOE), responsible for sabotage and espionage in occupied Europe during the Second World War: recruits were sometimes referred to internally as '*the Baker Street Irregulars*' after the streetwise urchins who operated 'under cover' for *Sherlock Holmes*. **Ian Fleming** knew some of the personnel and is said to have based *James Bond's* boss, known as 'M', in *Casino Royale* (released without much enthusiasm by publisher, Jonathan Cape in 1953: see Walk 10), on the head of SOE, who was known as 'CD'. The SOE has subsequently been imagined in many other films and novels, such as **Ken Follet**'s *Jackdaws* (2001).

Baker Street is where many fans from all over the world come to celebrate **Sir Arthur Conan Doyle** and his 'most notorious character', *Sherlock Holmes*.[6] There are few times in any day when you will not see people in the street, some of whom wear deerstalkers and puff at usually empty pipes, staring intently at maps and guidebooks.

However, other authors also jostle for attention as you walk up the street. Just a few yards along Baker Street, on your right, is a block of flats – Chiltern Court – and here are two plaques, one to **H.G. Wells** (1866–1946) who lived here from 1930–36, and the other to **Arnold Bennett** (1867–1931) who lived here for the last year of his life.

H.G. Wells

H.G. Wells (see also Walk 11 under 'Bromley' for more details of his early days) led an extraordinary life, and is seen not only as a prominent writer but also, to some extent, as a social and scientific prophet. He was born in Bromley, Kent, the last of four children to Joseph, a gardener and legendary fast bowler who once took four wickets in four balls – the first man ever to do so, according to official records – when playing for Kent against Sussex in 1862.

After stints as a draper's assistant, a junior in a chemist's shop and a schoolteacher, he published his first hugely successful book, *The Time Machine*, in 1895. In *War of the Worlds* (1898), he referenced Baker Street itself in a memorable scene in Book II, Chapter VIII, *Dead London*:

> And as I emerged from the top of Baker Street, I saw far away over the trees in the clearness of the sunset the hood of the Martian giant from which this howling proceeded.... A couple of hundred yards out of Baker Street I heard a yelping chorus, and saw, first a dog with a piece of putrescent red meat in his jaws coming headlong towards me, and then a pack of starving mongrels in pursuit of him.

Other novels include *The Invisible Man*, initially serialised in *Pearson's Magazine* in 1897, *The Island of Doctor Moreau* (1896), *The First Men in the Moon* (serialised alongside *Sherlock Holmes* stories in *Strand Magazine*, 1900), *The Shape of Things to Come* (a future history that ends in 2106, published in 1933) and *When the Sleeper Awakes*, originally published in 1899 and revised with the title *The Sleeper Awakes* for publication in 1910 – Wells regarded it as originally rushed and he was also able to revise certain parts and update the science to some degree. It tells the story of Graham who falls into a coma in 1897, having taken drugs for insomnia, and awakes in 2100 to find he is incredibly rich and powerful.

One of Wells' greatest influences was T.H. Huxley, whose lectures he attended: Huxley was known as 'Darwin's bulldog' and he fired up the young author's imagination, especially regarding evolution, history and man's ability to effectively shape the world. Wells saw writing as a wonderful chance to be free and adventurous in thought, and he knew many of the eminent thinkers and writers of his day, including **Joseph Conrad, Ford Madox Ford, Henry James, Arnold Bennett, George Gissing, Arthur Conan Doyle, Wilfred Owen,** and **George Bernard Shaw.** The idea of freedom for Wells also extended to love and he had many affairs.

Wells travelled extensively, visiting President Franklin D. Roosevelt and interviewing Joseph Stalin for the *New Statesman*: he found his subject, he subsequently wrote, 'fair, candid and honest', if a little unimaginative in his thought processes. He left liking the man and was to die before the worst of Stalin's excesses came to light in the west.[7] He predicted a world war before 1940 and was critical of Hitler, which resulted in his books being banned in public libraries in Germany from 1933. He wrote: 'The man who raises a fist has run out of ideas.' He was on the list of people subject to immediate arrest in the event of a successful Nazi invasion of Britain. He was to defy the bombers during the blitz, refusing to move his small household from his last home in nearby 13 Hanover Terrace, where he died in his four-poster bed having seen the war out (see below, this Walk).

Arnold Bennett

Arnold Bennett was a prolific writer, considering it important not to decry the 'two guineas apiece' he regularly received for his articles. He wrote for over 100 different newspapers and magazines. His most convincing works highlighted the lives of working people in the Staffordshire Potteries. *Riceyman Steps*, published in 1923, and winner of the James Tait Black Memorial Prize[8] for fiction, is possibly his most renowned novel.

Virginia Woolf wrote an essay in 1924, *Mr Bennett and Mrs Brown*, which has damaged his legacy and this is only fairly recently being revised. She divided writers into two camps – the rather fusty Edwardians, which included Bennett and Wells, and Georgians such as **Eliot, Forster** and **Joyce**, only the latter being capable of penetrating a character's inner life in all its fragmentedness. It is hard not to think that class-consciousness has something to do with Woolf's categorisation.

Returning to Baker Street from his beloved Paris, where he had possibly drunk a glass of infected tap water, Bennett died of typhoid in the Baker Street flat on 27 March 1931.

An Arnold Bennett Society, established in 1954, exists to promote and discuss his work. In 2017 the society instituted an annual Arnold Bennett Prize for a work written by an author who was born, lives or works in North Staffordshire, or one which features the area. The 2020 Prize was won by *It's Gone Dark Over Bill's Mother's* by **Lisa Blower**.

Arnold Bennett is one of a very select band who has had a food dish named after them. He used to frequent the Savoy Hotel in Strand and had the 'Omelette Arnold Bennett' specially made for him by chef Jean Baptiste Virlogeux – it is an omelette containing haddock, hard cheese and cream, and, at the time of writing, it remains on the Savoy's breakfast menu.[9] (see also Walk 3 – Dame Nellie Melba).

For most people, however, this street is associated with **Sir Arthur Conan Doyle** and his famous creation, *Sherlock Holmes*. Sir Arthur was a man who knew many of the great and good of his day, including H.G. Wells, Arnold Bennett, King Edward VII and several Prime Ministers, including H.H. Asquith, who went to school just up the river at the City School, next to the Millennium Bridge (see Walk 3) – he very much enjoyed his conversation but remarked that he was not very good on the golf course – and Arthur Balfour, whom he considered one of the greatest men that he met in his lifetime. Balfour was Prime Minister 1902–5, and served in various cabinet posts spanning 27 years under Prime Ministers Asquith, Lloyd George and Baldwin. In his autobiography, *Memories and Adventures*, Conan Doyle recounts that he was once a guest on Balfour's estate in Scotland and thought how moving it was to see Balfour, a very religious man, gather all his staff of about 20 together of a Sunday evening, to pray as one, from the most junior stable boy to the master of the house. He writes that there was one thing that Baldwin despised above all else, and that was cowardice.

Youth would be an ideal state if it came a little later in life

H.H. Asquith

Conan Doyle was also very struck by the qualities of Theodore Roosevelt, who at the age of 42, remains the youngest ever man to take the office of President of the United States (he was 26th President, 1901–9). He was to use the church where Roosevelt married in London, St George's, Hanover Square, as the setting for the wedding of *Hatty Doran* and *Lord St Simon* in *The Adventure of the Noble Bachelor* (see below, this Walk). Roosevelt is described by Conan Doyle as not a big or powerful man, but one who had 'a tremendous dynamic force and iron will'. He had 'the simplicity of real greatness, speaking his mind with great frankness and in the clearest possible English', and 'a quick blunt wit'.[10] On one occasion, Conan Doyle recounts, when Roosevelt was awoken to address some people who had assembled at a wayside railway station, his assistant remarked that they had travelled 60 miles to see him. 'They would have come 100 to see a cat with two heads,' Roosevelt replied.

The London Press of the early twentieth century was not in general impressed with the crop of authors that followed Dickens and Thackeray. However, it was seen by Sir Arthur Conan Doyle as just as talented and varied as at any other time in Britain's history. He wrote in his autobiography that he admired **Bram Stoker, Oscar Wilde, Rudyard Kipling, Hall Caine, Anthony Hope, Stephen Phillips, Bernard Shaw, Grant Allen, James Matthew Barrie, H.A. Jones, Arthur Wing Pinero, Marie Corelli, Stanley John Weyman, Winston Churchill** and **H.G. Wells.**

Rudyard Kipling

Rudyard Kipling (1865–1936) was immensely popular in the early years of the twentieth century. He twice refused a knighthood but accepted the Nobel Prize in 1907, in the words of the committee, given 'in consideration of the power of observation, originality of imagination, virility of ideas and remarkable talent for narration…' He was seen as the unofficial poet laureate of the British Empire and his writings for adults rapidly lost favour as the world and its values changed after the First World War. His children's stories, however, such as the *Just So Stories for Little Children*, have always maintained their popularity. Today he is seen as one of the most authentic voices of the British Empire and its values.

Sir Arthur Conan Doyle always regarded his writing on *Holmes* as not quite in the top tier of English literature and, while he tried to rectify matters with works such as *The White Company* and *Brigadier Gerard*, what the general public worldwide seemed to want above all else was more of the great consulting detective. Ironically, the preservation of his home 'Undershaw' was later in doubt (although saved from being demolished to make way for flats in the end) as the authorities expressed the view that Conan Doyle was not quite in the same literary league as Dickens…

The Sherlock Holmes Museum, which is on your left about three-quarters of the way along the street, attracts fans from all over the globe: often it is easily visible at the head of an uncharacteristically chatty and happy queue snaking back down the street. Usually, outside there is a 'policeman' who will lend you his helmet for a photo. It is worth checking out YouTube for videos of former visitors to the house to have an idea of what to expect. At the time of writing, tickets are only available on the door and it is worth coming along as early as you can for a quicker entry.

The Great Game

That *Holmes* is a real person, *Watson* his biographer and Conan Doyle merely a literary agent who ensured publication, and using these assumptions to resolve anomalies in the canon, is the basis of the Great Game, the Sherlockian Game, the Holmesian Game or simply the Game, and helps to some extent to explain why fact and fiction regarding *Sherlock Holmes* intermingle. The first essays on this subject saw the light of day in 1902. **Dorothy L. Sayers**, creator of Lord Peter Wimsey, writes that the Game 'must be played as solemnly as a county cricket match at Lord's; the slightest touch of extravagance or burlesque ruins the atmosphere.'

Walking the extent of Baker Street and then keeping the park to your right will bring you to Clarence Terrace which curves off to the left. **Elizabeth Bowen** (1899–1973), author of *The Heat of the Day*, lived at number 2 – there is a blue plaque. Continue to edge the park on your right as you walk.

The next but one terrace, Hanover, was the home of **Wilkie Collins** (1824–1889) who lived at number 17. This was the family home in which he lived as a young man in considerable opulence: he had a writing room and his brother, Charles, a painting room. He is said to have been inspired to write his most famous novel, *The Woman in White*, by a genuine incident when he followed a lady in flowing white clothes who was rushing away from some unseen, and he assumed distressing, incident. Subsequently, it is claimed that he took the lady, named Caroline, as his mistress, an arrangement that lasted happily for the rest of his life. The story is one that has subsequently been embellished by multiple retellings over brandy and cigars in the gentlemen's clubs of London: the unromantic claim that the lady owned a shop selling second-hand goods nearby and was just rushing from A to B on a route that passed his house.

Hanover Terrace is also noted for several other writers. **Sir Edmund Gosse** (1849–1928), author of *Father and Son*, lived at number 17; also, **Alfred Noyes** C.B.E. (1880–1958), prolific poet and novelist, possibly best known for *The Highwayman,* lived at number 13 before selling the house to H.G. Wells. In 1995, the BBC launched a poll to find Britain's favourite poem; *The Highwayman* (1906) came in 15th. Later, converting the house from the then nominated number 12A back to 13 again, was an increasingly defiant, deaf and irascible **H.G. Wells**, whose loud radio-playing often startled the neighbours. During the Second World War, with most of the Hanover Terrace occupants opting to escape the bombing, Wells and his small loyal staff remained. He died here, in his four-poster bed on 13 August 1946.

> My stepmother …was never a tower of strength to me,
> but at least she was always a lodge in my garden of cucumbers.
> Edmund Gosse, *Father and Son*, 1907

Regent's Park

You can cut into Regent's Park by a number of entrances. The park is one of the Royal Parks, named after the Prince regent (1762–1830). A wonderful picnic spot, it has walkways and lakes and is home to over 100 species of wild bird – feeding them is now discouraged as this inadvertently does more harm than good. For the energetic there is a 10km sign-posted walk. The park also houses London Zoo and an open-air theatre featuring a range of plays from May to September; a favourite for many visitors is watching a **Shakespeare** play in the open air on a summer's evening.

…the greatest genius the world ever knew

Noël Coward, talking about
Shakespeare in an interview
with Edward R. Murrow
on American TV, 1956

The Zoo itself has a number of literary connections. **Edward Lear** (1812–1888) worked here when he was 18, sketching animals and also the people who came to see them. He was living close by at number 61 Albany Street at the time. **George Bernard Shaw** (1856–1950) lived locally for a time and the Fabian Society, of which he was a prominent member, was founded in 17 Osnaburgh Street (there is a plaque) in 1884. **William Makepeace Thackeray** (1811–1863) liked to visit and wrote about the Zoo for various magazines, including *Punch*. In her poem, *The Zoo*, **Stevie Smith**, who was born in 1902 and died of a brain tumour on 7 March 1971, wrote of the caged lion's 'ruby rage' and his lovely teeth and claws which were designed to eat little boys.

North of the zoo and park is Primrose Hill, famous for its wonderful views over London. It is associated with many writers, including **Kingsley** and **Martin Amis**, **Claire Tomalin, Alan Bennett** – who lived at number 23 in nearby Gloucester Crescent, 'Britain's cleverest street', for forty years – and **Ian McEwan**.

Some of the filming for the very successful *Bridget Jones* films, adapted from novels by **Helen Fielding**, took place around Primrose Hill.

Alan Bennett

Alan Bennett was one of the original members – along with Peter Cook, Dudley Moore, and Jonathan Miller – of *Beyond the Fringe* in 1960. Numerous plays and screenplays include *Forty Years On* (1968), *A Day Out* (1972), *An Englishman Abroad* (1983), *Talking Heads* (1992 and 2002), *The Madness of King George III* (play 1991, film 1994), *The History Boys* (2004), a very funny and tender look at what constitutes a real education and which won three Olivier Awards and six Tony Awards on Broadway, *The Lady in the Van*, which was based on a real-life situation where a lady lived in a series of dilapidated vans on his driveway in Gloucester Crescent for 15 years and which became a film starring Dame Maggie Smith (2015), and *Allelujah!* (2018), a tale of an NHS hospital faced with closure. He refused a knighthood in 1996 saying that he has nothing against the monarchy and, indeed, enjoys writing about the Queen, but it would be a bit like 'wearing a suit every day'.[11]

Sylvia Plath and Ted Hughes

This area is also known for the tragic story of Sylvia Plath and Ted Hughes. No 3, Chalcot Square (3rd floor flat) is where the pair settled in February 1960, and, two years after the marriage ended, Plath moved with her children to 23 Fitzroy Road, which is only a few hundred yards away (**W.B. Yeats** had also previously occupied the address). Both of the above have blue plaques. On Monday 11 February 1963 she took some food and milk up to her two children, Frieda and Nicholas, opened their window and taped up any gaps under the entrance door. She went to the kitchen, once more blocked the gap under the door, turned the gas oven full-on, put a cloth on the bottom of the oven, lay down and placed her head on the cloth. This was just after 6 am.

Three hours later, a nurse sent by her doctor, Dr Horder, unable to gain any response at the front door, secured the help of a local builder who broke in. They discovered her body which failed to respond to resuscitation. A message to 'Please call Dr Horder' was found in the hall. The children were discovered, crying and cold but otherwise unharmed, upstairs.

Her *Collected Poems*, posthumously published in 1981, was awarded the Pulitzer Prize.

In 1998, Ted Hughes published *Birthday Letters*, a book of 88 poems about Plath and their lives. They were written over 25 years and all except two are addressed directly to Plath. Having previously kept his silence on the subject, the book was unexpected and instantly very successful in publishing terms. Hughes died nine months later.

Leaving Regent's Park and heading south towards Wimpole Street

This walk leaves the park and environs by the York Bridge exit to the south. Cross into York Gate. **William Macready**, manager of the Drury Lane Theatre and friend of **Charles Dickens**, lived at number 1. **Frances Palgrave**, compiler of *Golden Treasury of English Songs and Lyrics* (1861), lived for a time at number 5. Make your way south past the Royal Academy of Music Museum and into Devonshire Place, which continues as Upper Wimpole Street and is parallel to the world-famous Harley Street. At number 2 Wimpole Street, you will see a plaque to Sir Arthur Conan Doyle.

Conan Doyle wrote that, when looking for rooms for a surgery following his studies in ophthalmology in Vienna, he searched the doctors' quarters and at last found

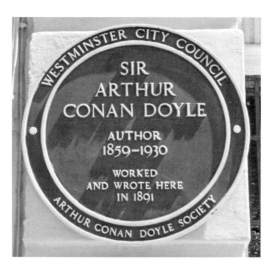

suitable accommodation not too far from Harley Street. There, for £120 a year, he had the use of a front room and part use of a waiting room. He was soon, he writes, to discover that they were both, in fact, waiting rooms. It was here that he began to while away the hours by writing short stories featuring the adventures of a new kind of consulting detective whom he christened *Sherlock Holmes* (at first favouring the name Sherringford Holmes).

Devonshire Place leads into Wimpole Street, 'the most august of London streets', according to **Virginia Woolf,** where **Elizabeth Barrett** lived from 1838–46. Other famous residents of Wimpole Street have included Sir Thomas Barlow, doctor to Queen Victoria (no 10), **Wilkie Collins** (no 82), Sir Paul McCartney 1964–66 (no 57), **Henry Hallam** (no 67) and, in fiction, *Henry Higgins* from *My Fair Lady* (Number 27a).

Above, right and below: *50 Wimpole Street.*

Whilst here **Elizabeth Barrett** conducted an extensive correspondence with a great many people, including **Robert Browning**, who had initially written to her saying how much he loved her work and with whom she was to conduct a secret relationship.

Poetry has been as serious a thing to me as life itself; and life has been a very serious thing: there has been no playing at skittles for me in either.

> **Elizabeth Barrett**, Preface to the 1844 edition of her poems, quoted in
> *The Poems of Elizabeth Barrett Browning*, The 'Albion Edition',
> Frederick Warne and Co, London, New York

Just below the York Gate, at 17 Marylebone Road, is St Marylebone Parish Church, where on 12 September 1846, Robert Browning and Elizabeth Barrett were secretly married – the church still has their marriage certificate. Six days later Elizabeth and her new husband set sail, settling in Italy. She expressed her love for her husband in one of her most famous poems:

> How do I love thee?
> Let me count the ways.
> I love thee to the depth and breadth and height
> My soul can reach, when feeling out of sight
> For the ends of being and ideal grace.

> **Elizabeth Barrett Browning**, from *How Do
> I Love Thee?* Sonnet 43, Sonnets
> from the Portuguese (1850)

There are several other literary associations to this St Marylebone Parish Church. **Lord Byron** was baptised here in 1788. One of **Richard Brinsley Sheridan**'s two marriages, that to Elizabeth Anne Linley, took place here. Sheridan was a long term owner of the Theatre Royal, Drury Lane and gained fame in his lifetime (1751–1816) for plays such as *The Rivals* and *School for Scandal*. He is buried in Poets' Corner, Westminster Abbey (see Walk 6).

St Marylebone Church is also the setting for Tom Rakewell's marriage to an old but rich maid in number five of Hogarth's *The Rake's Progress* (more details are in Walk 2).

Mrs David Ogilvy, who rented the floor above that of the Brownings in Italy 1849/50 has painted a vivid description of Elizabeth. She writes of her profuse feathery curls half hiding the small face and 'something unutterably pathetic' looking out from soft eyes. The overall impression, she says, was of a King Charles Spaniel.[12]

Elizabeth Barrett Browning's dog had a book written about it by **Virginia Woolf**: *Flush: A Biography* (1933) was cross-genre, part fiction and part non-fiction, and was inspired by Browning's own poems about her dog. In the book, Browning is largely regarded as an analogue for other female literary figures, including Woolf herself. Woolf wrote the book after the emotionally draining *Waves* (1931) and by the end regretted it, even dreading its forthcoming publication.

Elizabeth Barrett Browning died in Florence on 29 June 1861. A tablet was placed on the walls of Casa Guidi, her home. Translated, it reads: 'Here lived and wrote E.B.B. who united to a woman's heart the science of the learned, and the spirit of the poet, and made by her poetry a golden ring, uniting Italy and England. Grateful Florence places this memorial, 1861.'

The Barretts of Wimpole Street is a 1930 play by Rudolf Besier. It was made into a film starring Norma Shearer, Frederic March and Charles Laughton and directed by Sidney Franklin in 1934: the production was generally critically acclaimed, a big box-office hit and nominated at the Academy Awards for Best Picture, and Norma Shearer was nominated for Best Actress. In 1957 Franklin once more produced almost exactly the same film, except that this time it was in colour – the stars were Jennifer Jones, John Gielgud and Bill Travers. Both films were for MGM.

Walk onto Queen Anne Street. **James Boswell** (1740–1795) reputedly wrote some of his *Life of Samuel Johnson* here (see also Walk 7). There is a blue plaque to him nearby at 122 Great Portland Street, where he died.

The book was an immediate commercial and critical success and hundreds of editions, both complete and selective (it is very long) have followed. However, some critics have pointed out that it is not strictly a biography at all on account of a patchy account of Johnson's early years and the fact that Boswell makes changes to **Johnson**'s quotations and alters some of his observations.

Proceed into Bentinck Street which is where **Edward Gibbon** (1737–1794) lived while writing *The Decline and Fall of the Roman Empire*.

Drop down into Oxford Street. **Thomas Hardy** (1840–1928) wrote the poem *Coming up Oxford Street: Evening* in which he describes the despairing life of a city clerk walking up the street, with no interest in anything… 'wondering why he was born'.

Hardy adds at the end of the poem 'As seen 4 July 1872' and it is believed that, deeply unhappy himself, he considered changing the poem to the first person. This would have been two years before he found literary success with *Far From the Madding Crowd* (1874). The book was published first in *Cornhill Magazine* and it is believed that Hardy took the title from **Thomas Gray**'s poem '*Elegy Written in a Country Churchyard*' (1751):

> Far from the madding crowd's ignoble strife
> Their sober wishes never learn'd to stray;
> Along the cool sequester'd vale of life
> They kept the noiseless tenor of their way.

Almost opposite is Bond Street tube station: take a walk down South Molton Street which is alongside it, and at number 17 you will see a square blue plaque commemorating **William Blake**. Blake crops up all over the city and he came here in 1803, excited to be back in London, having spent two years in Felpham, Sussex. Sadly, this period in his life was excruciating as financial and artistic success eluded him.

Come back again to Oxford Street and turn right towards Oxford Circus: this grand thoroughfare claims to be Europe's busiest shopping street with over half a million visitors daily.[13] Originally a Roman road through the city, the fields in this area started

to be bought up by the Earl of Oxford in the eighteenth century. Until this time, it had not been seen as a desirable place for home or business with public hangings at one end – Marble Arch – and the notorious St Giles slums at the other. It was redesigned in conjunction with Regent Street by John Nash from 1810.

Sir Arthur Conan Doyle was one author who used Oxford Street in his stories – Latimer's, where *Watson* buys his boots and Bradley's, where *Holmes* sources his strongest shag tobacco, are here. Often, however, it is a place where people rush and cabs clatter in order to reach somewhere else. In *The Adventure of the Blue Carbuncle* for example, where a goose is the central feature, *Watson* reports that, as they go in search of the said bird's origin, 'our footfalls rang crisp and loudly', and he and *Holmes* travel through 'Wimpole Street, Harley Street and so through Wigmore Street into Oxford Street.' Also, *Holmes* is certain in *The Final Problem* that *Moriarty* is at the root of the affair when:

> I went out about midday to transact some business in Oxford Street. As I passed the corner which leads from Bentinck Street on to the Welbeck Street crossing a two-horse van furiously driven whizzed round and was on me like a flash...[14]

E. M. Forster also writes of Oxford Street in *Howards End* (1910), in a cheerier tone than **Thomas Hardy** (above): the 'electric lights sizzled and jagged in the main thoroughfares, gas lamps in the side streets glimmered a canary gold or green...'

Forster, in his 1937 essay *London is a Muddle* says that he disliked London in his youth but grew to like it, primarily by walking around it.

I'd better add I am quite sure I am not a great novelist because I have only got on to paper really three types of people – the person I think I am, the people who irritate me and the people I would like to be…

E.M. Forster talking about his life on the BBC, 1958

Towards Oxford Circus, on the left, just before John Lewis department store, is Holles Street, where **Lord Byron** was born, although the houses here were demolished in 1889. English Heritage say that there is no definitive evidence as to exactly which house was his but nonetheless a plaque, the first ever, was put up in 1867. Since that time over 900 plaques have been added all over London to celebrate a wide variety of achievements, literary and otherwise: the public can make suggestions as to suitable plaques.[15]

Lord Byron

Lord Byron was born on 22 January 1788 and died, aged just 36, on 19 April 1824 in Missolonghi, Greece. He was the only son of 'Mad Jack' Byron, a naval captain who deserted Byron's mother two years after his birth. The death of a relative led to Byron becoming a Lord at the age of ten. He was educated at Harrow and Cambridge.

Mad, bad and dangerous to know

Lady Caroline Lamb's assessment
of Byron. He called her his
'little volcano'.

He became known, through a succession of affairs with, most biographers believe, both men and women, as a sexually precocious man and very much his father's son. He was dark and striking to look at but was born with a club foot, refusing, it was said, to sleep in the same bed as his lovers for fear of them remarking upon it. He was also protective of his image much in the way of a modern celebrity, only approving certain depictions and paintings.

In 1812 he published *Childe Harolde's Pilgrimage*, which became an overnight sensation.

He was famously dismissive of **Southey, Wordsworth, Walter Scott** and especially **John Keats**, whom he referred to as 'Jack Keats' or 'Ketch', while at other times claiming he could not remember his name at all, but he and **Samuel Taylor Coleridge** were on occasions passionate about each other's work, if not always about each other. He also wrote enthusiastically about the poetry of **Percy Bysshe Shelley**.

In 1815 he married the wealthy socialite, Annabella Milbanke, with whom he had a child, Ada: she became a noted mathematician being particularly involved in the development of early computer theory. They split, very acrimoniously and publicly the following year, during which time Byron was reported to be having an affair with his half-sister and others. He then travelled abroad, never to return to England.

Byron began to publish his most famous work. *Don Juan*, from 1819 and it was still unfinished upon his death. He died of fever and infection while waiting to fight for the Greeks in their battle against the Ottoman Empire.

If you turn left at Oxford Circus, you will come to the campus of the University of Westminster. This is where **Edmund de Waal** C.B.E. worked as Professor of Ceramics from 2004–2011 when he published *The Hare With the Amber Eyes: A hidden inheritance* (2010), the extraordinary success of which, he wrote, 'changed my life' as thousands of letters started arriving, and it was translated into 30 languages.[16] It tells the story of de Waal's relatives, with reference to a collection of 264 Japanese netsuke – miniature wood and ivory sculptures. The book took many awards including the *Ondaatje Prize*. His second book, *The White Road* was published in 2015 and called 'a mighty achievement' in the *Guardian*;[17] the third, *Letters to Camondo*, was released in 2021.

A little to the north is Langham Street where **Doris Lessing** (1919–2013) lived, 1958–62 while writing *The Golden Notebook*. She rented the flat from her publisher. She later lived in West Hampstead where she was based when awarded the Nobel Prize in Literature for 2007, the oldest-ever woman recipient. 'I've won all the prizes in Europe, every bloody one', she said to the press on her doorstep (you can see the interview on YouTube) adding that this one was being given to her this year, at the age of 89, in case she should 'pop off' before the next round. She also said that there was more to life than prizes.

Regent Street

Return to Oxford Circus and walk straight ahead into Regent Street, which has a number of very interesting literary connections.

Regent Street is today branded as a prestigious lifestyle destination – a mixture of fashion, wellness, dining and lifestyle. To many, it is seen as the London home to some of the world's most exclusive shopping brands such as Coach, Hamleys, Apple, Mappin and Webb and Burberry. Originally designed by John Nash and James Burton from 1810, it was to have been straight to look triumphal, but land ownership issues resulted in its now-famous curve. One idea at the time was that the street would act as a divide between the upper classes in Mayfair and the lower classes in Soho. Much of it has always been owned by the Crown Estate on behalf of the monarch,[18] although some parts have been sold to finance regeneration.

Turn right into Hanover Street leading to Hanover Square which is a pleasant leafy oasis in which to take a rest or eat a snack – there are benches – and is the first stop as we head down Regent Street. It was built in the early eighteenth century to provide exquisite houses for the upper classes, now mostly offices, and it appears that many were snapped up by top military men such as Lord Cadogan and members of the government. There was discontent at the time as the square was deemed to be too near Tyburn, place of the hanging of malefactors who also trundled up to their execution, often drunk, in open carts along nearby Oxford Circus, both of these factors being of great inconvenience to the good folk who occupied the new houses.

St George's Hanover Square Church is a short distance to the south of the square, built at the same time as the houses. It has an impressive portico supported by six Corinthian columns which extend out over the pavement.

Laurence Sterne and Ignatius Sancho

Land being very scarce, the church was constructed without a graveyard and people in the parish, which included **Laurence Sterne** (1713–68), author of *Tristram Shandy*, were buried in the grounds of the nearby workhouse.

Subsequently, Laurence Sterne's body was possibly the victim of grave-robbers, being sold to anatomists at Cambridge University and was only reinterred after being recognised by someone who knew him in life. In the 1970s over 11,000 skulls were taken from this area when the land was redeveloped, and one, with marks that would have been caused by anatomists and which was consistent with the size and shape of his bust, was found. This, and other remains, were reinterred at Coxwold churchyard in North Yorkshire. Sterne was what is termed 'perpetual curate' here from 1760–8: incumbents of Church of England parishes were vicars, rectors or perpetual curates, the last most likely to be, to use a more modern term, 'economically challenged' and quite probably of lower social standing than their vicar and rector colleagues.

Although he often lived elsewhere, Laurence Sterne spent part of each month in London revelling in his fame following the success of *The Life and Opinions of Tristam Shandy, Gentleman*, the first parts of which were published in 1759. He said that he wrote not to be fed but to be famous. It was during the writing of an episode of this book that he received a letter from former slave, Ignatius Sancho, pleading for his help and influence to put an end to the slave trade. His reply and their subsequent correspondence was widely publicised and are considered important documents in the abolitionist campaign.

Ignatius Sancho (1729–80) became a celebrated figure in his own right, known for his literary talents – *The Letters of the Late Ignatius Sancho, an African* was published posthumously in two volumes in 1782. These reflected on his experiences of slavery and the problems of being an educated person of African origin living in eighteenth century London. In 1780, he also wrote a dramatic first-hand account of the Gordon Riots. He and his wife were right at the centre of town when, from 1774 until his death, they ran a shop, bustling by Sancho's accounts, in nearby Charles Street selling tobacco, sugar, soap, rum and general commodities. Following his death, his son, William, ran the shop before deciding to turn it into a printing house which, in 1803, published the fifth edition of his father's letters.

St George's was the parish church of George Frideric Handel who lived in nearby Brook Street where he composed *The Messiah*. He had much to do with the new church, initially being consulted about the purchase of the organ and helping to examine applicants for the post of inaugural church organist. He became a regular worshipper here, for the last few years of his life, attending church although totally blind and crippled with arthritis. He died in what is now number 25 Brook Street in 1759.

It is a very beautiful building, designed by John James, and it rapidly became a fashionable wedding church, one of the weddings, many years later, being that of future President of the United States, Theodore Roosevelt, aged 28, and Edith Carow, aged 25, on 2 December 1886: Roosevelt qualified, for residence purposes, by staying at Brown's Hotel in Dover Street. According to the Church's official website,[19] weddings of figures noteworthy in a literary sense include those of of Benjamin Disraeli to Mary

Anne in 1839, **George Meredith** to Mary Ellen Nichols in 1849, **George Eliot** to John Walter Cross in 1880, **Lord Alfred Douglas** to Olive Custance in 1902 and **John Buchan** to Susan Grosvenor in 1907.

In popular culture, the church in the song '*Get me to the church on time*' from *My Fair Lady*, the classic film starring Sir Rex Harrison and Audrey Hepburn, is St George's. In fiction it is also the location of *Lord St Simon*'s proposed marriage to American *Hatty Doran*, only to have her run away during the wedding breakfast in **Sir Arthur Conan Doyle**'s story, *The Adventure of the Noble Bachelor*. **Jane Austen** mentions a possible trip to London to see the interior of the church in *Mansfield Park*.

Walk back to Regent Street where the walk continues towards Piccadilly. **Dickens** houses *Lord Verisopht* here in *Nicholas Nickleby*. We first meet this debauched aristocrat at three o'clock in the afternoon, reclining listlessly on a sofa, his slippered foot dangling to the ground. He is yawning and comparing notes on the previous night's excesses with his constant companion, *Sir Mulberry Hawk*.

On the left-hand side, not far from the Eros statue in Piccadilly, is Café Royal. In the 1890s this was already a famous meeting place for the great and the good of the day, including **George Bernard Shaw, Sir Max Beerbohm, Sir Arthur Conan Doyle** and **Oscar Wilde**, who famously met his friend Frank Harris here on 24 March 1895 to discuss what to do about Lord Alfred Douglas' father, the Marquess of Queensbury, against whom Wilde had issued a charge of criminal libel (see Walk 10 regarding the confrontation between the Marquess and Wilde in Tite Street, Chelsea and the subsequent trial).

Turning left at Piccadilly Circus will lead you to Leicester Square. *Mr George*'s shooting gallery in Dickens' *Bleak House* was somewhere around here. **William Blake** had lodgings in Green Street (off the southern side of the square but no longer existing) for two years following his marriage to Catherine Boucher. This was a fashionable location for artists and painters in the eighteenth century – **William Hogarth** and **Sir Joshua Reynolds** had lived here before Blake.

The name derives from the 2nd Earl of Leicester, Robert Sidney, who had a house built here in the mid seventeenth century.

Panton Street links Leicester Square and Haymarket and a short way down next to Oxendon Street is the **Harold Pinter** Theatre. Built in just six months by Thomas Verity in 1881, it was previously called The Comedy Theatre until it was given its present name on 8 September 2011: it subsequently put on a marathon season of Pinter plays called 'Pinter at the Pinter'.

Pinter was born in 1930 in Hackney, East London. His first play was a student production, *The Room*, in 1957, and his second, *The Birthday*, in 1958 received reviews, most of which the British Library define as 'spectacularly negative'.[20] His plays from the late sixties, known as 'the memory plays', include *Old Times* (1971), and *Betrayal* (1978). He won the Nobel Prize in Literature 2005: the nomination said that he, 'in his plays uncovers the precipice under everyday prattle and forces entry into oppression's closed rooms'.

You are now in the very centre of one of the prime tourist areas of London – Piccadilly Circus, Trafalgar Square, Leicester Square and Haymarket with, practically speaking, a never-ending array of restaurants, take-away outlets, cinemas, theatres, galleries and pubs. Leicester Square, with a fountain and a statue of **William Shakespeare** in the middle, is a good place to take a rest on the free public seating and is where this walk ends.

WALK 2

Trafalgar Square, National Gallery, Leicester Square, Charing Cross Road and Soho

In This Walk: The lives and works of the following people and *fictional characters* are highlighted: Rudyard Kipling, Sir Harold Nicholson, Sir John Betjeman, Osbert Lancaster, Joseph Conrad, J.B. Priestley, Joe Orton, Muriel Spark, Sir J.M. Barrie, Sir Ian McKellen, Sir Noël Coward, William Hogarth, Alice Oseman, Frank Doel, Helene Hanff, Dame Agatha Christie, Thomas De Quincey, Mary Seacole, Charles Dickens, Dr Johnson, Casanova, Oscar Wilde, Lord Alfred Douglas, John Logie Baird, Mary Russell Mitford, William Hazlitt, Karl Marx, Charles De Gaulle, Brendan Behan, Dylan Thomas, Augustus John, Sir Max Beerbohm, Sylvia Plath, Anthony Powell, Fanny Burney, Percy Bysshe Shelley, William Blake, Dorothy L. Sayers, T.S. Eliot, Arnold Bennett, C.S. Lewis.

Distance: *See page 32; about 3.7 kilometres (2.3 miles)*

Time to allow: A morning, afternoon or evening.

Walking conditions: Flat but generally very busy, especially in the evening. The pavements can be quite narrow. There are cafés and pubs all along the route.

Route

Trafalgar Square
National Gallery
Irving Street
Leicester Square
Charing Cross Road
Soho Square
Greek Street
Romilly Street
Old Compton Street
Dean Street
Oxford Street
D'Arblay Street
Wardour Street

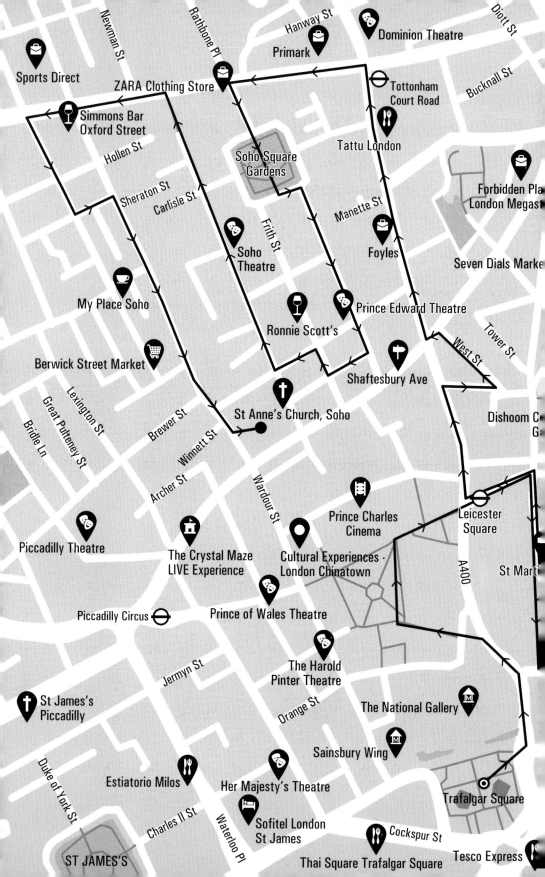

This walk heads off from Trafalgar Square (the square itself is discussed in more detail in Walk 3). Keeping St Martin-in-the-Fields to your right, walk into Charing Cross Road. Just past the National Portrait Gallery turn left into Irving Street where number 9 was home to the Beefsteak Club from its foundation in 1896. Members, who included **Rudyard Kipling, Sir Harold Nicholson, Sir John Betjeman** and theatre designer, Osbert Lancaster, dined primarily on beefsteaks, cheese, port and whisky.

Irving Street is also thought to be Brett Street in **Joseph Conrad**'s 1907 novel *The Secret Agent*. It centres on *Adolf Verloc* who owns a porn shop and is also a secret agent for an unspecified power. Conrad's gloomy view of London, especially Soho, was influenced by **Dickens'** *Bleak House*. Conrad's novel is dedicated to **H.G. Wells**.

The Garrick Theatre, which you will see just before turning into Irving Street, is at 2 Charing Cross Road and was the home of one of the most successful productions of modern times, **J.B. Priestley**'s *An Inspector Calls*. Priestley was a prolific writer, notably of plays and novels, until his death at the age of 90 on 14 August 1984.

Just up the road is Wyndham's Theatre, which opened in 1889, and was the venue for **Joe Orton**'s *Entertaining Mr Sloane* (1964) and **Muriel Spark**'s *The Prime of Miss Jean Brodie* (1966).

Walk straight on to Leicester Square. The cinemas here have been the venue for the premieres of very many famous blockbuster films.

Leave by Cranbourn Street – top right as you look at the square from where you entered – and you will see Leicester Square tube station ahead of you.

St Martin-in-the-Fields.

St Martin's Lane with the London Coliseum on the right.

It is interesting to cross the junction in front of you and turn first right to take a walk down one side of St Martin's Lane and back up the other to where you are now once again. St Martin's Lane is a little quieter than Charing Cross Road and significant for a number of reasons. You will pass the Duke of York's Theatre: **Sir J.M. Barrie**'s

Peter Pan, or The Boy Who Wouldn't Grow Up debuted here on 27 December 1904. More recent productions have included *King Lear* starring Sir Ian McKellen in 2018, *The Girl on the Train* (2019), Noël Coward's *Blithe Spirit* in 2020 and *The Glass Menagerie* (2022). The Lane is also home to the English National Opera at the London Coliseum and the Noël Coward Theatre, originally called The New Theatre and then The Albery, being renamed after 'The Master' in 2006.

Sir Noël Coward

Noël Coward was born in 1899 in Teddington (see Walk 10) and was on the stage for a great deal of his life, making his debut at the age of eleven. He was knighted in 1970, apparently having his original nomination for that honour by George VI in 1942 blocked by Sir Winston Churchill who, it is said, disapproved of his flamboyant lifestyle. He was not popular with Hitler either being, along with H.G. Wells (see Walk 1), one of those on the list to be immediately arrested in the event of a successful Nazi invasion of Britain.

His famous clipped accent and staccato-like delivery were the result, so he said, of trying to ensure that he was understood when talking to his increasingly deaf mother, Violet, who died in 1954.

He said that he had 'a talent to amuse' and he became the toast of London following the success of *The Vortex* in 1924 and soon had three more plays running at the same time – *On with the Dance, Hay Fever* and *Fallen Angels.*

In all, he wrote and produced comedies, dramas and musicals for the stage, the best known of which are probably *Private Lives, Blithe Spirit* and *Calvacade*. He also wrote or co-wrote about 281 songs: *Mad Dogs and Englishmen, Mad About The Boy* and *Someday I'll Find You* have become classics. Of his films, two of the most popular are *Brief Encounter* and *In Which We Serve*, both today being lampooned and loved in almost equal measure. He also had a very popular cabaret act which was recorded for the gramophone by CBS in 1955, the success of which led to a great deal of work in America.

It is of little help at the first rehearsal to be able to translate Cicero.

Noël Coward rejoinder to **T.S. Eliot** who was slighting about his education and remarked that he lacked a knowledge of the classics.

Sir Noël died of a heart attack on 26 March 1973 in his villa, *Blue Harbour* in Jamaica, as he was preparing to have morning coffee.

William Hogarth

St Martin's Academy was formed and attended by a number of artists, including William Hogarth, and initially operated from St Peter's Court, an alley off St Martin's Lane. Following its demise probably through financial scandal in 1724 – the records have been lost – it transferred to Salisbury Court in Fleet Street. Membership was by annual subscription and there are records to say that at one time it had 29 members and

at another 54, and they all came together principally to practise life-drawing.

Hogarth was very successful in his lifetime, initially famous for *The Harlot's Progress*, a series of six paintings originally published by private subscription in 1733 and witnessing a country girl's fall into prostitution, venereal disease and death at the age of 23: *The Rake's Progress*, a series of eight paintings was produced two years later, with the rake, *Tom Rakewell*, being the male equivalent of the harlot. It is believed that the idea for *The Harlot's Progress* came to Hogarth when he was painting a prostitute in her garret in Drury Lane and began to wonder about her life prior to this moment and afterwards. Both series of paintings were incredibly successful, making Hogarth a great deal of money as they were reproduced as prints and were very popular. **Charles Lamb** (see Walk 4) compared the individual paintings to a book, so remarkable and detailed is the story being told in each. In many ways, they were the forerunner of comic books and graphic novels.

The term 'graphic novel' first gained wide use in the 1960s and '70s and to the chagrin of some traditionalists, there have been some very successful and critically acclaimed authors in the genre. One such is **Alice Oseman** whose *Heartstopper* books have gained many fans by presenting relatable and upbeat stories of teenage life, particularly regarding the LGBTQ+ community. In 2022 Netflix brought out a hugely successful first TV version; series two and three were rapidly commissioned for 2023/4.

Once back in Charing Cross Road, walk up this interesting street of theatres, shops and restaurants, keeping an eye on the numbers on the right-hand side. After a busy junction, you will come to a shopfront, at the time of writing a small McDonalds restaurant, and on the left-hand side, as you look at it from the roadside, quite high up and easy to miss, there is a plaque saying that this is 84 Charing Cross Road. A stage play, TV play and a film have been made featuring this address for it was, in 1949, the antiquarian bookshop run by Frank Doel, called Marks and Co, that an American book collector, **Helene Hanff**, charged with obtaining all manner of classics for her library in New York. Over time and many letters, a friendship developed between Doel, the other staff and Hanff, that Hanff put into the best-selling book *84, Charing Cross Road*, in 1970. The authors requested by Hanff included **Jane Austen, Chaucer, Catullus, John Donne, Horace, Samuel Johnson, Samuel Pepys** and **Virginia Woolf.**

Dame Agatha Christie and London

Lichfield Street, on your right, leads to West Street which is the location of St Martin's Theatre where **Dame Agatha Christie**'s *The Mousetrap* has been running, continuously apart from the pandemic 2020/21 when all theatres had to close, since March 1974.

Dame Agatha Christie published 66 novels and 14 short story collections: some estimates put her total sales at between 2 and 4 billion, on a par with **Shakespeare** and probably only slightly less than the Bible. She is the creator of *Miss Marple* and *Hercule Poirot*.

Born in Torquay, Agatha Mary Clarissa Miller (1890–1976) came up to London as a young girl to stay with her Auntie Grannie in Ealing and found the experience quite thrilling. She married Archie Christie in 1914 and set up house in St John's Wood; a decade and divorce later, she purchased 22 Cresswell Place, Chelsea, and although she bought and sold several other London properties, she never let this one go (to visit, see section on Chelsea below, Walk 10). She married Max Mallowan in

The Ritz Hotel.

September 1930. Other homes included number 58 Sheffield Terrace, Notting Hill and, during the Second World War, 22 Lawn Road Flats, Hampstead (now Isokon Flats). The central Brown's, Claridge's, The Ritz and Savoy hotels feature in her works. There is a memorial to her, in the form of a book in bronze, 2.4 metres high, on Cranbourn Street.

Walk up to the top of Charing Cross Road and turn left into Oxford Street. Turn left again after a short while into Soho Street which will bring you to Soho Square, a green oasis with plenty of seats and a favourite of the lunchtime office crowd.

The origins of the word 'Soho' are contested but the most usual view is that it was once a hunting cry: this area of London was rural in the sixteenth century.

It is here that **Thomas De Quincey** (1785–1859) collapsed with hunger and his companion, a 15–year-old prostitute called Ann, rushed to Oxford Street to find sustenance. **Dickens** places *Dr Manette* and his daughter here in *A Tale of Two Cities*.

Mary Seacole

It was also here, at number 14 – look for the blue plaque – that Mary Seacole lived in 1857, having been forced to move from better accommodation at nearby 1 Tavistock Street. She had just returned from her legendary nursing work in the Crimea in poor health and was being chased by debt collectors.

Her autobiography was called *The Wonderful Adventures of Mrs Seacole in Many Lands* and it was released by James Blackwood in July 1857. The book was positively reviewed in the main and sold very well.

In the same year, her dire financial state was highlighted in the press and soldiers wrote in to say how wonderful she had been in their service and that of England. A fund-raising gala was held for her on the banks of the Thames over four nights and was attended by 80,000 people.

Mary Seacole died in 1881 and was, incredibly, 'lost' to the world for 100 years. The Mary Seacole Trust now leads a huge revival of interest in her life and writing. In 2004 she was voted the Greatest Black Briton and in 2016 a statue to her was unveiled in the grounds of St Thomas' Hospital on the South Bank.

Greek St leads off to the south. The Pillars of Hercules pub here is reputed to be that featured in **Dickens'** *A Tale of Two Cities*. Dr Johnson started a weekly literary club here. **Casanova** (1725–98) stayed in the street and his ghost is said to roam the area.

Off to the right, near the end of Greek Street, is Romilly Street. This was the location of Kettner's Restaurant, opened in 1867 by Auguste Kettner, chef to Napoleon III. It was one of **Oscar Wilde**'s (1854–1900) favourites, and we know that he ate here in October 1892 with his lover, Lord Alfred Douglas. Edward VII often wined and dined his mistress, Lillie Langtry, here. **Agatha Christie** was a regular.

Turn right at the first junction and walk up Frith Street, home of the world-famous Ronnie Scott's jazz venue. **William Hazlitt** (1778–1830), essayist and critic, lived at number 6. He died there in delirium and great pain but took advantage of his more lucid moments to write of it; his final words, apparently, were to say that he had lived a happy life. He was 52.

Take a left into Old Compton Street which has several claims to fame: John Logie Baird first demonstrated television in an upstairs room of a café here. Legend has it that he approached a man in the street and paid him one shilling to sit in one room whilst he went into another to see if the image had transmitted – several people have subsequently claimed to have been this first-ever man on television.

Mary Russell Mitford (1787–1855) completed *Our Life: Sketches of Rural Life* in this area.

Turn right into Dean Street. **Karl Marx** (1818–83), wife, maidservant and three children lived above the *Quo Vadis* Restaurant 1851–56, whence he travelled to the British Museum to work on *Das Kapital*.

At 49 Dean Street is the famous French House, 'a no music, no machines, no television, no mobile phones'[21] drinking and eating establishment. It is probably the most famous pub in Soho. Charles de Gaulle met with Resistance colleagues upstairs after the fall of France. Originally opening as York Minster in 1891, characters who met, ate or drank here have included **Brendan Behan, Dylan Thomas** – he accidentally left the manuscript of *Under Milk Wood* beneath a seat whence it was rescued by the pub's manager – **Augustus John**, **Sir Max Beerbohm** and **Sylvia Plath**. The pub specialises in fine wines; you can have a beer but only by the half-pint – a custom introduced by the legendary manager, Gaston Berlemont, who was born in the pub in 1914 and worked there until his retirement in 1989 – in order to make the place more continental and classier.

On the upper floors at 69, Dean Street was the Gargoyle Club, founded in 1925 by David Tennant, son of 1st Baron Glenconner. It was a members-only club with an initial membership of 300 which included **Noël Coward, Gladys Cooper, George Grossmith** and **Virginia Woolf.**

A celebrated member of the club was **Anthony Powell** (1905–2000) who was introduced by **Evelyn Waugh**. Considered by some as the English Proust, he wrote the 12 volume, million-word *A Dance to the Music of Time*: it took him 30 years in all.

At the top of Dean Street turn left into Oxford Street again, and left again into Berwick Street. D'Arblay Street is off to your right and is a rarity in being named after a female author: **Fanny Burney,** English novelist and diarist, who married General D'Arblay and lived at 50 Poland Street, opposite D'Arblay Street. **Percy Bysshe Shelley** (1792–1822) lodged at number 15 in 1811 after he had been sent down from Oxford. **William Blake** (1757–1827) lodged at number 28.

Blake's birthplace is marked by a plaque at 28 Broadwick Street, originally Broad Street, which is between Poland and Berwick Streets (see Walk 9 for more details of his life and work).

At the T-junction at the end of this street turn right and wander down Wardour Street until you come to the final stop on this walk which is on your left – St Anne's Church. Novelist and avid Sherlockian, **Dorothy L. Sayers**, a former churchwarden for many years, is buried here. It was at least partially designed by Sir Christopher Wren and consecrated on 21 March 1686. In 1743, Prince William Henry, younger brother of George III, was baptised here.

Following destruction in a German air raid on 24 September 1940, restoration was helped by many literary figures who either lent money or their names to the cause. These include **Dame Agatha Christie, T.S. Eliot** and **C.S. Lewis.** To celebrate the 25th anniversary of the rebuilding, a new entrance to Dean Street was officially inaugurated on 8 December 2016.

WALK 3

Trafalgar Square, Strand, Fleet St, St Paul's, Southwark Cathedral, Guy's Hospital, Lant Street, Shakespeare's Globe, Royal Festival Hall, Northumberland Avenue

In This Walk: The lives and works of the following people and *fictional characters* are highlighted: George Orwell, Virginia Woolf, John Masefield, Charles Dickens, *Aunt Betsy, Uriah Heep, Mealy Potatoes*, *David Copperfield*, Samuel Pepys, *Sherlock Holmes*, Oscar Wilde, Rudyard Kipling, G.K. Chesteron, Christopher Isherwood, Thomas Hood, Sir J.M. Barrie, John Galsworthy, George Bernard Shaw, Thomas Hardy, William Blake, Voltaire, William Makepeace Thackeray, H.G. Wells, William Terris, Jane Austen, Dame Ellen Terry, Dame Edith Evans, Sir Charlie Chaplin, Sir Noël Coward, Boris Karloff, Dame Gracie Fields, A.A. Milne, Lord Byron, Edgar Wallace, P.G. Wodehouse, Somerset Maugham, John Dryden, Wilkie Collins, William Harrison Ainsworth, Sir Arthur Conan Doyle, Richard Bean, Richard D'Oyly Carte, John Donne, Dante Rossetti, Samuel Johnson, Benjamin Motte, Jonathan Swift, *Martin Chuzzlewit*, Thomas Hughes, Oliver Goldsmith, Sir Walter Scott, Charles Lamb, Izaak Walton, William Tyndale, *Sweeney Todd*, Mark Twain, Keith Waterhouse, Sir John Betjeman, Samuel Richardson, John Milton, Francis Beaumont, John Fletcher, William Strachey, Sir Walter Raleigh, Alfred Noyes, John Keats, Julian Barnes, Sir Kingsley Amis, John Bunyan, John Gower, William Shakespeare, Geoffrey Chaucer, William Caxton, *Little Dorrit, Arthur Clennam*, Sir Walter Besant, Benjamin Disraeli, *Richard III, Henry IV, Macbeth, King Lear*, Robert Greene, Thomas Nashe, Christopher Marlowe, Thomas Kyd, Lemn Sissay.

Distance: *See pages 42–43; about 9.8 kilometres (6.1 miles)*

Time to allow: A complete day, at least. If you wish to check out all the fascinating alleys and courts of Fleet Street, St Paul's Cathedral, Shakespeare's Globe (perhaps taking in a tour or a production), the Royal Festival Hall and maybe have a drink or meal at one of the many drinking establishments which include the Sherlock Holmes pub, the walk can take several full days and evenings. The walk can, however, be split easily into two – north of the river (up to St Paul's) and south of the river (the remainder).

Walking conditions: It is quite flat with never more than a slight upward gradient (for example along Northumberland Avenue) but it is always busy with locals and tourists going about their business. Some of the buildings and vistas are amazing, so take a camera or smartphone.

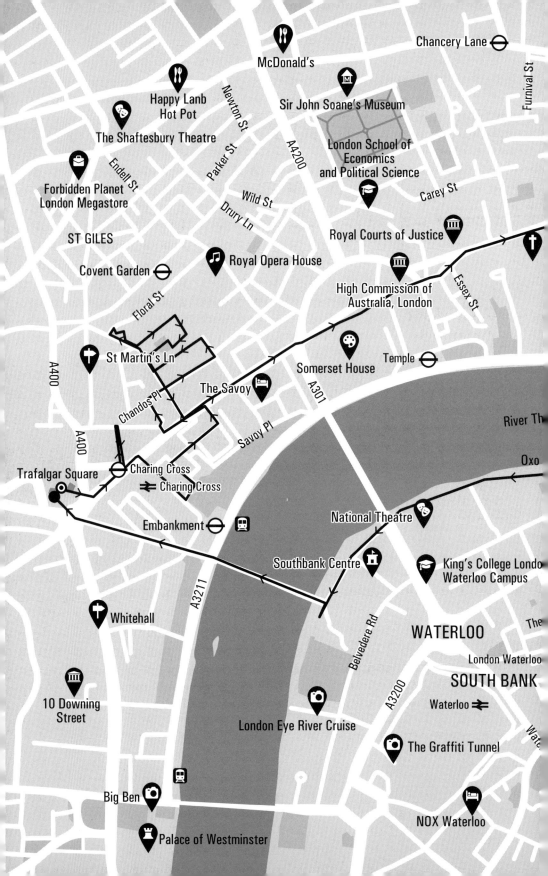

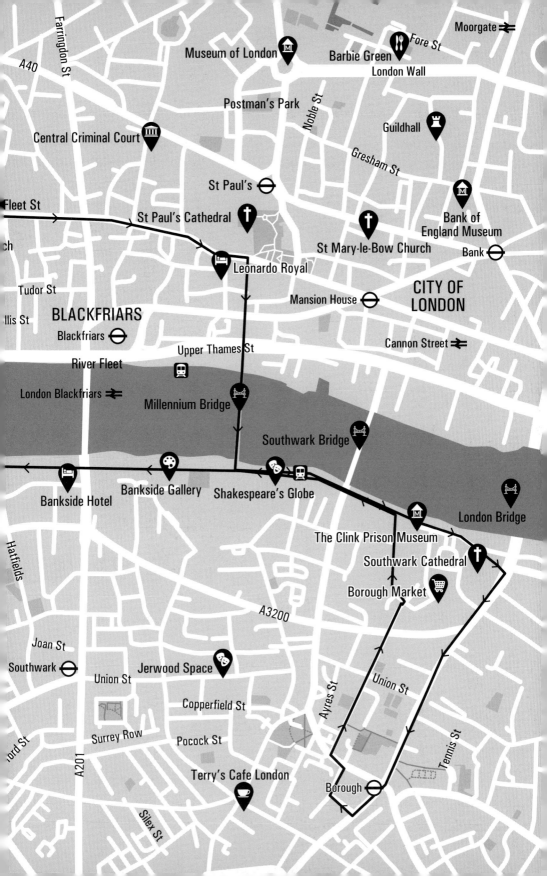

Route

Trafalgar Square
Strand
Charing Cross
Adelaide Street
Villiers Street
Buckingham Street
Durham House Street
John Adam Street
Robert Street
King William Street
Maiden Lane
Henrietta Street
St Paul's Church
King Street
Garrick Street
Rose Street
Strand again
Adelphi Theatre
The Savoy
Burleigh Street
Somerset House
Fleet Street
St Paul's Cathedral
Bread Street
Millennium Bridge
Southwark Cathedral
Guy's Hospital
Borough High Street
Lant Street
Church of St George the Martyr
Shakespeare's Globe
Royal Festival Hall
Embankment tube station
Northumberland Avenue
Trafalgar Square

You can reach Trafalgar Square easily from several central tube stations: Charing Cross is nearest – Northern (black), Bakerloo (brown) and Jubilee (grey) lines – but it is a short walk from Leicester Square and Piccadilly stations also. All manner of bus routes have stops around the square.

George Orwell (1903–50) stayed overnight in the square in August 1931, barely catching a wink of sleep, before shaving in the fountains and heading for Kent in the morning. The material would be used in his first published essay *The Spike* and the book *Down and Out in Paris and London* (1933). He had been a policeman in Burma and said he wished to know if the poor of England were treated the same as their counterparts there. Before setting out on his fact-finding missions into poverty and low-life experiences, Orwell used several 'safe houses' in which to change into the shabbiest clothes he could find – he apparently found the transformation quite difficult as he looked anything but poor no matter how hard he tried.

Orwell said that he wanted to make political writing an art. He was to depict the square in *Nineteen Eighty Four* where it has been renamed 'Victory Square'; adjacent 'St Martin's' as St Martin-in-the-Fields had been renamed, was 'a museum used for propaganda displays of various kinds'.

The National Gallery, fronting Trafalgar Square, is a convenient spot for meeting up – either outside, sitting along the low walls or inside where there are seats among the paintings, ideal for resting tired legs in magnificent surroundings; it has a café with prices for a coffee or meal that are not ridiculous for central London. It is free to enter.

The square was built to celebrate the victory of Nelson over the combined French and Spanish fleets at the battle of Trafalgar in 1805. The column of Dartmoor granite, and designed by William Railton, took three years to build and was finally finished in 1843 at a cost of £47,000, an incredible sum. Nelson has another column to his name, only slightly shorter than this one, in Great Yarmouth in Norfolk, where he used to land before visiting his wounded men in hospital (unusual at the time and one reason why he was followed so avidly by an adoring Norfolk press which regarded him, and still does, as one of their own) before proceeding to London. The fountains were added in 1841, partly to reduce the heat resulting from the sun baking down onto such a large stretch of asphalt and also to reduce the amount of space for potentially riotous gatherings.

Turn left down Strand (often known, although incorrectly, as 'THE' Strand). The traffic – private cars, taxis and buses – and the throngs of people is pure bedlam, so it is essential to cross the roads using the pedestrian crossings. Once into Strand, the pavements are slightly less crowded and also flat.

Strand takes its name from the old English word 'strond', meaning the edge of a river; here, from the twelfth to the seventeenth centuries the rich and powerful owned mansions that stretched down to the river, each with a private mooring. Thereafter it became very much as we see it today, a street of fashionable coffee shops, restaurants, taverns and theatres. It has always fascinated writers. **Virginia Woolf**, who knew the great streets of London intimately, was struck by its character – she writes in *Mrs Dalloway* (1925) that Strand was 'quite different from Westminster', being 'so serious; it was so busy'; **John Masefield**, Poet Laureate from 1930 to his death in 1967, in his poem *'Growing Old'* writes of 'jostling in the Strand'.

Hereabouts, if we are playing the Sherlockian 'Great Game', is the location of the 'worn and battered tin dispatch box' entrusted to *Watson*'s bank, Cox and Co, which contains many adventures not as yet released to the public. This would be the Holy

Grail for Sherlockians and many are the pastiches – new tales of *Holmes* – that begin by pretending that the author has somehow come by the mystical box. From 1888, the HQ of Cox and Co. was at the junction of Trafalgar Square and Strand, 16–18 Charing Cross, subsequently moving to Pall Mall.

Charles Dickens and this area

Charles Dickens placed the adult *David Copperfield* and his *Great-Aunt Betsey* in this location following their temporary fall from financial grace following the treacherous machinations of *Uriah Heep*. In fact, the whole of this area – Embankment, Villiers Street, Strand and Covent Garden – were *Copperfield*'s world as a youngster growing up while his father was imprisoned for debt. These events in the novel are largely autobiographical. The hopelessly grim blacking factory to which *Copperfield* – i.e. Dickens – was sent was near where Embankment tube is now (at the bottom of what was Hungerford Stairs). He worked with other boys, including *Mealy Potatoes*, so-called because of his complexion, and:

> No words can express the secret agony of my soul as I sunk into this companionship; compared these henceforth everyday associates with those of my happiest childhood – not to say with Steerforth, Traddles and the rest of those boys – and felt my hopes of growing up to be a learned and distinguished man, crushed in my bosom…

On a happier note, *Copperfield* tells us that he became an expert in where to buy bread pudding in this area – the 'flabby' sort with currants widely spaced was half the price of his favourite which was much more fruity and could be had in a shop on Strand – and he would eke out his meagre pay as best he could. Once, he thinks it might have been on his birthday, he dared to enter a pub somewhere around here called 'The Lion or The Lion and something', and ask the landlady for a pint of 'your very best ale'. She gave it to him, no doubt considerably diluted, along with a kiss, refusing to take his money.[22]

Dickens worked in this area while a reporter in the Houses of Parliament and produced many sketches from local life which were gathered together and published under the title *Sketches by Boz*. They were enough of a success to encourage the publishers Chapman and Hall to offer the talented 24–year-old authorship of a new publication based on the adventures of a certain *Mr Pickwick*.

Dickens records that upon receiving acceptance of his first-ever story, which was *A Dinner in Poplar Walk*, he wandered around in a daze for several hours, unable to talk to anyone.

The public was initially unaware of the identity of 'Boz' as was made plain in *Bentley's Miscellany* of March 1837:

> Who the Dickens Boz could be
> Puzzled many a learned elf,
> Till time unveiled the mystery
> And 'Boz' appeared as Dickens' self.

A brief Charles Dickens timeline

Charles Dickens crops up all over London and consequently in various of the walks described here, aged from a young boy of 12, referred to immediately above, up to his death during dinner at the age of 58, in Rochester, Kent. He had tumultuous energy, walking great distances and sometimes all night (see Walk 7), swimming in the Thames (see Walk 11) and travelling all over England, as well as to Italy, France and America, and it is sometimes difficult to place him at any given time. So here is a timeline of some of the main events in his life.

1812, Charles Dickens is born in Portsmouth (7 February).

1815, His family move to St Pancras, London.

1817, The family settles in Chatham, Kent.

1824, Charles is sent to work at Warren's Blacking Factory. His father is incarcerated in Marshalsea debtors' prison. It was at this time that Charles lodged in Lant Street so that he could visit his father (see below, this Walk).

1825, John Dickens, now released from prison, retires on a pension, which is never going to be enough to keep him in the style to which he would like to have become accustomed, and financial demands upon Charles, and, embarrassingly, his friends sometimes, are to continue until John's death. Charles is sent back to school (at Wellington House Academy).

1827, The family are evicted for non-payment of rates. Charles finds a job as a clerk to Charles Malloy, solicitor (see Walk 4).

1829, His family moves to Fitzroy Square and Charles works as a freelance reporter, having taught himself shorthand.

1831, Charles begins work as a reporter for *The Mirror of Parliament* and other journals.

1834, Charles becomes a reporter on *The Morning Chronicle* and meets Catherine Hogarth, having given up his initially ardent courtship of Maria Beadnell (although this would briefly flare up again, with the boot very much on the other foot, later in his life).

1835, Catherine Hogarth and Charles Dickens become engaged. He is by now gaining increasing acceptance for his articles in various magazines such as *Bell's Weekly.*

1836, He marries Catherine Hogarth at St Luke's, Chelsea (see Walk 10). He now lives in Furnivals Inn, which is quite prestigious for a young man.

1837, The first child is born (Charles) and the family move to 48 Doughty Street. *Pickwick Papers* is published in November. International fame is quick in coming.

1838, Second child (Mary) is born. He visits Yorkshire schools and begins working on *Nicholas Nickleby. Oliver Twist* published.

1839, Third child (Kate) is born. The family moves to Devonshire Terrace.

1840, *The Old Curiosity Shop* is published in 40 weekly parts; also, the first edition of *Master Humphrey's Clock*. *The Old Curiosity Shop* is one of Dickens' novels seen by many at the time and since as emotionally manipulative and best summed up in a quote which Oscar Wilde possibly never said: 'One must have a heart of stone to read the death of *Little Nell* without laughing.'

1841, Fourth child (Walter) is born. *Barnaby Rudge* is published in weekly instalments.

1842–3, Charles Dickens visits America which results in *American Notes*. He publishes *Martin Chuzzlewit*, as usual in sections. He regards this as his finest work to date although disappointing sales suggest that the public disagrees.

A Christmas Carol is published on 19 December 1843. It is an immediate and unprecedented commercial success. The redemption of *Scrooge* forever becomes a symbol of the healing power of kindness at Christmas. 'Scrooge' enters the English language defining someone mean and cruel, especially when it comes to money.

1844, A fifth child, Francis, is born. Charles Dickens writes and performs *The Chimes* to his friends, including John Forster, in Lincoln's Inn Fields (see Walk 4). There is not a dry eye in the house.

1845, He visits Italy. *The Cricket in the Hearth* is published on 20 December. The sixth child, Alfred, is born.

1846, *Pictures from Italy*, *Dombey and Son* and *The Battle of Life* are published.

1847, Seventh child, Sydney, is born. Dickens works with Miss Coutts and her *Home for Homeless Women*.

1849, Eighth child, Henry, is born.

1849. *David Copperfield* begins serialisation in monthly parts.

1850, Ninth child, Dora, is born. He begins *Household Words*, a weekly journal (see Walk 7).

1851, *A Child's History of England* begins serialisation in monthly parts.

1852, Tenth child, Edward, is born. *Bleak House* is released in monthly sections.

1854, *Hard Times* comes out in serial form.

1855, *Little Dorrit* is released in installments.

1856, Charles Dickens buys Gad's Hill Place in Rochester, Kent, a house he used to dream about owning when he was a boy.

1858, Charles separates from Catherine and, worried about his reputation (and sales) is forced to issue press statements in his 'defence'. It is rumoured (and still is) that he was having an affair with 18–year-old Ellen Ternan, whom he met the year before when she was performing at the Haymarket Theatre. He begins public readings.

1859, *A Tale of Two Cities* is serialized.

1860, First instalment of *Great Expectations* is released in December.

1864, *Our Mutual Friend* begins serialisation in May. Charles Dickens continues his public readings, against Doctor's advice.

1865, Charles Dickens is featured in the national press as he has been involved, travelling with Ellen Ternan it is pointed out, in the terrible Staplehurst Railway accident.

1867, He takes his second reading trip to America.

1870, Farewell Reading Tour of London begins. He is received by Queen Victoria. He begins *The Mystery of Edwin Drood* and only produces six of twelve intended parts before he dies on 9 June at Gad's Hill Place. On the day of his death he put in a full session of work on the novel. It has subsequently been 'finished' by many people with varying degrees of feasibility.

His last words are 'On the ground' as he had suffered a stroke and wished to lie down. Despite an expressed wish to have a local funeral, he is buried five days later in Westminster Abbey.

This author has written *The World of Charles Dickens*, Halsgrove (2012), which contains more details of his life and works.

Charing Cross Station in literature

In the front of Charing Cross station is a copy of a medieval 'cross' erected in 1291–4 by Edward I as a memorial to his wife, Eleanor of Castile (such crosses were granted by the monarch to mark something or somebody special and they were edifices of any shape, the bulk of the structure rarely in the form of an actual cross). This was destroyed on the orders of Oliver Cromwell in 1647, and a reimagining of the original, designed by E.M. Barry and made of stone and Aberdeen granite, was erected in 1865.

The name may derive from this cross, preceded by 'Charing' which was once a hamlet in this place that would have been rural and outside London until comparatively recent times – take a look at the buildings around you: they are not that old.

In 1554 Wyatt's troops passed the station and marched into Fleet Street and on to Ludgate – exactly the same route as this walk. The reasons for the uprising are not entirely clear but the rebels were opposed to Queen Mary's stated wish to marry Philip of Spain for both political and religious reasons and were led by Sir Thomas Wyatt who owned land in Kent. Wyatt was betrayed. He surrendered, was tortured, beheaded and his body quartered; 90 of his men were hanged, drawn and quartered. The Wyatt family lost their titles and land including Allington Castle in Kent. However, Elizabeth I restored these upon her accession in 1558.

Charing Cross was also one of many places in London where executions took place in the seventeenth century. **Samuel Pepys** witnessed one on 13 October 1660. Charles II entered England on 29 May 1660 to reclaim his throne on his 30th birthday. Thomas Harrison

The Queen Eleanor Memorial Cross.

had sat as one of the judges of Charles I. Pepys says that he went to Charing Cross to see Major-General Harrison hanged and thought he looked 'as cheerful as any man could do in that condition.' His head and heart were cut from his body and shown to the people whereupon 'there were great shouts of joy'. His last words were that he would come again at the right hand of Christ to judge those that now judged him.[23]

About two and a half centuries later, *Sherlock Holmes* is here, too. The thrilling end of *The Bruce Partington Plans* takes place in the smoking-room of the Charing Cross Hotel, an enterprise fronting the station itself, still thriving and looking much the same on the outside as in *Holmes'* day. *Oberstein* is tricked by a dictated note from *Holmes* to come to the hotel in order to collect the final tracing of the plans for £500 and here he is duly arrested before being 'engulfed for fifteen years in a British prison'.

Opposite the station, in Adelaide Street, is a statue of **Oscar Wilde** by Maggi Hambling called 'A Conversation with Oscar Wilde' and on it is engraved the quote: 'We are all in the gutter but some of us are looking at the stars.' It is in the form of a sarcophagus with Oscar Wilde rising up, smoking, from one end. The press has reported that some people have been reprimanded by passers-by for using it as a bench; however, the sculptor has been reported as saying that it is designed to be sat on so that you can have a chat with Wilde. He lived not far from here, across Strand and nearer the river in the now-demolished Salisbury Street, when he came down from Oxford in 1879.

'Always forgive your enemies; nothing annoys them so much'

Oscar Wilde

Charing Cross Station and Hotel.

The streets to the south

At this point, it is well worth the effort in literary terms to explore the slightly jumbled array of streets to the south of the main highway. So, immediately after Charing Cross Station turn right down Villiers Street, which leads to the Embankment. **Rudyard Kipling** lived at number 43 – the first large block on your right – from 1890–91. He said that his rooms were small and not 'overly clean' but he was thrilled to be here. The trains from Charing Cross Station, he said, 'rumbled through my dreams'.

Gordon's Wine Bar is on your left a little way down, at number 47. This vaulted and atmospheric establishment has seen many literary personalities, including **G.K. Chesterton** and **Hilaire Belloc**, escape the general bedlam of this part of town by coming in for a – sometimes extended – drink.

Immediately after Gordon's Wine Bar, turn left into Buckingham Street. This is where, in *David Copperfield*, *Great-aunt Betsey* finds possible accommodation for her beloved '*Trot*' as she calls him:

'With this brief introduction, she produced from her pocket an advertisement, carefully cut out of a newspaper, setting forth that in Buckingham Street'

'…there was let to be furnished, with a view of the river, a singularly desirable, and compact set of chambers, forming a genteel residence for a young gentleman… Terms moderate, and could be taken for a month only, if required.

"Why, this is the very thing, aunt" said I, flushed with the possible dignity of living in chambers.'

Bellingham Gardens in **Christopher Isherwood**'s *All the Conspirators* (1928) is likely based on the Buckingham Street/Victoria Gardens area, exactly where you are now standing: Isherwood knew the area well as he had a grandmother who lived in a flat here and he visited often. This novel, published when he was 24, was the only one of Isherwood's to be set primarily in London and was not a success: he later wrote that the reviews were even worse than he had anticipated in his moments of gloom. Shortly after the novel was published, he moved to Berlin.

Samuel Pepys lived at both numbers 12 and 14 during his busy life. Turn right into John Adam Street. Note Durham House on your left: this was the site of Durham House, occupied, between his stays at her majesty's pleasure in the Tower of London, by **Sir Walter Raleigh**. You will pass Robert Street on your right. Here is the Adelphi, which was once a prestigious residential address although much was pulled down in the 1930s. **Dickens** talks of walking in its many alleys and passageways in the period when he was working nearby at the blacking factory. Well-known literary figures to have lived here include **Robert Adam, Thomas Hood, J.M. Barrie** and **John Galsworthy**: there is a square blue

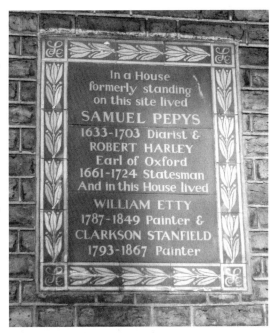

14 Buckingham Street.

Buckingham Street leads into Victoria Embankment Gardens, which has seats.

London County Council plaque to these four at 1–3 Robert Street. **George Bernard Shaw** lived nearby toward the end of the First World War, for which he considered all the involved nations culpable. **Thomas Hardy** worked at number 8 Robert Street as an architect from 1862–7. Although literature was to demand his time, especially following the publication of *Far From the Madding Crowd* in 1874, he was to design his own house, Max Gate, dismissed by some disappointed critics at the time as 'shockingly suburban'.

Walk along keeping the river to your right until you come to Adam Street. Turn left and follow the street back to Strand again.

The streets to the north

Before proceeding along Strand proper, this walk makes a small detour around the streets to the north of where you are standing now.

William Blake attended Mr Par's Drawing School when he was ten – this was situated at what is now the corner of Agar Street, just north of Strand.

Carry on to Maiden Lane. **Voltaire** (1694–1778) lived here for a time – there is a plaque. The Cider Cellars here were a drinking haunt of **William Makepeace Thackeray** while the famous Rules Restaurant has seen a constant procession of the great and the good, including some writers, fictional characters and literary enthusiasts: **Thackeray, Charles Dickens, John Galsworthy,** *Sherlock Holmes,* **Oscar Wilde,**

King Edward VII (reputedly a big *Sherlock Holmes* fan) and H.G. Wells are amongst them.

A little farther along, you will see a plaque marking the spot where the Victorian actor, William Terris (1847–97) was stabbed to death by a maniac. His ghost has been seen around here.

At the end of Maiden Lane, turn right into Bedford Street and right again into Henrietta Street. Number 11 is one of the addresses of Chapman and Hall, **Dickens'** first publishers; Dickens himself would sometimes dine locally, maybe at

François-Marie Arouet, known by his pen name, Voltaire, is celebrated by a plaque in Maiden Lane.

Rules, just mentioned, or at one of the steak houses for which this street was – and still is – famous. **Jane Austen** stayed here with her brother, when he worked in a local bank, from 1813–14. According to her letters, whilst here she did a great deal of shopping for poplin and gowns (including seven yards of material that would become a gown for her Mother). She also went to plays and watched the jugglers and the many other street entertainers.

A gate on the left a little way along will lead you into the courtyard of Inigo Jones' St Paul's church, finished in 1633 at a cost to the Bedford estate of £4,886. The first known victim of the Plague outbreak of 1665, Margaret Ponteous, is buried here. Unsurprisingly, given its location, many famous actors have their ashes scattered here or are commemorated in memorials. These include, in the former case, Dame Ellen Terry and Dame Edith Evans and in the latter, Sir Charlie Chaplin, **Sir Noël Coward**, Boris Karloff and Dame Gracie Fields.

Garrick Street lies off to the right of adjacent King Street. A short walk north will bring you, on your right, to Rose Street. This is significant as it is the location of The Lamb and Flag, known in the seventeenth century as 'the bucket of blood' as bare-knuckle fights took place here. On 18 December 1679, in Rose Alley behind the pub, **John Dryden**, Britain's first Poet Laureate, was attacked while strolling home from Will's Coffee House to his home at 43, Gerrard Street – a short distance away in Chinatown, where you can look for the blue plaque. The attack was probably by thugs paid by the Earl of Rochester, with whom he had a bitter relationship: Dryden had published a poem, *An Essay Upon Satire*, in which he attacked both King Charles II and the Earl for their many mistresses. Despite the offer of a huge reward of £50 leading for information, the culprits were never apprehended.

John Dryden

Quickly gaining favour with the newly restored king, Charles II, he produced several works in which the period is seen as restorative, following the chaos of Cromwell's years.

He married Lady Elizabeth Howard in 1663 and they had three sons, Charles, John and Erasmus, none of whom was to produce an heir.

His play-writing gained attention with *The Wild Gallant* in 1663 but this was not commercially successful. His most famous play was *Marriage a La Mode* (1673) and he made a lot of money with *All For Love* in 1678.

From 1688 Dryden lost favour – and, more importantly, his public offices and the income that went with them – as he refused to take an oath of allegiance to the new King and Queen, William and Mary, who succeeded the deposed James II. In 1689 **Thomas Shadwell** was appointed Poet Laureate in his place.

Dryden is seen as the dominant literary figure of his age, although he was not, and is not now, devoid of critics, and these have included **William Wordsworth**, who was scathing about some of his translations. Others defended him, including **Alexander Pope**, while **Henry Fielding** quotes him in *Tom Jones* (see below, chapter 7). He developed the heroic couplet as a standard form in English poetry.

He invented the phrase 'blaze of glory' which comes from his 1686 poem, *The Hind and the Panther*:

> But, Gracious God…
> Thy throne is darkness in th' abyss of light,
> A blaze of glory that forbids the sight.

Schoolchildren everywhere are now taught not to end sentences in prepositions – this 'rule' is attributed to Dryden who took Ben Jonson to task for this practice.

He now rests in Westminster Abbey. Lady Elizabeth lived until 1714 but went mad shortly after his death.

> There is a pleasure in being mad which none but madmen know.

John Dryden

Make your way southward towards Strand once again – there are all sorts of interesting streets, alleys, cafés and shops on your way there.

Turn left and, a short distance away you will see the Adelphi Theatre. It is the fourth building to stand on the site and was originally opened in 1806 as The *Sans Pareil* by a merchant called John Scott and his daughter, Jane. Jane was a prolific writer of comedy pieces, farce, and melodrama and in these early years, the theatre was famous for what were called *Adelphi Screamers*. Much of **Dickens'** work, adapted either by himself or others, fitted perfectly as his work is very visual and dramatic, and he came to use the theatre for exposure, sometimes making a great deal of money out of his productions. One of the greatest successes for Dickens was an adaptation of his Christmas story *No Thoroughfare* which he wrote with his good friend, **Wilkie Collins**, and put on at the Adelphi in December 1867 where it ran to over 150 performances and made a fortune.

Dickens was also a friend of **William Harrison Ainsworth** (1805–1882) who initially trained as a lawyer but, not taking to the profession, wrote articles and

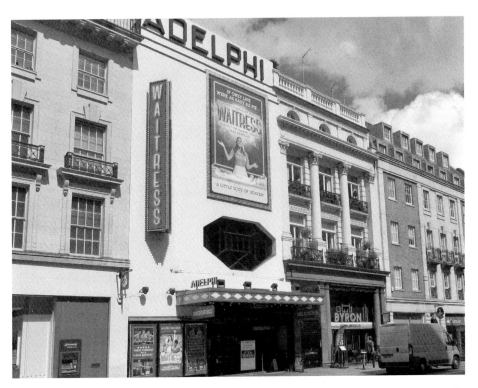

books, his first great success being *Rookwood* in 1834; this was followed by 39 other novels.[24] He is credited with introducing Dickens to the illustrator, George Cruikshank, as well as to **John Forster** who became Dickens' lifelong friend and first biographer. In 1872, two years after Dickens' death during dinner at Gads Hill Place, Rochester, Ainsworth put on a play called *Hilda* at the Adelphi: it was based on his work, *The Miser's Daughter*, but all did not go well as

Cruikshank wrote to the *Times*, aggrieved at not being mentioned in the show's credits.

Someone else who put on plays here was **Sir Arthur Conan Doyle** who had similar success with *The Speckled Band* which premiered here on 10 June 1910. Conan Doyle writes that it was a very quick job – two weeks, in fact, was all it took to convert the story – and this was necessary because his previous play at the venue, *The House of Temperley,* had been forced to close despite financial success, as a mark of respect, agreed by all West End producers, on the death of King Edward VII. This in effect ended the play's run. Conan Doyle, however, having leased the theatre could not afford to have it standing empty, and luckily the new play quickly made up any losses – when full, the theatre could house 1,500 people plus another 500 standing, and a successful season could enrich all concerned very quickly. He writes that he purchased a live snake for the production – 'the pride of my heart', he says in his autobiography, *Memories and Adventures* – a feature not appreciated by all critics, one of whom wrote that it was 'a palpably artificial serpent'; Conan Doyle was tempted to offer the critic a good sum of money to go to bed with it.[25]

The theatre has run many memorable recent productions and these include *My Fair Lady* (1981), *The Jungle Book* (1984–5), *Chicago* (1997–2006), *Made in Dagenham* (2014–5: based on the book by **Richard Bean** which centres on the Ford sewing machinists' strike of 1968), and *Back to the Future: The Musical* (premiered 2021).

The theatre is said to be haunted by the ghost of William Terris, referred to above, who regularly appeared at the theatre and was stabbed to death when entering by the back entrance in Maiden Lane on 16 December 1897.

Walking on from the Adelphi you will soon see, on the other side of the road, one of London's legendary hotels: the Savoy, the main gilded entrance tucked back from the main thoroughfare in its own private street. The Savoy was the idea of Richard D'Oyly Carte, who financed the hotel from the proceeds of his shows and wanted the stars of the day to find a home there whilst in London. Early bookings came from Sarah Bernhardt with her Red Setter, Tosco, Lily Langtry, who later kept a permanent flat there, and Dame Nellie Melba for whom the hotel invented Melba Toast and Peach Melba (see also **Arnold Bennett**'s Omelette, Walk 1).[26]

Just past the Savoy, turn right into Savoy Buildings. This is the former site of Fountain Court where **William Blake** had rooms in 1821 and where he died six years later. Turn left into Savoy Way and past Savoy Chapel: here, **John Donne**, having eloped, secretly married Ann More, the niece of Lady Egerton.

A little farther along is Simpson's in the Strand. **Conan Doyle** and **Dickens** were regulars here at the peak of their respective careers, as were, in the fictional world, *Sherlock Holmes* and *Dr John Watson*.

Burleigh Street branches off the northern side of Strand a short distance along from Simpson's. This was the original home of *Strand Magazine* which ran to 711 issues from 1891 to 1950. It settled down at sales of about 500,000 copies an issue for several decades up to the 1930s.

Adjacent to the imposing Somerset House was, from 1829 to 1897 when it moved to Wimbledon, Kings College School. Early masters included the water-colourist, John Sell Cotman and **Gabriele Rossetti** who sent his son, **Dante**, there, in 1837.[27]

Plaque in Carting Street by the Savoy Hotel.

Simpson's was a favourite restaurant of Sherlock Holmes *and* Dr Watson. *At end of* The Adventure of the Dying Detective, Holmes, *after fasting for three days, tells* Watson *'something nutritious at Simpson's would not be out of place'. Their creator, Sir Arthur Conan Doyle, was a patron as had been Charles Dickens before him.*

William Blake would have come here, too, as Somerset House was at the time the location of the Royal Academy to which he was admitted in 1779: he was one of the poorest students.

After passing the disused Aldwych Station, turn right into Surrey Street and right again into Surrey Steps – here you will find the baths, possibly Roman, about which *David Copperfield* talks of plunging coldly into many times. *David Copperfield* was Dickens' personal favourite of all his novels.

Back again in Strand, St Clement Danes hoves into view, stranded on an island between two roads: here alongside is a famous statue of **Samuel Johnson**. A little farther along is Middle Temple Lane on your right. This was once the business premises of Benjamin Motte, bookseller, and purchaser for the sum of £200, of the copyright of **Jonathan Swift**'s *Gulliver's Travels*.

Gulliver's Travels or Travels into Several Remote Nations of the World. In Four Parts. By Lemuel Gulliver, First a Surgeon, and then a Captain of Several Ships was published to almost universal acclaim in 1726 and went through several editions extremely quickly. Like all of Swift's works, it was initially published using a pseudonym. Some later writers, such as **William Makepeace Thackeray**, considered it blasphemous. It regularly features in all manner of charts listing the greatest novels in the English Language.

Swift was born in 1667, wrote his own epitaph in Latin, encouraging the 'Voyager' to go forth and emulate this vigorous champion of Liberty, and died in 1745. The word *Lilliputian*, meaning a small or delicate person, has entered the English Language.

As previously remarked, **Dickens** used many areas of London in his novels. One such is here where, in a happy scene after terrible deprivations and problems in *Martin Chuzzlewit*, *Martin* secures:

> ...two garrets for himself and Mark situated in a court in the Strand not far from Temple Bar... and it was with a glow of satisfaction, which as a selfish man he never could have known and never had, that, thinking how much pains and trouble he had saved Mark, and how pleased and astonished Mark would be, he afterwards walked up and down, in the Temple, eating a meat pie for his dinner.[28]

On your left, at number 17 Fleet Street, you will see one of the few heavily timbered houses to have escaped the Great Fire of London in 1666.[29] It is called Prince Henry's Room and has some rare and exquisite ceiling plasterwork – it has had many uses through the centuries and, at time of writing, the future is under review. At number 22 is the still-thriving Ye Olde Cock Tavern.

Prince Henry's Room.

Temple Bar, which used to be where Strand meets Fleet Street, is the setting for Tellson's Bank in *A Tale of Two Cities*. Dickens describes it as a 'triumphant perfection of inconvenience'. When recruiting a new young employee, Dickens writes, they keep him somewhere until he was old, …' until he had the full Tellson flavour and blue mould upon him', and only then was he permitted to be seen.

The dragon on the top of Temple Bar was described by *Martin* in **Virginia Woolf**'s *The Years* as 'something between a serpent and a fowl'.

Almost opposite is St Dunstans-in-the-West with its magnificent clock which dates from 1671. It was the first clock in London to have a minute hand. The two giants which you can see at the front strike the quarters and hours and turn their heads. The clock is mentioned in many works of literature, including **Thomas Hughes'** *Tom Brown's Schooldays*, *The Diary of Samuel Pepys* (in 1662 and 1667), *The Vicar of Wakefield* by **Oliver Goldsmith**, *The Fortunes of Nigel* by **Sir Walter Scott**, *Barnaby Rudge and David Copperfield* by **Charles Dickens**, *Elia and the Last Essays of Elia* by **Charles Lamb** and a book actually published in 1653 in St Dunstan's Churchyard called *The Compleat Angler* by **Izaak Walton**.

The two giants on the clock may depict Gog and Magog.

The Church is named after St Dunstan, probably the foremost saint in English folklore before the story of St Thomas Becket caught hold of people's imagination. Notable personages who have worshipped in the church include the poet, **John Donne**, who held a benefice here from 1624–31 and **Samuel Pepys**. **William Tyndale**, translator of the Bible into English, lectured here: he was to die, strangled and burnt at the stake around October 1536, his purported crime being heresy. His last words are reported in *Foxe's Book of Martyrs* (published 20 March 1563) to have been a cry for God to open the eyes of the King of England. William Tyndale is credited with creating some expressions in English that have entered the everyday: 'my brother's keeper', 'a moment in time', 'seek and ye shall find', 'the salt of the earth', 'let there be light', and 'filthy lucre' being some.

There is no proof but the church is also believed to have been the place of worship of the *Demon Barber of Fleet Street*, Sweeney Todd, who, after setting up shop in 1785, is believed to have cut the throats of over 100 of his customers, selling their bodies to make pies (there was a very popular pie shop in nearby Bell Yard).

Fleet Street was once the centre of the newspaper and publishing industry; you will see references to famous newspapers, publishers and, indeed, writers wherever you go. **Lord Byron**'s publishers, John Murray, to whom he entrusted *Childe Harold* – it caused a sensation and made Byron a household name – occupied an office at number 33. Again, ahead of you at number 37 is the site of the Mitre Tavern, where **Boswell** and **Johnson** shared many a cup.

A tavern chair is the throne of human felicity.

James Boswell, *The Life of Samuel Johnson LL.D* (1791)

At the corner of Hare Place is El Vinos, a famous watering hole for journalists during the period when Fleet Street was the centre of the newspaper industry. Turn right into Bouverie Street and number 10 is where *Punch*, one of the most famous and influential magazines of the nineteenth century, was headquartered. The famous *Punch* lunches attracted many influential writers, including **Mark Twain** and **James Thurber** from America, all of whom were invited to carve their initials in the huge deal *Punch* table, and some who agreed to do so are **Keith Waterhouse**, author of *Billy Liar*; **A.A. Milne**, author of *Winnie-the-Pooh*; and **Sir John Betjeman**. **Charles Dickens** attended some of the lunches, too, but for some reason was never invited to 'sign'. Mark Twain famously declined declaring that, as **W.M. Thackeray** had already signed, 'two-thirds of Thackeray' would suffice as far as he was concerned.

Turn left into Dorset Rise and you will see Salisbury Square to your left. **Samuel Richardson** (1689–1761) lived at number 1 writing *Pamela* which is usually regarded as the first modern English novel. A little up the street, a plaque marks **Pepys'** birthplace (in Salisbury Court).

Ye Old Cheddar Cheese is a small pub at 145 Fleet Street, on the left-hand side as you walk. It has been frequented by many literary figures, including **Dickens, Conan Doyle** and probably once or twice – he is reputed to have forsworn alcohol in his later years, preferring tea – by **Dr Johnson** who lived just behind it in Gough Square, where at number 17 he completed his famous Dictionary in 1755.[30] He worked in the garret with six assistants.

Nip up the alleyway at the side of the pub, Wine Office Court, to take a look at this and some of Dr Johnson's 'innumerable little lanes and courts'.

Walking down Fleet Street once more, turn into Bride Lane which will bring you to St Bride's Church, 'the journalists' church'. Pepys was baptised here and **John Milton** is thought to have lived for a while in the churchyard.

The walk continues through Ludgate Hill to St Paul's Cathedral. St Paul's has been on this site for 1,400 years and has been built and rebuilt five times. The task of designing the present structure was assigned to Sir Christopher Wren in 1668 – he had already begun the task of replacing over 50 churches destroyed in the Great Fire of London in 1666. It was consecrated in December 1697.

The poet, **John Donne**, was Dean to the Cathedral 1621–31 and his white marble tomb, scorched by the Great Fire of London, can be seen in the south aisle.

Take a look, too, at St Vedast's church nearby. This was another built by Wren following the Great Fire. **Sir John Betjeman** loved it, having been a churchwarden here.

St Paul's Cathedral.

St Paul's Churchyard was, at the time of **Samuel Pepys**, a centre of the bookselling trade and he tells us of being in a quandary about which books to choose from his bookseller here on 10 December 1663. He was torn between **Chaucer**, **Dugdale**'s *History of St Paul's*, **Stow**'s *London*, **Gesner**, *History of Trent*, besides **Shakespeare, Jonson,** and **Beaumont's** plays.[31]

Paternoster Row was part of this bookselling area as well as the site of coffee houses and boarding establishments: **Charlotte** and **Anne Bronte stayed** at the well-known Chapter Coffee House in 1847 when they came to London to visit a publisher.

If you would like to see where **John Milton**, author of *Paradise Lost*, was born, travel down St Paul's Churchyard, which becomes the very busy Cannon Street and turn left into Bread Street where he was born on 9 December 1608: there is a square blue plaque here. The name of the street is quite simply because, at the time of Milton's birth, this had been the city's bread market for at least 500 years.

John Milton

John Milton was born in 1608 and lived through turbulent times until 1674. He was educated at St Paul's School and Cambridge by which time he reputedly spoke ten languages. He was completely blind from 1652, although the exact cause is not clear. Having argued for the necessity of Charles I's execution, he lived in constant danger after the monarchy was restored in 1660.

He began writing in his teens and published his first volume of poetry, *Poems of Mr John Milton, Both English and Latin*, in 1645. *Paradise Lost* was published in ten volumes in 1667. His other works included *Samson Agonistes* and *Paradise Regain'd* (both 1671). *Paradise Lost* was republished in 12 volumes in 1674. Many regard him as second only to **Shakespeare** as the finest writer in the English Language.

William Blake was inspired by Milton and his work, especially *Paradise Lost*. He wrote the poem *Milton* in which Milton returns from Heaven and embarks on a quest to save Albion – a name for Britain – and in his quest Blake's body becomes infused with Milton's spirit. The preface to this poem contains the words that subsequently became the favourite poem and hymn of many, *Jerusalem*, which begins 'And did those feet in ancient time…' *Milton* was written and illustrated by Blake 1804 -11 and the British Library holds one of only four hand-coloured copies in the world.

The corner of Bread Street and Friday Street is the location of the Mermaid Tavern, which was a real alehouse but has been subject to so many mythical tales that it is difficult sometimes to separate fact from fiction. The building itself was destroyed in the Great Fire of London in 1666.

The Mermaid Tavern is the supposed site of The Fraternitie of Sireniacal Gentlemen which met on the first Friday of every month, and eminent writers included **Thomas Coryate** – seventeenth century writer and wit – **Ben Jonson, Francis Beaumont, John Fletcher, John Donne** and **William Strachey.** It is fancied by some to have been founded by **Sir Walter Raleigh** in 1603 but, if so, he had very little time in which to enjoy it as he was imprisoned in the Tower of London in that year.

There is a well-known painting by John Faed, 1851, which shows **Shakespeare** at the tavern and another by an unknown artist depicting Shakespeare and **Jonson** debating together. **Alfred Noyes** (see Walk 1) wrote *Tales of the Mermaid Tavern* (1913), a long poem with chapters dedicated to users of the tavern, including **Shakespeare, Jonson** and **Marlowe. John Keats** wrote *Lines of the Mermaid Tavern* (1818) in which he asks if Elysium is better than the Mermaid Tavern: many other writers have also featured it in their works.

From here the walk crosses the river on the Millennium Bridge – known for a time upon its initial opening in 2000 as the Wobbly Bridge as it swayed alarmingly in the wind (until it was closed for a time while the fault was rectified). It is not difficult to find your way as you just need to head towards the river – you can even use your sense of smell to direct you. There is a fabulous view of the Thames, up and downstream, as you cross towards the big oblong structure with a huge chimney that is now the Tate Modern.

Note the long red-brick building on your right as you approach the bridge – this is the City of London School. It has some distinguished old boys – called 'Old Citizens' – and these include **Julian Barnes**, who won the Man Booker Prize for Fiction in 2011 for *Sense of an Ending*. His other novels include *Flaubert's Parrot* (1984), shortlisted for the Booker Prize, *A History of the World in 10½ Chapters* (1989), *Arthur and George* (2005), *The Noise of Time* (2016) and *The Only Story* (2018). He has won many awards including *Commandeur de L'Ordre des Arts et des Lettres* (2004) and, in 2021, *The Jerusalem Prize*, first awarded to **Bertrand Russell** in 1963 and given to writers who have explored human freedom in society.

Sir Kingsley Amis (1922–1995), author of *Lucky Jim* (1954) is another 'Citizen', as are Mike Brearley, England Cricket Captain 1977–81, H.H. Asquith, Prime

Minister 1908–16 and actors Daniel Radcliffe, who played *Harry Potter* in the blockbuster films, and Skandar Keynes who starred in the three *Chronicles of Narnia* outings.

Once on the other side of the river, turn left and take the ten-minute stroll along the river bank to Southwark Cathedral. You will see the extraordinary shapes of the tall new buildings on the north shore which do not, however, prevent St Paul's dominance of the skyline. This is an airy, exhilarating walk and one which is also interesting for historic reasons. You will weave in and out a little from the shoreline, under tunnels, into ancient cobbled streets and, in one instance, through a food market.

There are two major tourist attractions *en-route*. The first is a replica of Sir Francis Drake's *Golden Hinde*. The ship was originally called *Pelican* but Drake changed the name to honour his patron, Sir Christopher Hatton, on whose crest was a golden hinde (red deer). You, and the kids, can go on board for a moderate fee. The second is a little nearer Southwark Cathedral – the Clink Prison. This prison, under the sway of the Bishop of Winchester rather than the king, probably dates from the twelfth century – a much smaller prison, probably little more than a cell, has been here, under the same bishop's jurisdiction, from about 860. Debtors, heretics or practically anybody who had fallen out with the bishop could be incarcerated here, to be clapped in irons – the name

Southwark Cathedral with The Shard in the background.

'Clink' is thought to derive from the sound of hammer and metal 'clinking' as this was done. It is reasonably priced and an interesting way to spend an hour or so: most of the 1,000-plus reviews on TripAdvisor are enthusiastic.

You will soon reach Southwark Cathedral or, to give it its full name, The Cathedral and Collegiate Church of St Saviour and St Mary Overie: it has been a cathedral since 1905, although the site has been one of worship for over 1,000 years. There is a memorial to **John Bunyan** here (his grave is in Bunhill Fields Burial Ground, literally a few yards from those of **William Blake** and **Daniel Defoe** – ten minutes' walk from Old Street tube: see Walk 9) and to Chaucer's friend, **John Gower**, who died in 1408. It has connections to **Shakespeare** whose brother, Edmund, was buried here in 1607. John Harvard, one of the founders of the American university that bears his name, has a chapel here and his father is reputed to have been a business associate of Shakespeare. Much more recently, it was also home to a stray cat who took a shine to living here in 2008: the cat was nicknamed Doorkins Magnificat and she has spawned a popular children's book *Doorkins The Cathedral Cat*. Dorkins died on 30 September 2020 and a memorial service was held for her several weeks later, which is a first.

Tooley Street runs from London Bridge station. In the 1930s, **George Orwell** lived as a destitute here while researching *Down and Out in Paris and London*: he took notes and wrote them up in Bermondsey Library (demolished in the 1980s).

In **John Keats'** lifetime, Tooley Street met what is now Weston Street opposite the site of Hay's Galleria today. Keats was a medical student at Guy's Hospital at the time and this would have been a very down-at-heel neighbourhood. Coming home early one daybreak after a long night in October 1816, he wrote *On First Looking into Chapman's Homer* which he had finished and despatched for his friend, **Charles Cowden Clarke** who lived nearby and had introduced him to Homer, to see before 10 am.

> Then felt I like some watcher of the skies
> When a new planet swims into his ken
>
> **John Keats**, *On First Looking into*
> *Chapman's Homer*

Guy's Hospital, where Keats worked, now has a statue of him, seated at one end of a semi-circular bench. The site is a few yards from The Shard – you can walk there from here. Alternatively go by train: head for London Bridge tube station on the Northern and Jubilee lines. On leaving the tube train, follow the signs to the Shard and turn right along St Thomas Street. After about 50 metres turn left into an imposing courtyard and go straight across. You will find the statue in an inner garden: it was given a voice by Talking Statues in 2016, activated by QR Code.

Geoffrey Chaucer and the Canterbury Tales

Chaucer begins his tales in the Tabard Inn, which was on the east side of Borough High Street, Southwark, not far from Southwark Cathedral; the inn burnt down in 1669 but you can gain a good impression of how it looked by visiting a similar establishment which exists nearby in the same street – the galleried George Inn which found fame when visited by **Charles Dickens** and was featured by him in *Our Mutual Friend.*

> Bifil that in that seson on a day,
> In Southwerk at the Tabard as I lay
> Redy to wenden on my pilgrymage
> To Caunterbury with ful devout corage …

> **Geoffrey Chaucer**, The General Prologue,
> *Canterbury Tales.*

The Canterbury tales, comprising one of the most significant and popular works in literature, are written in Middle English and follow a group of pilgrims as they make their way to Canterbury Cathedral. All the world is here – the tales are successively descriptive, rude, funny, moral and philosophical. The host of the Tabard Inn suggests that in order to while away the time, each pilgrim tells two tales on the way out and two on the way back; the winner of what is considered the best tale will receive a free supper. The tales are probably unfinished as Chaucer planned 100 tales but only 24 exist, some written by him for other works beforehand. The original manuscript in Chaucer's hand does not exist – he worked on it from 1387 up to his death in 1400 – but there were over 80 copies made in the next century alone, a sure sign that the tales were very popular. This would also account for the many variations in the texts.

Chaucer himself was born about 1345 into a well-to-do family of wine merchants. Still in his teens, he fought in Edward III's army in France where he was captured and ransomed back. He entered royal service, working for the king's son, the powerful John of Gaunt, and he did very well, indeed, gaining some lucrative appointments. Towards the end of the century, however, court machinations may have resulted in his influence waning.

William Caxton

William Caxton (1415–1492) introduced the printing press to England and one of his first major works was a magnificent edition of the *Canterbury Tales*. He followed this up with another, including woodcuts, in 1483. These are known as 'Caxton's Chaucer' and are held by the British Library.

William Caxton was originally a merchant who spent time in Bruges and Cologne before settling in Westminster in 1476. He produced many documents, including Letters of Indulgence, which were letters issued by the church or authorised person remitting sins and which could sometimes be obtained in return for a fee. This work would have provided a cash flow when undertaking his major projects. The British Library has much fascinating information about Caxton's life and work which members can access on request.

The first 'books'

The first 'books' were pieces of stone or bark and primarily factual – recording goods, food supplies etc. Stories were probably passed on verbally or through paintings. The Egyptians, as far back as the First Dynasty, were the first to use pages in the form of papyrus sheets which were attached to form a scroll. About ad500, parchment, made of animal skin and hence tougher than plant-based material, became fashionable, leading to the production of some exquisitely illustrated manuscripts. The Chinese are generally credited with inventing paper, initially utilising hemp, which was very practical and relatively cheap. Thereafter, Johannes Gutenberg invented the first printing press in about 1450; this meant that, for the first time in history, the written word could be widely disseminated.

This walk proceeds down Borough High Street, past Little Dorrit Court on your right, and the crossroads with Marshalsea Road. Just before the crossroads, on your left, is the Church of St George the Martyr, known as 'Little Dorrit's Church' as it is where, in the novel by **Charles Dickens**, she is christened and also where she marries *Arthur Clennam*, 'with the sun shining on them through the painted figure of Our Saviour shining on the window.'[32] Her father was to be incarcerated, as was Dickens', in nearby Marshalsea debtors' prison and his financial affairs are in such a tangle that no one can work out how to get him released.

Carry on down Borough High Street and, after a short while, turn right into Lant Street. The street is named after Thomas Lant who owned much of the area and let it out, in the eighteenth century. This is where a 12–year-old Charles Dickens lodged, in a dismal back attic, when he was working at the blacking factory across Blackfriars Bridge, and is close to where his father had been incarcerated for debt – Marshalsea Prison. These events are fictionalised in *David Copperfield* and the fear of debt was never to leave Dickens for the rest of his life, no matter how successful he became.

The prison was privately run and was a blatant extortion racket, with a better room, food and drink and even freedom being available for a price. Many hundreds of prisoners, with no access to money, died of starvation and torture. The prison was closed in 1842 and Dickens visited what was left of it as an adult in 1857, just before *Little Dorrit* was published, where 'I found the outer front courtyard, often mentioned here, metamorphosed into a butter shop…'.[33] Dickens does, however, proceed to find parts of the prison wall still standing – see photographs.

Twenty years later a great admirer of, and recognised contemporary expert on, Dickens, **Sir Walter Besant**, took a trip to see the remains of the Marshalsea which he described in his very popular book *South London*:

I think it was in the year 1877 or 1878 or thereabouts that I walked over to see the Marshalsea before it was pulled down. I found a long narrow terrace of mean houses—they are still standing: there was a narrow courtyard in front for exercise and air: a high wall separated the prison from the Churchyard: the rooms in the terrace were filled with deep cupboards on either side of the fireplace: these cupboards contained the coals, the cooking utensils, the stores, and the clothes of the occupants. My guide, a working man employed on the demolition of another part of the Prison, pointed to certain marks on the floor as, he said, the place where they fastened the staples when they tied down the poor prisoners. Such was his historic information: he also pointed out Mr Dorrit's room – so real was the novelist's creation.

The wall to the left is all that remains of the Marshalsea Prison. The headstones are those of some richer prisoners who had been able to make financial provision for them.

Message marking the site of Marshalsea Prison: 'But whosoever goes into Marshalsea Place will find his feet on the very paving-stones of the extinct Marshalsea jail... and will stand among the crowding ghosts of many miserable years.'

Now all that is left of the prison is a wall, which adjoins the churchyard of St George the Martyr, and a circular plaque in the ground as depicted in the accompanying photograph.

Sir Walter Besant

Sir Walter Besant (1836–1901) was a prolific novelist, social critic and antiquarian – although his stock has diminished today, he was among the most famous men of his time. A prominent Freemason, he was also one of the founders of the *Society of Authors* in 1884: the society has prospered and is prominent today in promoting the best interests of authors. He was knighted in 1885.

Walter Besant was born in Southsea, Hampshire and aimed to take holy orders upon leaving Cambridge University with First Class Honours. As mentioned above, he was a great fan of Charles Dickens, celebrated for his knowledge of the novels and in 1876 co-wrote, with **James Rice** with whom he was to collaborate a great deal in the future, a short story entitled *The Death of Samuel Pickwick*.

He wrote over 40 novels himself as well as numerous biographies, histories and other works. The late Victorians ranked him alongside **George Meredith** and **Thomas Hardy** as one of their finest three living men of letters. In 1882 he wrote *All Sorts and Conditions of Men*, a didactic and melodramatic tale, the main subject matter of which was life in the slums, and it sold an incredible 250,000 copies. He additionally published a popular series of books on the history of London.

> I've been walking about London for the last 30 years, and I find something fresh in it every day.
>
> **Sir Walter Besant**

His elder brother was the prominent mathematician, William Henry Besant, and another brother, Frank, married Annie Wood who, as **Annie Besant,** became a feared campaigner for women's rights and was seen as a champion of human freedom: she wrote over 300 books and pamphlets and died in 1933, aged 85.

If you died in prison

The prisoners who died in the Marshalsea were buried anywhere and everywhere, often in shallow graves which would contain the remains of others whose bodies had been treated with quicklime to hurry on decomposition. Some gravestones of those whose relatives could afford one can be seen around the present churchyard of St George the Martyr. The remains of hundreds of others who could not afford an actual grave with a stone memorial were found during road widening works around the church: samples were sent to the Natural History Museum where at the time of writing they are being digitised and analysed.

The Charles Dickens Primary School was built very close by and there is also a Weller Street, named after *Sam Weller* in *The Pickwick Papers*.

This walk makes its way back to the river, along Mint Street, then Marshalsea Road and into Redcross Way. A short distance up, inspect Little Dorrit Park on your right, a very pleasant small green oasis. When you come to Bankside, turn left along the riverbank.

The story of Shakespeare's Globe

> All the world's a stage,
> And all the men and women merely players;
> They have their exits and their entrances;
> And one man in his time plays many parts,
> His acts being seven ages.

William Shakespeare, *As You Like It*
(1599), Act 2, Scene 7

Soon, before reaching the Tate Modern, you will see Shakespeare's Globe Theatre on your left. It is a modern replica of the Globe Theatre, originally built in 1599, destroyed by fire in 1613, rebuilt and then demolished in 1644. Shakespeare wrote plays for this theatre, which in his day could seat 3,000 although health and safety issues today mean that only 1,400 people can be accommodated safely. No metal was used in construction – it is made entirely of English oak with mortise and tenon joints. The seats are also oak which can sometimes be a problem over a long production unless you hire a cushion.

This part of London was not at all for the respectable of seventeenth century society: it had numerous brothels and a bear-baiting pit as well as at least four other theatres which, particularly in the upper balconies, were the scenes of all sorts of immoral and drunken goings-on.

The Globe is not quite on the original site as there are now houses on that, but it is only about 230 meters (750 feet) away. The at times complex and difficult project owes most to one man, the American actor and director, Sam Wanamaker (1919–1993).

He came to Britain in 1950 and, thinking he could be ostracised in Hollywood because of his communist views, he decided to stay. He battled an unenthusiastic local authority, and obstructive officials from other bodies (who would much rather have seen the site be developed into lucrative offices), raised over 10 million dollars and saw his 'obsession' well on the way to fruition by the time he died. He was awarded the C.B.E. (Commander of the Order of the British Empire) in July 1993: he died of prostate cancer on December 18 of that year, aged 74.

Largely thanks to his vision and energy, there are now replicas or interpretations of Shakespeare's Globe in many countries, and these include Canada, Argentina, Germany (there are 3), Italy, Japan (there are 2), New Zealand and the United States (there are no fewer than 8).

You will pass a plaque that reads 'In Thanksgiving for Sam Wanamaker, Actor, Director, Producer, 1919–1993, whose vision rebuilt Shakespeare's Globe Theatre on Bankside in this parish.'

You can have a tour, or, of course, see a play. Details of each season's productions are given on the theatre's website www.shakespearesglobe.com

Shakespeare's London

The population of London in Shakespeare's day[34] was possibly about 200,000 and growing every day: today it is about 9.5 million.[35] It was very diverse, across the board from the Royal Court of about 1,000 to scholars, teachers, businessmen, merchants, craftsmen, labourers, beggars, thieves and spies. London also attracted traders from Germany, the Netherlands and elsewhere so the place was a jumble of accents and customs. Disease was rife and the huge army of the poor was regarded as a main cause and feared: Queen Elizabeth initiated a limited amount of poor relief not out of the goodness of her heart but from a worry that the plague, or something similar, would reoccur at any moment. For many, to quote Thomas Hobbes in 1651, life was 'solitary, poore, nasty, brutish and short'.

Life was also very smelly. The Thames was used for the disposal of every conceivable type of waste, and this was not to be rectified until 'The Great Stink' led to Sir Joseph Bazalgette's 'cathedral of sewage' and the embankment of the Thames after Benjamin Disraeli called time on the problem in 1858. Human waste was also a problem for everyone at home. Neolithic man used a form of flushing latrines but the technology was not practical for everyday use until Sir John Harington – some believe that the American word for 'toilet', which is 'john', derives from his name – wrote an article on the subject in 1596, and installed a flush system in his Somerset house.

One theory as to why the Royal Court of about a thousand regularly moved on from place to place is that there came a time when the sewage built up around them to such an extent that life became unbearable.

When Shakespeare came down to London from Stratford-upon-Avon, of the many professions, producing the printed word was quite a booming business and going to plays (as Pepys constantly did) was very much the form of intelligent entertainment favoured by royalty and the educated classes. We are not quite sure exactly when Shakespeare left Stratford but it would have been following his hurried marriage to the pregnant Anne and after the birth of his twins (Anne had first given birth to their first child, Susanna in 1583) Judith and Hamnet, two years later.

In 1594 he became a shareholder in a theatre company, The Lord Chamberlain's Men, and they produced plays around Shoreditch and what we now call the South Bank: these included *A Midsummer Night's Dream, The Merchant of Venice, Richard III* and the *Henry VI* plays.

He was becoming increasingly famous at this time and his plays were performed for Elizabeth's court. The Globe Theatre came into existence in 1599 after The Lord Chamberlain's Men ran into problems with the leases of their existing theatres. More royal approval followed upon the accession of James I in 1603 when the theatre company began calling themselves The King's Men. *King Lear* and *Macbeth* date from this period.

Where did he live?

It is known that he stayed in various parts of London, including Blackfriars and probably Silver Street near St Giles Cripplegate (see Walk 9); we also know something of his business ventures and that he, or someone of the same name, may have defaulted on his taxes in 1597. However, further details about his everyday life are few. In addition, despite two famous images of him, one from The First Folio and the other from his memorial in Stratford-upon-Avon, we are not sure what he looked like – both were posthumous and conceivably intended to flatter.

What's in a name?

In documents he signed, his name is signed in various ways, such as Willm Shakp, Willm Shakspere and William Shakespeare (which is on his Will). In a further variation, it is interesting that James **Boswell**, in his many discussions with **Johnson** about the theatre in *The Life of Samuel Johnson LL.D* spells the playwright's name 'Shakspeare'.

A rose by any other name would smell as sweet

William Shakespeare, Romeo and Juliet

The details of Shakespeare's personal life are scarce, infuriatingly so, although we know the dates of the plays and a surprising amount about the circumstances of their productions.

It is not clear why he moved back to Stratford-upon-Avon after the disastrous fire which started in the Globe when, in 1613, a cannon in a production set the thatched roof alight. Some scholars think that, perhaps, his health was failing. He died in April 1616.

The Sonnets

The first almost complete volume of Shakespeare's sonnets was published in 1609. The first 126 are addressed to an adored young man, socially superior to the poet. The remaining sonnets, 127 to 152, seem addressed to the so-called 'Dark Lady'. The sonnets have a mysterious dedication 'To W.H.' Who is this? William Herbert, third Earl of Pembroke? Henry Wriothesley, Earl of Southampton? We do not know – it is even possible that it was the printer who dedicated the collection and that it has nothing to do with Shakespeare at all.[36] Whoever the young man was that so besotted Shakespeare may never be universally agreed, but he expresses his feelings towards him in one of the most famous of the sonnets:

> Shall I compare thee to a summer's day?
> Thou art more lovely and more temperate:
> Rough winds do shake the darling buds of May,
> And summer's lease hath all too short a date;
> Sometime too hot the eye of heaven shines,
> And often is his gold complexion dimm'd;
> And every fair from fair sometime declines,
> By chance or nature's changing course untrimm'd;
> But thy eternal summer shall not fade,
> Nor lose possession of that fair thou ow'st;
> Nor shall death brag thou wander'st in his shade,
> When in eternal lines to time thou grow'st:
> So long as men can breathe or eyes can see,
> So long lives this, and this gives life to thee.

William Shakespeare, Sonnet 18

One reason why this sonnet resonates so strongly with people today is that it is clearly being addressed to future readers – in 10 years, 100 or 1,000, in fact, 'so long as men can breathe or eyes can see'.

The British Library has much excellent material on the sonnet as a form of expression and on Shakespeare's sonnets in particular.

Contemporary opinion of Shakespeare

Shakespeare, the finest writer in the English Language, has had his plays produced in all sorts of forms worldwide, more often than those of any other dramatist. Commonly called 'The Bard'[37], it is interesting to hear how he was seen by his contemporaries, which was not always favourably. Fellow dramatist Robert Greene, for example, called him 'an upstart crow' in his *Groats-Worth of Wit* of 1592 – this is probably aimed at him as a man who presumed to compete with his university-educated fellow dramatists like Christopher Marlowe and Thomas Nashe, two of the famous 'University Wits'.

Samuel Pepys was a prolific theatre-goer and went to many Shakespeare plays, thinking some good, others not so fine. It has already been seen how he debated whether or not to buy works of Shakespeare on one occasion, 10 December 1663, at his booksellers in St Paul's Churchyard (he decided against it this time). Here are his thoughts on several visits to the theatre to see Shakespeare.

1 March 1662: *Romeo and Juliet*, 'it is a play of itself the worst that ever I heard in my life, and the worst acted that I ever saw these people do'.[38]

7 Nov 1667: Pepys went at noon with Sir W. Pen to see *The Tempest*. The House was full and the King and Court were there. He wrote that the play 'has no great wit, but yet good…'

31 August 1668: Pepys went to the Duke of York's Playhouse, and saw *Hamlet*… 'and mightily pleased with it'.

20 Jan 1669: Again he is at the Duke of York's and saw *Twelfth Night*… 'I think, one of the weakest plays I ever saw on stage'.'

On this occasion, his evening is made worse by his wife noticing that Pepys' eyes had strayed to pretty women in the playhouse and she chastised him, 'which did vex me'.[39]

Dr Johnson was a great admirer but did not always favour going to the theatre, saying to **Boswell**: 'Many of Shakspeare's (as Boswell spelt the name in his *Life of Johnson,* 1791) plays are the worse for being acted: Macbeth for instance'. Words had a greater power for Johnson than for most people and Boswell says that when Johnson was at Oxford, reading the speech of the ghost in *Hamlet* terrified the great lexicographer when he was alone.

Christopher Marlowe

Christopher Marlowe was a contemporary of Shakespeare and shared lodgings for a period with Thomas Kyd. He was born in 1564 at Canterbury and died in 1593, possibly in a bar fight, at the age of 29. His flame burnt brightly in his short life.

… the first English poet whose powers can be called sublime was Christopher Marlowe

Algernon Charles Swinburne, *The Age of Shakespeare*, 1908

After a very bright time at school and a more chequered career at Cambridge he experienced brilliant success with his first play, *Tamburlaine the Great,* around 1587, and he produced a sequel a couple of years later. Historians are not sure of the sequence of his other plays but they, too, were very well received and enhanced his reputation: we have *Dr Faustus*, *The Jew of Malta*, *The Massacre at Paris* and *Edward II*, which depicted the love of two men – Edward and Gaveston – and has been seen as an indication that Marlowe was gay. There is also his alleged pronouncement when up in front of the Privy Council in 1593 that 'all that they that love not tobacco and boys were fooles', and *Hero and Leander*.

My God, my god, look not so fierce on me!
Adders and serpents, let me breathe a while!
Ugly hell, gape not! Come not, Lucifer!

Christopher Marlowe
The Tragical History of Dr Faustus
From the Quarto of 1604

When he was at Cambridge he was recruited into spycraft, probably for Sir Francis Walsingham, and the rumours about his activities did little to spoil his 'bad boy' image.

Many scholars think that Marlowe had a great influence on Shakespeare. For instance, it is easy to imagine *The Merchant of Venice* having been prompted in some way by *The Jew of Malta*. There is, in addition, the old chestnut about him writing Shakespeare's plays – some even say that he faked his death and somehow re-emerged as the 'bard' – and it seems fair to say that variations on this idea, fuelled by incomplete documentation about his often scandalous activities, will not be going away any time soon.

Walking for a few minutes, keeping St Paul's across the river to your right will bring you to the Tate Modern – there are three other Tate Galleries: Tate Britain, Tate Liverpool and Tate St Ives. For fans of **William Blake**'s astonishing paintings, Tate Britain is very much worth a trip (Pimlico tube). The museum to your left here puts on a huge array of exhibitions and artistic displays. The building itself was originally Bankside Power Station, designed by Sir Giles Gilbert Scott, who also designed Battersea Power Station. Some of the buildings behind it were the offices of the power company and have been converted to other uses; for example, the London School of Economics has converted one into a very large student hall.[40]

About ten minutes' walk farther on is the Royal Festival Hall. Originally built for the Festival of Britain and opened on 3 May 1951, here you will find book launches, popular musicals, films, photographic exhibitions, master classes on writing, lectures and lots of other things. There are also cafés and restaurants.

The Royal Festival Hall is one of several organisations that make up the Southbank Centre. **Lemn Sissay** O.B.E. was appointed artist-in-residence here in 2007. Among many other roles, he was official poet for the 2012 London Olympics, Chancellor of the University of Manchester from 2015 and in 2017 was appointed a trustee of the Foundling Museum in Brunswick Square (see Walk 8). In 2019 he published *My Name is Why*, the subject matter of which was his life in care homes as he grew up: it received extraordinary and positive reviews. He is the author of five poetry collections.

When you are ready to leave the South Bank, head for the Golden Jubilee Bridges and cross over to Embankment tube station. The views of the Thames as you walk across are fantastic: there are two bridges – one to go across and one to come back and some people spend a little while walking back and forth several times, perhaps also taking photographs.

This walk heads left – notice, on the riverbank to your left, the bust to Sir Joseph Bazalgette, one of the great, almost unsung, heroes of the Victorian age for his 'cathedral of sewage' which, although underground and thus invisible, still serves London and can be accessed for those firm of foot in a trip along the sewers – and turn right into the wide, leafy Northumberland Avenue.

This thoroughfare – 'street' seems not quite grand enough a term – was built in the 1880s on land owned by the Dukes of Northumberland. Expensive hotels, especially the Grand, the Metropole, and the Victoria, which had over 500 bedrooms and generated its own electricity through dynamos, vied for the business of the wealthy. Thomas

The Sherlock Holmes Pub.

Edison set up his UK headquarters here in late Victorian times with many politicians and famous actors coming along to make sound recordings.

In literary terms, it is probably the second most important street in London for *Sherlock Holmes* fans, after Baker Street. It features in several of the stories, perhaps most famously in *The Hound of the Baskervilles* when *Sir Henry Baskerville*, newly arrived to claim his inheritance, checks into the Northumberland Hotel where he has a boot stolen from outside his room. In *The Greek Interpreter*, we read that *Mr Melas* obtained clients from the wealthy orientals who used the hotels here; *Holmes* successfully narrows down his search for a man hereabouts in *The Adventure of the Noble Bachelor* based on the facts that not many hotels charge 'eight shillings for a bed and eightpence for a glass of sherry'; also, in *The Adventure of the Illustrious Client*, *Watson* is walking at the Trafalgar Square end of the avenue when he reads a newspaper hoarding on the side of the street containing the terrifying news that *Holmes* has been attacked. And around here is the Turkish Bath establishment used by *Holmes* and *Watson*.

About halfway up, on the right-hand side, is the Sherlock Holmes pub which serves traditional pints and food: it contains a fine collection of *Holmes* memorabilia and a reconstruction of *Holmes* and *Watson*'s sitting room at Baker Street which was set up, originally, for the Festival of Britain in 1951.[41]

Carry on towards Trafalgar Square where you will see Nelson standing atop his column. The walk ends here and you have come full circle.

WALK 4

Holborn, Lincoln's Inn Fields,
Temple Bar and Chancery Lane

In This Walk: The lives and works of the following people and *fictional characters* are highlighted: Mamie Dickens, Charles and Mary Lamb, Marcus Rashford, Samuel Taylor Coleridge, William Wordsworth, Percy Bysshe Shelley, Leigh Hunt, William Hazlitt, Wilkie Collins, Thomas Hughes, H. Rider Haggard, Arnold Bennett, Charles Dickens, *Sir Leicester Dedlock, Tulkinghorn, Lady Dedlock*, John Forster, Charles Dickens, Thomas Carlyle, Sir John Soane, Canaletto, William Hogarth, J.M.W. Turner, Sir Joshua Reynolds, George Soane, Giles Gilbert Scott, Oliver Goldsmith, *Pip, Magwitch, Mr Snagsby*, Thomas Chatterton, Henry Wallis.

Distance: *See page 81; about 2.4 kilometres (1.5 miles)*

Time to allow: half a day

Walking conditions: Flat but with all sorts of nooks, crannies and some narrow alleys to negotiate. Lots of people and traffic everywhere.

Route

Holborn tube station
Kingsway
Lincoln's Inn Fields
Sir John Soane's Museum
Portsmouth Street
Chancery Lane
Temple Church
High Holborn
Brook Street
Chancery Lane tube station

This walk, beginning at Holborn tube station (Central [red] and Piccadilly [blue] lines), is to some degree a celebration of **Charles Dickens** simply because of where it is – he placed some of his most striking characters around here. Some of his fiction based in this locality is dramatic and quite bleak but the area had a happy side for his family, too:

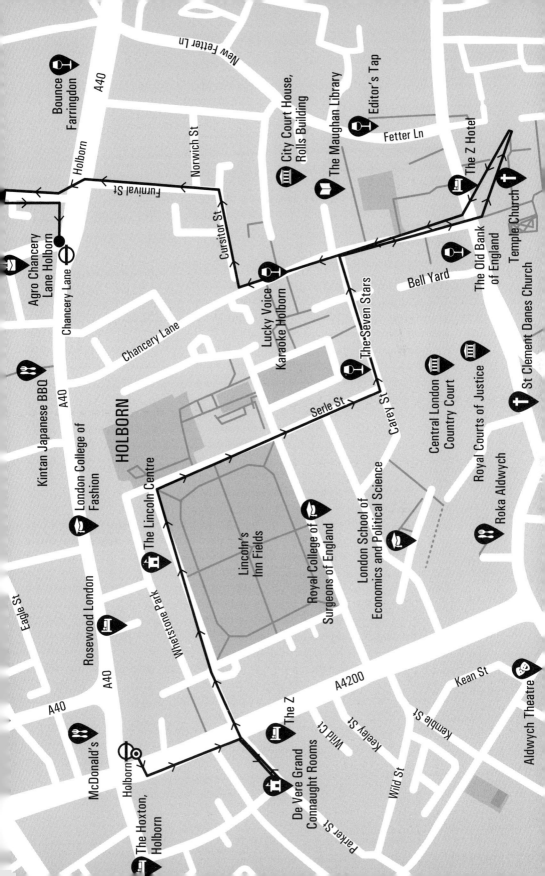

in the 1860s it was a prime shopping location and **Mamie Dickens**, in *My Father as I Recall Him*, talks of visiting a shop here on Christmas Eve:

> In our childish days, my father used to take us, every twenty-fourth day of December, to a toy shop in Holborn, where we were allowed to select our Christmas presents, and also any that we wished to give to our little companions. Although I believe we were often an hour or more in the shop before our several tastes were satisfied, he never showed the least impatience, was always interested, and as desirous as we, that we should choose exactly what we liked best.

Charles and Mary Lamb

Head straight down Kingsway. Great Queen Street leads off to the right and number 7, Little Queen Street, which ran off it more or less parallel to Kingsway, marks the site of Charles and Mary Lamb's house, 1792–6, although they lived in other parts of London also, such as Mitre Court and Covent Garden. It was here on 22 September 1796 that Mary Lamb, in a fraught state following an argument with a serving maid, took a kitchen knife and stabbed her mother through the heart. According to the *Morning Chronicle*, Mary was found by the landlord who rushed up on hearing the dispute, 'wildly standing' over her dead mother.

She was convicted but the jury returned a verdict of 'lunacy' which resulted in her being put in the charge and care of her brother. Mary was subsequently reported as saying that she had come to terms with her actions and considered that she had, on the whole, been a good and obedient daughter and was assured of her mother's forgiveness.

Charles Lamb had been at school with **Samuel Taylor Coleridge**: they were lifelong friends and the centre of a group that favoured political reform and would come to include **William Wordsworth, Percy Bysshe Shelley, Leigh Hunt** and **William Hazlitt.** It was to Coleridge that he wrote wanting to tell him of the tragedy himself as he did not wish to rely on newspaper reports or gossip. He pleaded with Coleridge to send a letter back, adding '– as religious a letter as possible'.

Charles Lamb was an essayist, critic, poet and novelist, possibly best known for *Essays of Elia* (1823). He co-wrote *Tales from Shakespeare* (1807) with his sister, Mary: it was an attempt to retell the stories for young people whilst using as little Shakespearean language as possible – Mary concentrated on the comedies and Charles took the tragedies: sexual references were removed.

They say in their introduction that 'It was no easy matter to give the histories of men and women in terms familiar to the apprehension of a very young mind'. It proved, however, remarkably influential in Victorian England, being adapted several times, and the original has never to this day been out of print.

Lawyers, I suppose, were children once.

Charles Lamb

There is a Charles Lamb Society of London.[42]

The idea of bringing history and literature especially to young people has been a constant in modern times. In 1851 **Charles Dickens** began serialising his '*A Child's History of England*' which he wrote primarily for his own children. This is how he begins his description of ancient England:

> In the old days, a long, long while ago, before Our Saviour was born on earth and lay asleep in a manger, these Islands were in the same place, and the stormy sea roared round them, just as it roars now. But the sea was not alive, then, with great ships and brave sailors, sailing to and from all parts of the world. It was very lonely.

In more modern times, the mantle has been taken up by many people, one of whom is the Manchester United and England footballer, **Marcus Rashford** M.B.E., who, in 2021, published, with Carl Anka, his book *You are A Champion: How to Be the Best You Can Be*, helped on its way by various crowd funding initiatives. He also established the *Marcus Rashford Book Club* which aims to encourage reading and literacy in children aged 8–12 years.

Lincoln's Inn Fields

Turn left into Lincoln's Inn Fields. This very grand square, laid out originally in the 1630s, is the largest in London. It takes its name from the adjacent Lincoln's Inn, one of four Inns of Court in London to which barristers are called. **Wilkie Collins** (1824–1889), author of *The Woman in White* and *The Moonstone*, **Thomas Hughes** (1822–1896), author of *Tom Brown's Schooldays*, and **H. Rider Haggard** (1856–1925), author of *King Solomon's Mines* which has reputedly sold well over 100 million copies, all studied here. **Arnold Bennett** (see Walk 1) briefly worked in a solicitor's practice here.

This is also the territory of **Dickens'** *Bleak House* (1852) and of interminable legal suits which caused people to despair and die. This, in particular, is the setting for the crushing and eternal legal proceedings known as 'Jarndyce and Jarndyce'. *Sir Leicester Dedlock*, one of the parties to the Jarndyce suit thought it was just fine being a 'slow, expensive, British constitutional kind of thing.' It had been designed by his forebears to be the summit of human wisdom. It cost him a fortune which he paid to his deceitful solicitor, *Tulkinghorn*, and in his increasingly sad existence, he eventually lost his wife, the beautiful *Lady Dedlock*, who died of a broken heart on the grave of her lover, *Nemo*, not far from where you now stand.[43]

Tulkinghorn's house is said to be based on number 58 which, in reality, was the home of Dickens' great friend and biographer, **John Forster** (1812–1876). Much of the house was, wrote Dickens, let out to members of the legal profession and, in consequence, inside, 'lawyers lie like maggots in nuts.' It was here that, on 2 December 1844, Dickens and Forster arranged a meeting of their closest friends, which included **Thomas Carlyle**, to hear the great man read his new Christmas story, *The Chimes*.

It was said that everyone wept with emotion but in the outside world the story was not able to replicate the unprecedented success of the story that he had published the Christmas before – *A Christmas Carol*.

Dickens was always ready to fight and satirise bureaucracy. Before *Bleak House*, he had written an essay, *A Poor Man's Tale of a Patent*, in which a man comes here to the Patent Office, goes to over a dozen other offices at a total cost of 'ninety-six pounds, seven and eightpence', only to be confronted with obfuscation at every turn. Later, in *Little Dorrit* (1855) Dickens introduces his readers to the immortal Circumlocution Office, a Kafkaesque place of no sense, no satisfaction and eternal paper trails.

At number 13 Lincoln's Inn Fields is Sir John Soane's Museum.[44] As the passageways are narrow, only a limited number of people are allowed in at any one time. It contains the architectural drawings and models of Sir John Soane (1753–1837) along with paintings, sculptures and antiquities collected over a lifetime. Paintings include works by Canaletto, William Hogarth, J.M.W. Turner (who Sir John knew personally), and Sir Joshua Reynolds. The collection was left to the nation upon Soane's death as he disliked his son, George, intensely and wanted to ensure that he be disinherited, which he ensured by a private Act of Parliament in 1833, four years before his death.

George Soane, Sir John's son, was constantly in debt and married against his father's wishes. Following a stint in debtor's prison in 1815, he published two articles in the *Champion* newspaper criticising English architecture and that of his father in a way

The shape of the iconic British red telephone box, designed by Giles Gilbert Scott, was reputedly inspired by the monument on Eliza Soane's grave. The boxes are being replaced in many places by ones of a more modern design, but this is an original still working in nearby Oxford Street.

that his family considered scurrilous and cruel. On reading them, his mother, Eliza, reportedly said that he had provided her 'death blow' and, already sickly, died two months later. Sir John lived for another twenty-two years but never spoke to George again. Sir John had the offending articles framed and put on the wall headed 'Death Blows given by George Soane.' The monument designed by Eliza's grieving husband and erected over her grave in Old St Pancras churchyard is said to have inspired the shape of the iconic red British telephone box – Giles Gilbert Scott, the designer, was a trustee of the museum for 35 years and he designed the famous box in the 1920s.

At the time of writing, it is planned to appoint two artists-in-residence to the newly restored Drawing Office.

Portsmouth Street leads off Lincoln's Inn Fields and down here you cannot miss a building with '1567' painted on it and which boldly states on the front that it is *The Old Curiosity Shop* as depicted by **Charles Dickens**. It is a lovely old structure and it is easy to imagine *Kit*, in the novel, coming upon it on 'a gloomy autumn evening…' – he thought the old place had never looked so dismal in its dreary twilight, the windows broken, 'the rusty sashes rattling in their frames…'[45] The location, however, is contested, some thinking that the original was either in Orange Street, behind the National Gallery or in Fetter Lane, off Fleet Street.

Leaving Lincoln's Inn Fields by Serle Street (bottom left-hand corner as you look south towards the river), turn left when you come to the junction with Carey Street. On your right, you will pass Bell Yard where, on 11 November 1661, **Samuel Pepys** was taken by Captain Ferrers to a gaming house for the first time in his life. He is shocked

by what he sees – men willing to lose so much money – and considers a gamester's life 'very miserable, and poor, and unmanly'. They go on to a dancing school in nearby Fleet Street where they watch a group of 'pretty girls' dance but Pepys does not approve of the girls being exposed to 'so much vanity'.

Go right, down Chancery Lane. This will bring you to Temple Church. The area around is called Temple after the church and houses two of the four Inns of Court, the Inner Temple and the Middle Temple. The original church on this site dates back to 1118 and the Knights Templar.

Among those buried in the church is **Oliver Goldsmith**, one of Johnson's inner circle of friends (a fact not always appreciated by **James Boswell** who found the man an irritant). He both delighted and appalled his friends (Horace Walpole nicknamed him 'inspired idiot') with his child-like ways and complete uselessness with money – on the rare occasions he had any, he would spend it on a lavish party, gamble it away or give it to the first good cause he encountered. He came to people's attention with *The Vicar of Wakefield* (1766), which Johnson helped him to sell to a publisher and, most famously perhaps, he wrote *She Stoops to Conquer*, first performed in 1773. He died in 1774 aged just 43 and Johnson said that he was one 'who touched nothing that he did not adorn'.

This area is also an important location for **Charles Dickens**, especially in *Great Expectations,* for it is around here, 'at the top of the last house' in 'Garden-court down by the river' (now gone), that *Pip* lodged a week after his 23rd birthday. It is eleven o'clock at night and the rain is dashing so hard about the windows that *Pip* says 'I might have fancied myself in a storm-beaten lighthouse.' There is a noise downstairs and a man appears. Pip speaks:

'Do you wish to come in?'
'Yes,' he replied; 'I wish to come in, master.'
I had asked him the question inhospitably enough, for I resented the sort of bright and gratified recognition that still shone in his face.

It is *Magwitch* who *Pip* is soon to learn is the source of his allowance, and not *Miss Havisham* as he had supposed and wanted. Pip feels embarrassed and humiliated and the tale takes a sad tone from this point. There were two endings, the first of which sees *Estella* married, Pip single and offers little hope of happiness. **Wilkie Collins** was one of the many friends of Dickens who requested another and the second ending, which Dickens described as 'as pretty a little piece of writing as I could', offers hope for *Pip* and *Estella*: Dickens finally came around to the belief that the second was, indeed, better.

Retrace your steps up Chancery Lane and turn right into Cursitor Street. In *Bleak House* **Dickens** writes: 'On the eastern borders of Chancery Lane, that is to say, more particularly in Cook's Court, Cursitor Street, *Mr. Snagsby*, law-stationer, pursues his lawful calling'. *Mr Snagsby* is a timid, bald-headed man, totally dominated by his wife and rumour has it that 'if he had the spirit of a mouse he wouldn't stand it.' He becomes tragically entwined with *Tulkinghorn* and *Krook*, a man with a rag and bone shop who dies spectacularly – by spontaneous combustion. This is a subject that fascinated Dickens, and he refers to it in *Martin Chuzzlewit* and *A Christmas Carol*, but was seen by some as sensationalism for its own sake.

This is an area of many twisting and narrow alleys: Snagsby's *shop could well have been in one of these.*

Turn left into Furnival Street. This will bring you to High Holborn. The large red building at 138–142 Holborn was the site of Furnival's Inn where Dickens had rooms when writing *The Pickwick Papers*, published in instalments from 1836. He knew this area because, as a very young man, he had been employed nearby by the solicitor, Charles Malloy, who was based here.

Thomas Chatterton

Just before reaching Chancery Lane tube station, on your right, is Brooke Street. Number 39, now part of an office block, was where 'the marvellous boy' (Wordsworth), Thomas Chatterton, poisoned himself with arsenic on the night of 24 August 1770: he was 17 years and 277 days old.

He became a romantic hero to many young people after he tried to pass off his work as that of an imaginary fifteenth century monk and poet called **Thomas Rowley**. He succeeded to some degree although not everyone was convinced. It was a general opinion, though, that even if the poems were 'fake', they had considerable merit.

Maurice Evan Hare, who wrote an introduction to the 1778 edition of Chatterton's poems, said that the young man produced 'ancient writings' in the following way. He would first of all write the lines in the English of the present and then translate them into fifteenth century verse by the use of an English-Rowley dictionary that he had compiled himself: he spent almost all of his scarce resources on books such as **Speght**'s *Chaucer* and possibly **Bailey**'s *Universal Etymological Dictionary*. Such efforts, however, were insufficient to convince Horace Walpole, who in his youth had himself committed mild fraud of a similar nature and to whom Chatterton subsequently sent his work: they developed a very frosty relationship in the end.

As to the making of an actual 'ancient' document, when it was necessary to produce one, a friend and local chemist named Rudhall claims that the methods Chatterton used involved rubbing the parchment with ochre or upon dirty stones, as well as using a candle flame to darken the document and change the hue of the ink.

While walking in St Pancras Churchyard with a friend on 21 August 1770, Chatterton failed to notice a freshly-dug grave and tumbled into it: on scrambling out he reportedly told his companion that he had been at war with the grave for some time. Three days later, depressed, broke and probably very hungry as he spurned the efforts of his landlady – according to an early biography, a Mrs Angell, maker of sacques (babies' jackets) – to get him to eat, he tore up all his works that he had in his room and took poison. The torn scraps were swept up by his landlady and sold to Dr Thomas Fry. There is some speculation that he may have been attempting to treat himself medicinally, possibly for sexual disease, and overdosed.[46]

This is the most extraordinary young man that has encountered my knowledge. It is wonderful how the whelp has written such things.

Dr Johnson, referring to the 'Rowley' verses of Chatterton having just been part of a lively discussion when some were read out and which he then pronounced a fraud (from *The Life of Samuel Johnson LL.D*, 1791, as recorded by James Boswell).

There is a square plaque about 12 feet up on the site of an office block denoting where number 39 once was.

Although his death attracted little contemporary attention, his fame grew afterwards. 'Oh Chatterton! How very sad thy fate!' wrote **Keats** in his sonnet *To Chatterton*. **Coleridge** composed *Monody on the Death of Chatterton* and **Oscar Wilde** was to lecture on him.

I weep, that heaven-born Genius should so fall

Samuel Taylor Coleridge

The Death of Chatterton is a famous painting by Henry Wallis, now in Tate Britain. It is dated 1856 and **George Meredith**, the novelist, is reputed to have been the model. The paintings – there are two other smaller versions – were immediately incredibly popular and the images of the dying/dead poet became some of the most reproduced artworks of the Victorian era.[47]

There is a Thomas Chatterton Society www.thomaschattertonsociety.com

Opposite Chancery Lane tube station you will find Staple Inn which **Dickens** describes in *The Mystery of Edwin Drood*: 'one of those nooks where a few smoky sparrows twitter in smoky trees, as though they called to one another, "Let us play at country".'

This walk ends here.

WALK 5

Pall Mall, Piccadilly and Mayfair

In This Walk: The lives and works of the following people and *fictional characters* are highlighted: Francis St John Thackeray, John Wilson Croker, Rudyard Kipling, Anthony Trollope, Matthew Arnold, Charles Dickens, William Makepeace Thackeray, Sir Yehudi Menuhin, Jules Verne, *James Bond*, Arnold Bennett, Hilaire Belloc, Sir Arthur Conan Doyle, Henry James, H.G. Wells, Sir Winston Churchill, Benjamin Disraeli, Beau Brummell, Evelyn Waugh, Oswald Mosley, David Niven. Randolph Churchill, Lord Byron, *Dr Watson*, Thomas Carlyle, Alfred Lord Tennyson, Virginia Woolf, E.M. Forster, Dame Agatha Christie, Sir Lawrence Olivier, Siegfried Sassoon, Sir Kazuo Ishiguro, Sir Henry Irving, Bram Stoker, Oscar Wilde, Richard Sheridan, William Gladstone, Sir Thomas Beecham, Sir Isaiah Berlin, Edward Bulwer-Lytton, Bruce Chatwin, Alan Clark, Edward de Bono, Malcolm Muggeridge, J.B. Priestley, Sir Terence Rattigan, Aldous Huxley, Sir Herbert Beerbohm Tree, Thomas Babington Macaulay, Marmion Savage, P.G. Wodehouse, Ian Fleming, *Raffles*, E.W. Hornung, *Bunny Manders*, William Blake, Robert Graves, Enid Blyton.

Distance: *See page 91; about 3.7 kilometres (about 2.3 miles)*

Time to allow: A morning, afternoon or evening.

Walking conditions: No steep slopes and, on the whole, wide, spacious thoroughfares. This has been an affluent area of London for hundreds of years and remains so today. Every type of food and drink is available, from takeaways to tea at the Ritz.

Route

Trafalgar Square
Pall Mall East
Waterloo Place
St James Street
St James's Square
Piccadilly
Berkeley Street
Bruton Street
Albermarle Sreet
Piccadilly again
St James' Church
Piccadilly Circus

This walk begins at Trafalgar Square, discussed previously in Walks 2 and 3.

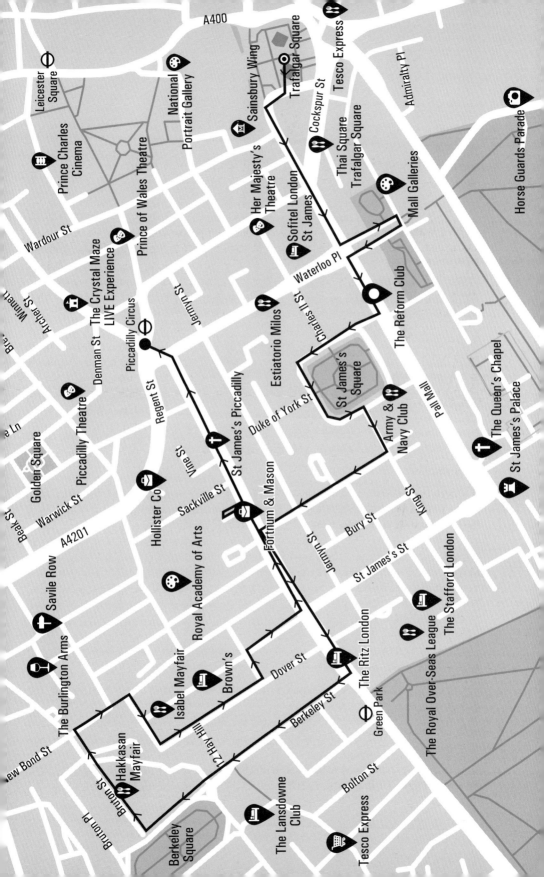

Buses from and to most areas of London operate from stops all around Trafalgar Square. It is also a good place to catch a bus for a sightseeing tour.

Pell Mell

From Trafalgar Square, turn into Pall Mall East which becomes Pall Mall. The name derives from pall-mall, or pell mell, a game, a precursor to croquet, that was played here in the sixteenth and seventeenth centuries. It possibly came from France. There are records of Mary Queen of Scots, Charles II and King James VI taking part in the game and **Pepys** mentions it in his diaries – he comes across the Duke of York playing it in St James' Park in 1661. Two years later, on 15 May 1663, he mentions a conversation he has with the 'keeper of the Pell Mell' who is sweeping the track and tells him that the secret to keeping the ground smooth is to mix the earth all over with 'cockle-shells powdered' but if the weather is too dry this mixture turns to dust and 'deads the ball'.

Land of the Clubs

Several members' clubs were based in this part of Pall Mall – the Athenaeum, the Reform and the Carlton among them.

Turn left into Waterloo Place and you will see the Athenaeum on your right, designed by Decimus Burton. The club was built of the site of Carlton House, a royal palace, and inherited some if its wine cellars.

Many writers have been associated with the club in various ways. Founded in 1824 by **John Wilson Croker**, editor of *Boswell's Life of Johnson*, it quickly gained fame for its gravitas and the number of eminent people who became members. **Rudyard Kipling** did not like it much but others, like **Anthony Trollope** found the atmosphere good for work, as did **Dickens**, who had his famous reconciliation with **Thackeray**, to whom he had not spoken for years, at the bottom of the main staircase: this was initiated by Thackeray who said afterwards 'I'm glad I have done this.'

> …there was something in his mind and character, larger and more spacious, more liberal, with less admixture of anything petty, or unreal, or affected than it has been my fortune ever to meet. In this respect I would compare him to Tennyson.
>
> **Francis St John Thackeray**, cousin to William Makepeace Thackeray
> writing in *Temple Bar*, '*Reminiscences of William Makepeace Thackeray*',
> 98th Volume, May to August 1893

A member and frequent visitor was **Matthew Arnold** (1822–88), author, poet, critic, journalist and, for 35 years, school inspector. He was the son of Thomas Arnold, famous at the time and since as Headmaster of Rugby School. His poetry received very mixed reviews during his lifetime. His 1869 prose work *Culture and Anarchy* attempted to present a definition of culture and was much discussed in Victorian social circles

Looking back from Pall Mall East, you can see the dome of the National Gallery, St Martin-in-the-Fields and, extreme right, the Canadian High Commission.

and this would have included the Athenaeum. As a newspaper man, he was strikingly successful and is credited with the term 'New Journalism'.

Today, on the club's official website, Sir Yehudi Menuhin refers to the 'cross-fertilisation' in the club that occurs quite naturally, 'a plurality of uniqueness, if I may invent so unlikely, yet so democratic, a word,' he says.

The Reform Club is not far away, on the corner of the next block, so to speak, at 104 Pall Mall. It features in several novels, notably **Anthony Trollope**'s *Phineas Finn* (1867), where the main character is a member of the club and, again, so is *Phileas Fogg* in **Jules Verne**'s *Around the World in Eighty Days* (1872). The club is the location of the fencing scene involving *James Bond* in *Die Another Day* (2002). Among the very many famous literary names associated with the club are **Arnold Bennett, Hilaire Belloc, Sir Arthur Conan Doyle, Henry James, William Makepeace Thackeray,** and **H.G. Wells.**

'Phineas belonged to an excellent club – the Reform Club – and went into very good society' wrote Anthony Trollope in *Phineas Finn* (1867). The Club had been open just over 25 years at that time and was the most palatial of establishments. It had a library of books donated by members that eventually came to number over 85,000 volumes. In more modern times Michael Palin began and ended his 1989 documentary *Around the World in Eighty Days* on the steps of the club.

The nearby Royal Automobile Club at 89, Pall Mall organised the Prince Henry Tour in July 1911, which was a race from Homburg in Germany to London. One of the drivers for the British team was **Sir Arthur Conan Doyle** who drove his own 16 horse-power Dietrich-Lorraine, called *Billy*. The British team won the race. Sir Arthur loved driving and several of the *Holmes* stories, such as *The Adventure of the Dancing Men* were inspired by his travels by car in Norfolk.[48]

The Carlton Club is nearby at 69 St James Street which you will come to further up on your right. Originally the home of the Conservative Party, the Duke of Wellington was a founding member. You must be nominated to join and thereafter elected. **Rudyard Kipling** was a member here but, generally, members with a literary reputation have mostly been politicians who 'also wrote', such as **Sir Winston Churchill** and **Benjamin Disraeli**.

Also on St James Street is the oldest gentleman's club in London, White's, established in 1693 as a hot chocolate house, with members today including Charles, Prince of Wales and some say, William, Duke of Cambridge (it is not always possible to know for sure). Past members include **Beau Brummell – Conan Doyle** was to use him as a character in his 1896 novel, *Rodney Stone* – **Evelyn Waugh**, **David Niven**, Randolph Churchill and David Cameron. There is a very long waiting list if you think of joining and then you might be blackballed anyway. **Disraeli** said that there are two things an Englishman cannot command – being made a Knight of the Garter and a member of White's.

About mid-way down St James Street is Bennet Street where **Byron** lodged at number 4 in 1813–14 (it's demolished now).

Turning right again into King Street will bring you to St James's Square and the London Library. It is to this library that *Watson* comes – not the British Library – when *Holmes* asks him to spend the next twenty-four hours in an intensive study of Chinese pottery in *The Adventure of the Illustrious Client*. He leaves, having consulted his friend

Lomax, the sub-librarian, with a 'goodly volume' under his arm, his studies leading to not entirely anticipated results at the beautiful house of *Baron Gruner* who lives 'just up the road' in Mayfair.

The London Library came into being as a result of **Thomas Carlyle** declaring on 24 June 1840 that London needed a new central library. It now has over a million books and periodicals and 6,500 members who in the past have included, **Kipling, Thackeray, Tennyson, Woolf, E.M. Forster, Dame Agatha Christie, Sir Lawrence Olivier, Siegfried Sassoon, Sir Edward Elgar, Sir Winston Churchill, Sir Kazuo Ishiguro** and **Sir Henry Irving**. Over time, five Poets Laureate and ten Nobel Prize winners have been members. Membership is available.[49]

In 2018 the London Library discovered 26 books that they believed contained notes – underlinings, crosses and even instructions to have sections typewritten – made by **Bram Stoker** while writing *Dracula*. Some of the books are *Book of Were-Wolves* by **Sabine Baring-Gould**, *Pseudodoxica Epidemica* by **Sir Thomas Browne** and *Transylvania* by **Charles Boner**. These have been examined by experts for handwriting and style; also, the period of Stoker's membership of the library and the writing of *Dracula* coincide: 1890–7.[50]

Walk on to Piccadilly. This street became famous for the manufacture of piccadills – large fancy collars often of lace that became fashionable in the 1600s – and hence was known as 'Piccadilly'. It is said to have inspired **Oscar Wilde**'s *The Importance of Being Earnest*. Here are some famous establishments – such as the Ritz Hotel, Burlington Arcade, Fortnum and Mason, Hatchards bookshop, and The Royal Academy of Arts.

Chapman and Hall, **Dickens**' first publishers, were located at 193 Piccadilly from 1850.

If you follow Berkeley Street, opposite the Ritz Hotel, it will lead you to Berkeley Square, at the bottom of which, off to your right, is Bruton Street, which was home to **Richard Sheridan**, author of *The School for Scandal*. **Anthony Trollope**, in *The Way We Live Now*, published in 1875, describes the *Longestaffes*' family house in Bruton Street:

> It was not by any means a charming house… It was gloomy and inconvenient, with large drawing rooms, bad bedrooms and very little accommodation for servants. But it was the old family town house, having been inhabited by three or four generations of Longestaffes.

Several chapters of the novel are set in Bruton Street.

You can cut through to two roads that run parallel to Berkeley Street, first Dover Street and then Albermarle Street where you will find much of one side of the thoroughfare occupied by the impressive block that is Brown's Hotel. This was a favourite of **Rudyard Kipling** who stayed here following his marriage to Caroline Balestier on 18 January 1892: the hotel gave them their rooms free as a wedding present. Other famous guests included **Sir Arthur Conan Doyle, Bram Stoker, Sir J.M. Barrie** and **Oscar Wilde**.

The Albany

Following Piccadilly along towards Piccadilly Circus will bring you, just before Sackville Street, to Albany Court Yard on your left. At the end is The Albany or just Albany.

The Albany was built 1771–76 and converted into apartments or 'sets' in 1802. From its inception, it became a prestigious place to live, especially for up-and-coming young men, or those already established in society. The astonishing list of people who have lived here includes **Lord Byron**, William Gladstone, Sir Thomas Beecham, **Sir Isaiah Berlin, Edward Bulwer-Lytton, Bruce Chatwin, Alan Clark**, Edward de Bono, **Malcolm Muggeridge, J.B. Priestley, Sir Terence Rattigan**, Aldous Huxley and Sir Herbert Beerbohm Tree.

It was the home for a time to **Thomas Babington Macaulay** (1800–1859) who wrote extensively about Britain and the Empire. His most famous work was *The History of England from the Accession of James II (1848)*. His poems, principally about heroic episodes in history, were extremely popular with the Victorians and collected in a best-selling edition of 1842. The following lines from *Horatius* are especially well-known and were uttered by **Churchill** and a passenger named *Marcus Peters* during a famous scene on the London Underground in the 2017 film *Darkest Hour*, directed by Joe Wright and starring Gary Oldman. In the scene, Churchill asks the passengers in his carriage if they thought that he should try to negotiate peace with Hitler and thus avoid war: the answer was an emphatic 'no'. Then he starts, and *Marcus Peters* completes, the following verse:

> Then out spake brave Horatius,
> The Captain of the Gate:
> 'To every man upon this earth
> Death cometh soon or late.
> And how can man die better
> Than facing fearful odds,
> For the ashes of his fathers,
> And the temples of his gods?'

In a subsequent scene in the film, and following the famous 'we shall fight them on the beaches' speech, Lord Halifax remarks that Churchill has just 'mobilised the English Language and sent it into war'.

The Albany is also well represented in fiction. The first novel to feature the sets was *The Bachelor of the Albany* (1847) by **Marmion Savage**, and writers who set characters here include **Benjamin Disraeli** (*Sybil*), **Charles Dickens** (*Our Mutual Friend*), **Oscar Wilde** (*The Picture of Dorian Gray* and *The Importance of Being Earnest*), **P.G. Wodehouse** (a short story, *Uncle Fred Flits By*) and **Ian Fleming** (*Moonraker*).

Raffles, Sir Arthur Conan Doyle and E.W. Hornung

It was also here that Sir Arthur Conan Doyle's brother-in-law, E.W. Hornung, set *Raffles: The Amateur Cracksman*. He first discussed the idea with Conan Doyle, who was intrigued. The 26 stories and one novel – about half of Conan Doyle's total *Holmes* output – were a great contemporary success and have stood the test of time more than Hornung's other writing. In many ways, *Raffles* is an inversion of *Holmes*.

A.J. Raffles first came to the public's attention with *The Ides of March* in 1898. He is living at the Albany and plays cricket as an 'amateur' for England and as he is very good at it he gains a fame that he uses to infiltrate the moneyed classes, whom he robs, although always according to a code of honour: as in cricket, it is the game that counts. He is joined by *Bunny Manders*, having saved him from financial disgrace. *Bunny* has idolised *Raffles* since they were at public school together where *Bunny* was *Raffles*' fag. E.W. Hornung had himself attended Uppingham School and the idea that the two were thus 'gentlemen' engaging in criminal activity was seen by **George Orwell** as a main factor in the fascination with which the general public held them.

> You may figure me as gazing on Raffles all this time in mute and rapt amazement. But I had long been past that pitch. If he had told me now that he had broken into the Bank of England, or the Tower, I should not have disbelieved him for a moment. I was prepared to go home with him to the Albany and find the regalia under his bed.

> **E.W. Hornung**, *The Criminologists' Club*,

Conan Doyle applauded the talent of his brother-in-law but regarded the key flaw to be the suggestion that a man who broke the laws of England should be a hero. In the end, *Raffles* dies in the Boer War having volunteered as you would expect a man of honour and patriotism to do and *Bunny* returns home to write tales of their adventures. Such a sad end was seen by most as just deserts.

Leaving the Albany, turn left and follow Piccadilly towards Piccadilly Circus. You will pass some famous stores, including Fortnum and Mason – take a look at the remarkable chiming clock above the entrance. It weighs four tons and was installed in 1964 – every hour four-foot-high models of the founders, William Fortnum and Hugh Mason, pop out and bow to each other – then pass Hatchards before coming to St James's Church on your right.

This church was designed by Sir Christopher Wren[51] and is also known as St James-in-the-Fields. **William Blake** was baptised here in 1757; and in 1918 **Robert Graves**, author of *Goodbye to All That*, married Nancy Nicholson in the church. Many well-connected people and some eminent in fields from botany and cricket to painting and travel, are buried here. The church also had another so-called 'detached burial ground' in Camden from 1790–1853 which in turn saw large scale excavations and reburials largely due to extension of the railway network. For the modern traveller, the church and yard offer an oasis in which to rest – there is a large space at the front and a garden at the rear, both with benches much used by the local shop and office workers to sit on and eat lunch; there is also a café.

The church also has connections to **Enid Blyton** (1897–1968), reputed to have sold over 600 million books and to have written so many – she was an amazingly quick writer, prompting accusations (which she vehemently denied) that she employed some ghost writers – that no one is sure of the total number. She is the fourth most translated author in the world behind Dame Agatha Christie, William Shakespeare and Jules Verne. Her eldest daughter, Gillian Baverstock, was married in St James's in August 1957 and the memorial service for Enid Blyton herself was held here in January 1969.

St James's Church.

Her most famous works are probably those featuring *Noddy*, *The Famous Five*, *The Secret Seven* and *Malory Towers*, the last being set in an institution based on daughter's school. She has received criticism for both the style and content of her stories but her main titles continue to be best-sellers today.

From here, the walk proceeds to Piccadilly Circus, where it ends.

WALK 6

At the centre of Government – a walk in Westminster, Victoria and Whitehall

In This Walk: The lives and works of the following people and *fictional characters* are highlighted: Benjamin Disraeli, 'Jack the Ripper', J.M.W. Turner, *The Daleks, Dr Who,* Jane Austen, Wilkie Collins, *David Copperfield, Pip,* Charles Dickens, *James Bond, Blofeld,* William Wordsworth, Lord Byron, Somerset Maugham, Zhang Yingyu, Thomas De Quincey, Shakespeare, *Macbeth,* John Williams, John Preston, Isaac Newton, Dan Browne, E.L. James, Ted Hughes, Philip Larkin, C.S. Lewis, Edward Bulwer-Lytton, Ben Jonson, Alfred, Lord Tennyson, Samuel Pepys, John Milton, William Caxton, Chaucer, Sir Walter Raleigh, Olaudah Equiano, Oscar Wilde, John Hollingshead, *Sherlock Holmes,* Guy N. Pocock, Tobias Smollett, George Bernard Shaw.

Distance: *See page 101; about 4.9 kilometres (3.1 miles)*

Time to allow: Half a day for the basic walking but longer if you wish to linger on the Embankment, and perhaps tour Westminster Abbey or Buckingham Palace.

Walking conditions: Flat along quite wide and spacious pavements for the most part, but with hundreds of people everywhere.

Route

Embankment tube station
Jubilee Foot Bridges
Victoria Embankment
Westminster Bridge
Big Ben and the Houses of Parliament
Westminster Abbey and Poets' Corner
St Margaret's Church
Little College Street
Buckingham Palace
Birdcage Walk
Whitehall
Axe Yard
Horse Guards Avenue
Trafalgar Square

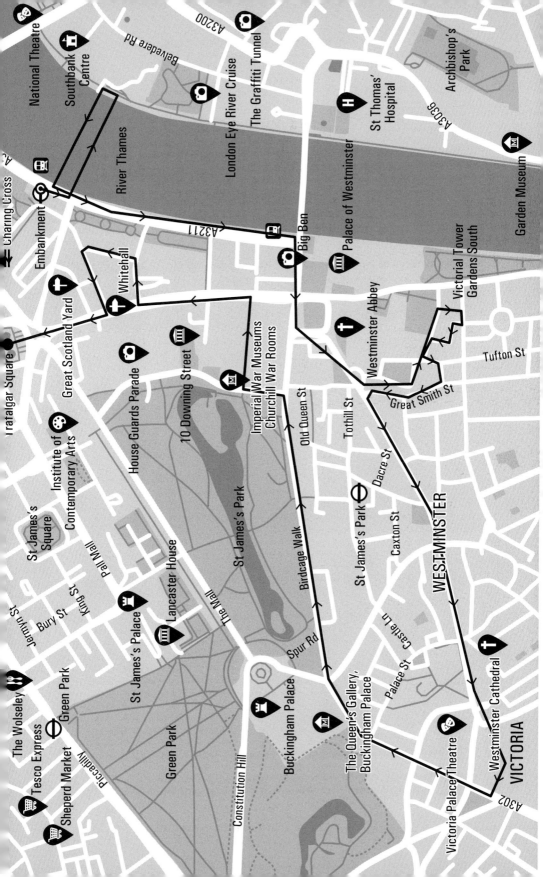

Embankment tube station.

At the beginning of this walk, on your right, you will pass the southern entrance to Northumberland Avenue, a very interesting Holmesian location discussed in Walk 3.

This walk begins at Embankment tube – District (green), Circle (yellow), Bakerloo (brown) and Northern (black) lines. This time, though, we are heading across the water to Waterloo and the reason for starting here is to experience the vistas from both sides of the Golden Jubilee Foot Bridges – the east side, to Waterloo and the west side on the way back. The views of London both down- and up-river are fabulous and make for one of the best free spectacles in the city. You gain an excellent view of many of the places discussed in this book as well as a sense of the scale of London.

The foot bridges were designed by Lifschutz Davidson Sandilands and won a specialist award from the Royal Fine Art Commission in 2003 in the 'Building of the Year' Awards. When you have crossed the river and returned, turn left as you leave the bridge by Embankment tube station and walk up the Embankment.

The Great Stink

The air along the Thames had long been foul and then it became so bad that the work in Parliament was brought to a halt: even the curtains soaked in chloride of lime were unable to hide the stench. This was at a time when people thought that disease was easily spread by fetid air. In 1858 Disraeli said that the Thames had become 'a Stygian pool reeking with ineffable and unbearable horror'. The problem was that for centuries human, and every other form of waste, had been dumped into the River Thames; it was seen as an Empire issue as well – the British Empire was stinking and rotting at its core.

Sir Joseph Bazalgette memorial.

Sir Joseph Bazalgette, a monument to whom you will pass as you walk on the river's edge, proposed the most ambitious urban engineering project ever undertaken – embanking the Thames to create the Victoria, Albert and Chelsea embankments and digging a vast underground sewage system which is still in use today.

The Victoria Embankment along which you are walking was begun in 1865. In 1878 this stretch became the first street in Britain to be permanently lit with electricity.

You will pass a very pleasant, even lush, park on your right – this has seats and one of the table-tennis tables in metal that have become a feature of London park life– just bring your own bats and balls. It also has statues of eminent Victorians.

On your right, you will see, not far from Big Ben, the Norman Shaw Buildings, unmistakable due to their 'stripes' of red brick and white Portland stone. This was New Scotland Yard until 1967, after which the building became government offices. During construction in 1888, the torso of a woman was discovered by workers – the rest of her was never found. At first seen as possibly a medical prank, the ghastly find was later linked to 'Jack the Ripper' but again, this theory was dismissed by the police. It became known as 'The Whitehall Mystery' and the case has never been solved.

Westminster Bridge and the Arts

Westminster Bridge links Westminster to Lambeth and is painted primarily green which is the colour of the seats in the House of Commons. On one side is the newly restored, gilded and painted Elizabeth Tower, known all over the world as Big Ben. It has been a Grade 2 listed structure since 1981. On the arches of the bridge are the coats of arms of Queen Victoria and Albert, Prince Consort, along with that of Lord Palmerston who was Prime Minister when the bridge was opened in 1862. It has long fired the imagination of writers, painters, poets and filmmakers. **J.M.W. Turner** painted a famous picture, *The Burning of the Houses of Lords and Commons*, in 1825 which features the previous bridge. *The Daleks* cross it in their invasion in the twenty-second century (*Dr Who* episode, 1964). **Jane Austen**, in *Emma* (1815) mentions a visit to Astley's Theatre which was situated just over the far side of the bridge (from where you are standing now) and **Wilkie Collins** recalled a visit to the same theatre; *Pip* mentions the bridge in *Great Expectations* and **Charles Dickens** mentions it in both *David Copperfield* and *Barnaby Rudge*:

> At the head of that division which had Westminster Bridge for its approach to the scene of action, Lord George Gordon took his post; with Gashford at his right hand, and sundry ruffians, of most unpromising appearance, forming a kind of staff about him.

> **Charles Dickens**, *Barnaby Rudge*, Chapter 49

Jim, played by Cillian Murphy, walks across the eerily deserted bridge in the film *28 Days' Later* (directed by Danny Boyle, 2002) and *James Bond* finds himself confronting his nemesis on the bridge after *Blofeld*'s helicopter crashes on it in *Spectre* (EON Productions 2015).

The most famous poem associated with the bridge, in fact, some claim the most famous poem about London in the English Language, is *Composed upon Westminster Bridge, September 3, 1802*, by **William Wordsworth**. He was travelling to Paris with his sister, Dorothy when his carriage stopped on the bridge. The poem ends:

> Ne'er saw I, never felt, a calm so deep!
> The river glideth at his own sweet will:
> Dear God! the very houses seem asleep;
> And all that mighty heart is lying still!

In 1807 **Byron** swam under the bridge on his way from Lambeth to Blackfriars.

On the far side of the bridge, in Lambeth Palace Road, is St Thomas' Hospital where **William Somerset Maugham** (1874–1965) trained as a medical man (although he was much more interested in keeping notebooks full of odd phrases heard and peculiarities observed when treating people). He would often go out as an obstetrician to the nearby slums of Lambeth and the characters he met are depicted in his first novel, *Liza of Lambeth* (1897), and the hospital became St Luke's in *Of Human Bondage* (1915). He had long periods as a writer when work did not go well at all but he also had periods of almost unprecedented success; for example, in 1908 he had four plays running simultaneously in the West End. A popular cartoon of the time depicted Shakespeare looking nervously at billboards and chewing his fingernails.

> There are three rules for writing a novel. Unfortunately, no one knows what they are.
>
> **William Somerset Maugham**

Big Ben looms straight ahead. Officially called Elizabeth Tower it was designed by Augustus Pugin and was his last commission before he succumbed to madness. On finally submitting the plans he is reported to have said about his creation '…it is beautiful'. Completed in 1859, it has 334 steps up to the belfry (a lift is being installed at the time of writing). It has developed a tilt – about 20 inches at the top – but it is estimated that this should not be a critical problem for a few thousand years. It was restored to its original bright blues and golds, glass panels repaired and replaced, and the clock taken apart, repaired and put back together again, before and after the pandemic of 2020–23.

This is the centre of government in the UK, and everywhere in the world the machinations of the powerful, the rulers, the rich, have always inspired writers. *The Book of Swindles* (c.1617) by **Zhang Yingyu** is an early book allegedly about real cases in which he illustrates 24 different categories of fraud perpetrated by the powerful which include 'False Relations', 'Scheming for Wealth', 'Marriage' and 'Monks and Priests'. **Thomas De Quincey** (see Walk 7) published an influential essay, *On Murder Considered as One of the Fine Arts*, in *Blackwood's Magazine* in 1827, which begins with an assessment of **Shakespeare**'s *Macbeth* and goes on to consider contemporary crimes, particularly those committed by John Williams in 1811, known as 'The Ratcliff Highway Murders', and which resulted in seven deaths.

One of the most successful of recent novels centring on a purported real crime – an unsuccessful murder attempt – is *A Very English Scandal* (2016) by **John Preston** which details the alleged affair of Jeremy Thorpe, leader of the Liberal Party, and his lover, Norman Scott; it was very enthusiastically reviewed and led to a well-received three-part TV series in 2018 starring Hugh Grant and Ben Whishaw.

Westminster Abbey

Westminster Abbey is here.[52] It gives its name to the general area, originally called 'Westmynstre'. The Collegiate Church of St Peter, Westminster, to give Westminster Abbey its correct title, is neither a parish church nor a cathedral but a 'Royal Peculiar', subject only to the sovereign and not any bishop or archbishop.

There was originally a monastery here around 960, which King Edward decided to greatly enlarge, and this included building a new church, dedicated to St Peter, which was consecrated just a few days before the King's death, on 28 December 1065 – he was buried in front of the high altar. Remnants of the original monastery can still be seen in the cloisters.

Two centuries later, King Henry III rebuilt the abbey in the then fashionable grand Gothic style. Except for Edward V and Edward VIII, all monarchs of England have been crowned in the abbey.

There are also 3,300 burials in the church and cloisters – you can see a cluster of medieval kings and consorts around the tomb of Edward the Confessor. 'The Tomb of the Unknown Warrior' is close to the West Door and a scene of pilgrimage.

To charge or not to charge

One man who failed to see the tombs upon a visit, as he could not pay the required entry fee, was the writer and poet, **Charles Lamb** (see Walk 4) who, in his essay *The Tombs in the Abbey,* published in 1833, recalls going along on a Wednesday to hear choral anthems after which he wished to reacquaint himself 'after lapsed years' with the tombs and antiquities, but:

> I found myself excluded; turned out like a dog, or some profane person, into the common street, with feelings not very congenial to the place, or to the solemn service which I had been listening to. It was a jar after that music.

He writes that the abbey should not be closed to 'the decent but low-in-purse enthusiast' who must 'commit an injury against his family economy' if he is to enter. Almost 200 years later, this is the dilemma still facing the UK's abbeys, museums and cathedrals – to charge or not to charge? Some have a compulsory entrance fee, in others such a fee is voluntary, in some you can enter for free but must pay to enter 'special' exhibitions or areas, and many have no charges at all. It is quite a muddle. To avoid any unpleasant (and costly) surprises when travelling in London, it is a good idea to check before visiting any historic church or building for costs – all have websites.

The tomb of Isaac Newton will be of interest to enthusiasts of American author, **Dan Brown** and in particular of *The Da Vinci Code* (book 2003, film 2006) as it is to this that Teabing, Langdon and Neveu rush to try to solve the cryptex's password. *The Da Vinci Code* has sold 80 million copies worldwide but in the UK has reportedly been pipped at the post in the best-seller stakes by **E.L. James'** *Fifty Shades of Grey* (see Walk 10).

Poets' Corner

Of particular note on this walk is Poets' Corner. Over 100 writers are either buried here or have memorials. There is much to see and many stories to learn. **Chaucer** was the first to be buried here in 1400, not because he was a lauded poet but because he worked for the king. Two hundred years later, **Edmund Spenser**, author of *The Faerie Queen*, asked to be buried near Chaucer. You will notice that the Shakespeare memorial is very similar to the one in the middle of Leicester Square. **Dickens** has a plain tablet. More modern tablets celebrate **Ted Hughes, Philip Larkin** and **C.S. Lewis**.

Some writers are not celebrated or buried in Poets' Corner but in other parts of the abbey – **Edward Bulwer-Lytton**, for example, and **Ben Jonson**, who has a memorial in the north aisle of the nave.

Alfred Lord Tennyson

Alfred, Lord Tennyson (1809–92) has a memorial here: he was Poet Laureate for 42 years, 'the grand old man of Victorian poetry', and beloved by the Victorian people but not very often by the critics – and his reputation was to fall further, before rising again, following his death. He minded the criticism he received very much and he undertook therapy for depression.

His fame grew particularly following *In Memoriam A.H.H.* which he composed over many years in tribute to his beloved friend, Arthur Hallam, who suddenly died at the age of 22: it was finally published in 1850. This was the year that he succeeded **William Wordsworth** as Poet Laureate. Queen Victoria was a great admirer, declaring his poetry, particularly the above, a great solace after the death of her adored Prince Albert, and on four occasions offered him a baronetcy which he declined. When he eventually accepted a peerage from Gladstone, he declared that he did so on behalf of literature.

Today, two of his most oft-quoted works are *The Lady of Shalott* (1833 and another version with a different ending in 1842) and *The Charge of the Light Brigade* (1854) about the charge of The Light Brigade at the Battle of Balaclava in the Crimean War. The poem celebrates the courage of British Light Brigade soldiers who, misinterpreting an order from their commander, roared into the enemy guns. The language used is thundering and relentless. Stanza II reads:

> 'Forward, the Light Brigade!'
> Was there a man dismayed?
> Not though the soldier knew
> Someone had blundered.
> Theirs not to make reply,
> Theirs not to reason why,

Theirs but to do and die.
Into the valley of Death
Rode the six hundred.

He is credited with some additions to the English Language and these include 'Tis better to have loved and lost / Than never to have loved at all'.

11,000 people applied for tickets to his funeral in the Abbey but there was room for only 1,000.

St Margaret's Church

St Margaret's Church stands alongside the Abbey. This was built in the twelfth century for a very unusual reason: the monks in the abbey found that the everyday and noisy incursion of citizens into the abbey for services and other church-related business detracted from their communion with God, and St Margaret's was built to give the people somewhere else to go and thus leave the monks in peace. It is dedicated to St Margaret of Antioch, of whom little is known. Rebuilt and restored many times over the years, it is nevertheless much as it was after some major changes led to its consecration on 9 April 1523.

St Margaret's is of particular interest in the context of this walk because of the people buried here. **William Caxton**, the first printer of Chaucer's *Canterbury Tales*, has a memorial here following his death in 1491. Following his execution in nearby Old Palace Yard on 29 October 1618, **Sir Walter Raleigh**'s head was embalmed and presented to his wife and his body laid to rest in the church: legend has it that she kept the head in a red velvet bag. This story maintains that 29 years later, following his wife's death, the head was placed in his tomb.

Raleigh's last last words are reported to have been to his executioner who was hesitant to complete his task. Having inspected the axe and remarked upon its sharpness, Raleigh reputedly said 'What dost thou fear? Strike, man, strike!'

Samuel Pepys held his wedding in the church on 1 December, 1655, when he was 22 and his wife, Elizabeth, 15.

Olaudah Equiano

Olaudah Equiano was baptised in the church in February 1759, aged 12. Born in what is today southern Nigeria, he was bought and sold as a slave several times and was given at least three 'new' names by those who paid the money, including 'Gustavus Vassa' by which he was known most of his life. Eventually able to purchase his freedom for the sum of 40 pounds when he was twenty, he became a successful businessman and campaigner for abolition. He eventually settled in England. In 1789 he published his autobiography, *The Interesting Narrative of the Life of Olaudah Equiano, or Gustavus Vassa, the African*, which became an enormous success, the first edition selling out almost immediately.

The book is dedicated 'To the Lords Spiritual and Temporal, and the Commons of the Parliament of Great Britain' and lists The Prince of Wales and the Duke of York among the subscribers. He writes that he desires to excite in their 'august assemblies' compassion for the miseries which the Slave Trade has inflicted upon his fellow countrymen, and that murder, torture and 'every other imaginable barbarity and iniquity' is being practised upon slaves without any recourse. He ends by hoping that abolition may be imminent.

The book was massively influential: here was an educated and intelligent man with direct and horrifying first-hand accounts of slavery. Equiano died in 1797 leaving behind his wife and two daughters. Ten years later, Britain formally abolished the slave trade.

A few yards from the Abbey is Little College Street in an area known once as 'Devil's Acre': **Oscar Wilde** may have used a male brothel here. **Dickens** was one of many writers who saw such an area, reeking of poverty and suffering a terrible cholera epidemic in the nineteenth century, as quite unacceptable, especially a few yards from the very heart of the British Empire: he wrote of it in his role as a young parliamentary reporter before his great fame and then, afterwards as the greatest novelist of the age, in his weekly publication, *Household Words*. John Hollingshead wrote an influential book about the area in 1861 called *Ragged London*.[53]

We are each our own devil, and we make this world our hell

Oscar Wilde, The Duchess of Padua

Two minutes from College Street is Barton Street and number 14 has a blue plaque commemorating **T.E. Lawrence**, 'Lawrence of Arabia', who became a sensation with the publication of his *Seven Pillars of Wisdom* in 1926: it was produced on a 'high-priced subscription' business model. The legendary film, *Lawrence of Arabia*, came out in 1962, directed by David Lean and starring Peter O'Toole. It won seven Academy Awards. Proceed down Victoria Street. From Victoria Station walk to Terminus Place and turn right into Buckingham Palace Road.

Here is Buckingham Palace. The Palace is an extended and modified version of Buckingham House, built for the Duke of Buckingham in 1703. It is the London residence of the monarch of the United Kingdom and has 775 rooms and the largest private garden in London. Tours are available from July to October, either of the grounds only or the palace also. You should allow about 3 hours for the extended tour and booking is essential. Tickets can be bought online.

When you are ready to leave Buckingham Palace, take Birdcage Walk – so-called because King James I kept many of his precious exotic birds in cages along this street – which is along the southern side of St James's Park. At the extremity of the park, turn left up Horse Guards Road and then right into King Charles Street. This will be familiar to *Sherlock Holmes* fans: *Percy Phelps* ran to the side door of his offices on this street, which he found unlocked after he had discovered that important documents were missing in *The Naval Treaty*. There was no one outside, although great activity in Whitehall. Turn left into Whitehall.

Passing the Cenotaph on your right, you will soon see Downing Street on your left. Number 10 is the official residence and office of the Prime Minister, one of the most famous addresses in the world. The original building on the site was the Axe brewery,

KING CHARLES STREET SW1

CITY OF WESTMINSTER

owned by the Abbey of Abingdon in the Middle Ages. This gave its name to Axe Yard which is where **Samuel Pepys** was living with his wife and a single servant in 1659–60, when the legendary *Diary* begins.

The Diary of Samuel Pepys

The Diary of Samuel Pepys is probably the most intimate book in history, alongside, perhaps, Boswell's account of the life of Dr Johnson. It is described by **Guy N. Pocock**, in the introduction to the influential edition published by J.M. Dent in 1925, as on a plane of intimacy more close than between living friends: there is silliness, weakness and fear here as we see him go to sleep in church, be scolded by his wife for his wandering eye during a **Shakespeare** play, and spend plentiful sums on fine clothes and wigs. We also watch him working extremely hard for the navy and mixing with the highest in the land over business and dinner. Then of course, and probably most famously, we hear his hour-by-hour account of the Great Fire of London and how it affected his household. In short, we experience an extraordinarily rich life in vivid detail.

The Diaries do not appear to have been written for posterity but purely for his own satisfaction as they were written in a kind of code. Between 1819 and 1822, John Smith, the vicar of Baldock 'decoded' the document.

Tobias Smollett, a surgeon as well as the writer of picaresque novels and many books, including *A Complete History of England*, which he wrote 1757–65 and considered his master work, established a practice in Downing Street at the end of his Navy commission. (see chapter 10 for details of Smollett's literary works)

A little farther up you will see Horse Guards Avenue to your right: turn up here and left into Whitehall Court where there is an enormous block of apartments looking out onto Whitehall Gardens and the Embankment. **George Bernard Shaw** owned number 4 from 1928 to 1945. Turning left again and walking up Whitehall Place will bring you back to Whitehall.

Turn right and proceed up Whitehall until you see Nelson on top of his column. This is Trafalgar Square where this walk ends.

Approaching Trafalgar Square with Nelson on top of his column, the dome of the National Gallery to the left and the spire of St Martin-in-the Fields on the right.

WALK 7

Tottenham Court Road, around the British Museum and Covent Garden

In This Walk: The lives and works of the following people and *fictional characters* are highlighted: Charles Dickens, Wyndham Lewis, Algernon Charles Swinburne, Dante Gabriel Rossetti, Samuel Taylor Coleridge, George Bernard Shaw, Virginia Woolf, William Makepeace Thackeray, Henry Baker, *Sherlock Holmes*, Wilkie Collins, J.K. Rowling, Dame Agatha Christie, Ian McEwan, Saki, E.M. Forster, H.G. Wells, John Mortimer, Weedon Grossmith, Robert Bridges, John Middleton Murry, George Orwell, Sir Hans Sloane, Ayuba Suleiman Diallo, Robert Haydon, John Keats, Karl Marx, Lenin, Bram Stoker, Charles Lamb, Lewis Carroll, Oscar Wilde, Henry Fielding, *Tom Jones*, Samuel Pepys, *Eliza Doolittle*, Thomas De Quincy, *Inspector Bucket,* John Gay, Henry James, John Dryden, Charles Macklin, Joseph Grimaldi, Alexander Pope, Tobias Smollett, William Congreve, James Boswell, Samuel Johnson, *Dracula.*

Distance: *See page 113; about 4.3 kilometres (about 2.7 miles)*

Time to allow: 2–3 hours for the basic walking, but as this trip includes visits to the British Museum as well as to Covent Garden with all its eateries, pubs, theatres and free street shows, there is, practically speaking, no upper time limit.

Walking conditions: Very busy with thousands of residents and visitors everywhere. Basically flat. Some narrow pavements.

Route

Tottenham Court Road tube station
Tottenham Court Road
Percy Street
Newman Street
Berners Street
Mortimer Street
Tottenham Court Road
Fitzroy Square
Tottenham Court Road again
Bayley Street
Bedford Square
Russell Square

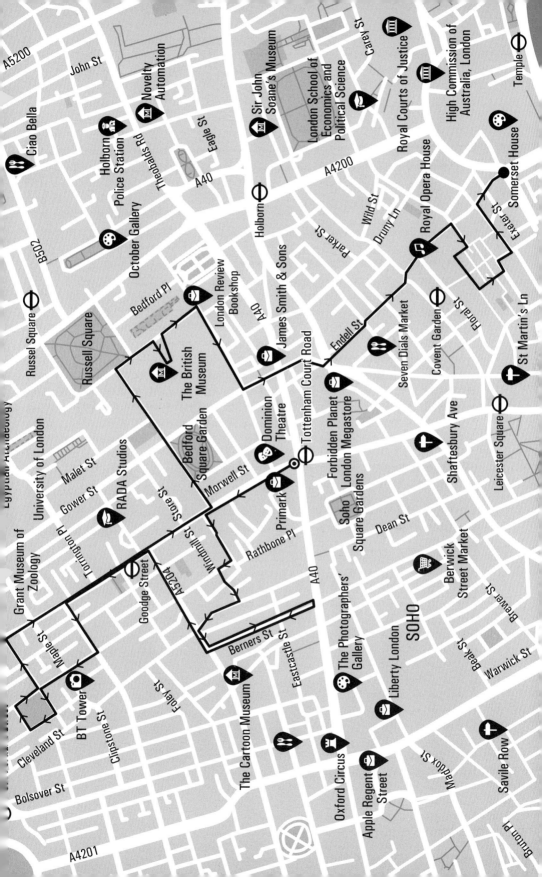

Montague Street
British Museum
Covent Garden

This walk begins at Tottenham Court Road tube station which is on the Central (red) and Northern (black) lines. Once you could travel from here to the next stop, 'British Museum', but that is closed now. In **Charles Dickens**' day, this was the station for St Giles, a dreadful slum which had been immortalised a few years previously by Dickens in *Bell's Life* where he wrote of 'dirty men, filthy women, squalid children, fluttering shuttlecocks, noisy battledores, reeking pies, bad fruit, more than doubtful oysters, attenuated cats, depressed dogs and anatomical fowls….' It had been through here in the eighteenth century that the carts full of those destined to be hanged would pass, as mentioned in Walk 1.

The name of the area derives from the manor estate of Tottenham Court. In the eighteenth century, a famous fair took place for fourteen consecutive days here, beginning on 4 August. There would be theatrical productions, not unlike a Georgian Edinburgh Fringe Festival, music, drinking, cock-fighting, bull-baiting and the settlement of 'bouts of honour' in the boxing ring between men and between women; the instigator needed to put up an advertisement beforehand according to a fixed set of rules.

On leaving the tube, the immediate area is dominated by Centre Point, a 34–storey skyscraper, completed in 1966 and built using pre-cast panels of crushed Portland stone originating in Dorset.

About three hundred metres along, turn left into Percy Street, home of the author and painter, **Wyndham Lewis** (1882–1957). Take, first, Percy Passage and then

Newman Passage and you will have cut through to Newman Street where both poets **Algernon Charles Swinburne** (1837–1909) and **Dante Gabriel Rossetti** (1828–1882) lived or worked. Walk up towards Goodge Street and, at the top, turn left and take the second left into Berners

Street, home briefly in 1812 to **Samuel Taylor Coleridge** – you will see a blue plaque at number 71. The Middlesex Hospital, where **Kipling** died, was once in this area but closed in 2005 and the site has been redeveloped.

At the top of Berners Street, turn right into Mortimer Street and carry straight on until you reach Tottenham Court Road where you turn left. Walk straight on, passing Goodge Street tube station on your left until you come to Grafton Way where a left turn will shortly bring you to Fitzroy Square. A plaque at number 29 denotes that this was home to **George Bernard Shaw**, with his mother, in 1887. **Virginia Stephen**, later Woolf, also lived here with her brother, Adrian, 1907–11. This is only one of eighteen houses in London to have two plaques; some individuals have more – **William Makepeace Thackeray,** for example, has three.

Leave the square by Fitzroy Street where **Charles Dickens** and his family stayed for a while, possibly at number 25 but the exact number is disputed, in 1832 when Dickens was 20 and an aspiring political correspondent. Turn left into Howland Street and re-join Tottenham Court Road.

Walk along Tottenham Court Road with Centre Point in front of you. It is not difficult to imagine being back in 1892 and walking along this street of plumbers, pawnbrokers, locksmiths, grocers and other small businesses, with a big postal sorting office at the Tottenham Court Road end. It is about four on Christmas morning and, about a kilometre along, just after Goodge Street tube station on the right, a tallish man looms out of the gaslight. His name, we later learn, is *Henry Baker*. He has a white goose slung over his shoulder. Staggering slightly as he is a little drunk, he is set upon by a gang of men, one of whom knocks off his hat. He raises his stick to defend himself but he only succeeds in smashing the shop window behind him. A man dressed in an official-looking commissionaire's uniform who goes by the name of *Peterson*, an honest fellow well known to the great detective *Sherlock Holmes*, is fortuitously passing by and runs forward to assist. The man, however, is scared by *Peterson* who in the relative gloom resembles a policeman, and fearing arrest for the damage he has caused, *Henry Baker* drops the goose. He runs as fast as he can towards Oxford Street and vanishes 'in the labyrinth of small streets which lie at the back of Tottenham Court Road'. This is how the favourite Christmas *Sherlock Holmes* story of many people, *The Adventure of the Blue Carbuncle*, starts.

Tottenham Court Road is mentioned in many books by a variety of authors, including Wilkie Collins, Virginia Woolf, J. K. Rowling, Dame Agatha Christie, Ian McEwan, Saki, E. M. Forster, H. G. Wells, Bernard Shaw and John Mortimer.

PICKERING [gently] What is it you want, my girl?
THE FLOWER GIRL. I want to be a lady in a flower shop stead of selling at the corner of Tottenham Court Road. But they won't take me unless I can talk more

genteel. He said he could teach me. Well, here I am ready to pay him – not asking any favour – and he treats me as if I was dirt.

Bernard Shaw, *Pygmalion* (1912).

Leading off the main thoroughfare, on your left once you have passed Goodge Street Station you will see Bayley Street which leads straight on to Bedford Square. Following the success of *The Diary of A Nobody*, **Weedon Grossmith** lived at number 1, 1902–19. The future Poet Laureate, **Robert Bridges** (1844–1930) lived as a young man at number 52.

Running down the side of Bedford Square is Bloomsbury Street, which is where **John Middleton Murry** set up *Adelphi* through which **George Orwell** initially came to public attention.

The Square leads to Montague Place at the end of which is Russell Square.

Montague Street – where *Sherlock Holmes* initially had lodgings when he came up to London, as we learn in *The Musgrave Ritual* – leads to a T-junction with Great Russell Street and turning right here will bring you to the main entrance of the British

Museum, which was founded in 1753, principally comprising the collections of Sir Hans Sloane. It now has over 8 million works, many acquired during the expansion of the British Empire. The Natural History Museum was formed as a branch institution in 1881. The British Library, which

is estimated to have between 170 and 200 million items, moved to its own site near King's Cross Station and was officially opened by Her Majesty the Queen in 1998. The ownership of some objects, such as the Parthenon Marbles, especially at the time of writing, is disputed. It is one of the greatest museums in the world, an essential visit for everyone, and is currently free to enter although a donation of £5 is encouraged; some parts and exhibition areas may levy a charge if you wish to include these in your visit. It is open every day from 10.00 am to 5.30 pm with a late-night on Fridays until 20.30.[54]

Ayuba Suleiman Diallo

One of the remarkable men to have played a minor part in the formation of the British Museum was Ayuba Suleiman Diallo (1701–73). He was born in Bundu, Senegal, son of a leader who traded in slaves until Diallo himself was captured and taken. He was shipped to America where his perceived nobility, piety and literacy encouraged his captors to ship him on to England. Here, during 1773–4, he was used by several people to translate Arabic, and this included Hans Sloane of the British Museum, who also had him catalogue and organise some of the collections. While in England, he was referred to as Job ben Solomon. Returning to Africa, he found that one of his two wives, thinking him dead, had remarried: he forgave her saying she could not possibly have known the circumstances of his life.

Thomas Bluett, a British judge who met Diallo in jail, encouraged him to tell his life story which was published in 1734 as '*Some Memoirs of the Life of Job, the Son of Solomon, the High Priest of Boonda in Africa; Who was a Slave About Two Years in Maryland; and Afterwards Being Brought to England, was Set Free, and Sent to His Native Land in the Year 1734*'. This was one of the earliest slave narratives.

A portrait of Diallo was painted by William Hoare in 1733. It was following a visit to see the Elgin Marbles in March 1817 with his friend, the painter, Robert Haydon, that **John Keats** wrote *Ode on a Grecian Urn*.

The Reading Room was constructed over three years, opening on 2 May 1857, and among those initially granted tickets to use it were **Charles Dickens, Karl Marx, Lenin** (studying under the name Jacob Richter), **Sir Arthur Conan Doyle** and **Bram Stoker**. In *Dracula*, the narrator, *Jonathan Harker*, writes 'Having had some time at my disposal when in London, I had visited the British Museum, and made search among the books and maps in the library regarding Transylvania…' and a short time later we learn that *Van Helsing* goes to the museum 'looking up some authorities on ancient medicine…' In *The Adventure of Wysteria Lodge*, Conan Doyle has *Sherlock Holmes* spend a morning here studying Eckermann's *Voodooism and the Negroid Religions*.[55] **Virginia Woolf** refers to the Reading Room in *A Room of One's Own*. **Charles Lamb** (see Walk 4) spent several years studying here and writing pieces for magazines following early retirement after working as a clerk for 33 years in The East India Company.

Lewis Carroll (Revd Charles Dodgson)

The Library holds many priceless and important literary manuscripts, some of which are available to view online and some available for members in the reading rooms.

One of the former is *Alice's Adventures Under Ground*, the original manuscript version of *Alice In Wonderland* by Reverend Charles Dodgson, better known as Lewis Carroll.

In 1856, Dodgson was teaching mathematics – he had received a First Class Honours Degree in the subject – at Christ Church, Oxford and he became friends with Henry Liddell, Dean of the College, and his children, Alice, Lorina and Edith. He originally told the tale to the girls when he took them on a trip along the Thames on 4 July 1862. Alice so liked the story that she asked Dodgson to write it down for her and this he did, presenting it to Alice as a Christmas present in 1864. It has 37 illustrations and a coloured title page.

Dodgson was encouraged to publish the story for a wider audience and, after almost doubling its size to 27,500 words and adding drawings by John Tenniel, he changed the title to *Alice in Wonderland* and this was published in 1865. It came to be seen as one of the greatest-ever children's tales; it has never been out of print and has been translated into 100 languages.

The original manuscript was held by Alice Liddell, who was forced to sell it to pay death duties when her husband died. It was then sold twice again before being bought by a group of wealthy Americans who donated it to the British Library as a 'thank you' to the country for standing up to Hitler; here it remains.

Charles Dodgson, or Lewis Carroll, was a multi-talented individual – a brilliant mathematician, writer, poet – *The Hunting of the Snark* (1874–6) is his masterpiece in the genre of 'literary nonsense' – and also a photographer: he photographed many

Royal Opera House.

famous people, including Alfred, Lord Tennyson, Dante Gabriel Rossetti and Michael Faraday. He stopped taking and developing pictures, however, in 1880 because it simply took up too much of his time.

From here the walk drops south towards Covent Garden (see map) which will take perhaps 10 to 15 minutes at a relaxed pace: the name may derive from 'Convent Garden', after the medieval religious institution of which it formed a part. Today, this is theatreland; the walk passes the magnificent Royal Opera House, sometimes itself referred to as 'Covent Garden'. It is the third theatre on the site as a result of disastrous fires, with the present building being the result of a comprehensive refurbishment in the 1990s.

On the opposite side of the street to the opera house, and a few yards to the north is an imposing building, still easily identifiable, that was once Bow Street Magistrates' Court: this was where **Oscar Wilde** was held pending his trial.

Nearby, at number 4 Bow Street, lived magistrate and author, **Henry Fielding** (1707–54) who, in 1749, recruited six men to become the famous Bow Street Runners, named after the courtroom, and often seen as Britain's first police force. They lasted until 1839 when the employees – who did not like their name as they considered that it lacked the necessary gravitas – were merged with the Metropolitan Police Force.

On 28 February 1749, Henry Fielding published *Tom Jones* (full title *The History of Tom Jones, A Foundling*), one of the earliest and greatest of English novels. Among its features is that the novelist, at the beginning of each chapter, has a word directly with the reader about what is going on and this creates an intimacy between the two. The novel has been produced for the stage and filmed several times and, at the time of writing, a new production, set in 1960s London with music from the period, has been announced.

Reader, I think proper, before we proceed any further together, to acquaint thee that I intend to digress, through this whole history, as often as I see occasion, of which I am myself a better judge than any pitiful critic whatever…

Tom Jones, **Henry Fielding**

Henry Fielding was succeeded by his brother, John, who continued his police work and then by Richard Ford who, in 1763, established a similar team on horseback, primarily to tackle highwaymen, at which it was startlingly successful. The Bow Street Horse Patrol, as it was officially called, wore bright scarlet waistcoats and almost inevitably became known to the press and public as the 'Robin Redbreasts'.

Covent Garden had been used since the seventh century as arable land but from 1654 a fruit and vegetable market took hold, followed by houses, taverns and brothels. Parliament took steps to control the area by legislation from the 1830s, leading to a huge growth in the market. By the 1970s traffic congestion was so great that the market relocated to Nine Elms and the area was developed as we see it today. Other attractions, such as the London Transport Museum, were added close by. The buildings are controlled by the Covent Garden Area Trust who pay a peppercorn rent for each lease of one red apple and a posy of flowers. Visitors find it an interesting place to linger, maybe for a drink and a bite, with some just sitting along the street curbs and watching the often-incredible street performers.

Covent Garden and writers

Many writers have used the area in their works or found inspiration here. **Samuel Pepys** mentions Covent Garden a good deal in his famous diaries. **Jane Austen** stayed at an apartment here in 1813–14. The central figure in **George Bernard Shaw**'s *Pygmalion*, *Eliza Doolittle*, sells flowers at a market stall. This was, of course, later turned into the famous musical *My Fair Lady*, starring Audrey Hepburn and Sir Rex Harrison.

James Boswell met **Samuel Johnson** here. It was in a bookshop kept by their mutual friend, the actor Thomas Davies in 'Russel-street'. It is Monday 16 May 1763 and Boswell describes the moment in his *Life of Samuel Johnson LL.D.* He had been having tea with Mr and Mrs Davies in the back room when through the glass door which led into the shop he saw Johnson enter. Mr Davies led Johnson towards Boswell 'somewhat in the manner of an actor in the part of *Horatio* when he addresses *Hamlet* on the appearance of his father's ghost, "Look, my Lord, it comes".'

William Hogarth sets scene 3 of *The Rake's Progress – The Orgy –* in the Rose Tavern, Covent Garden (see Walk 2). This was a tavern frequented by all manner of people but with a distinctly unsavoury reputation. **Samuel Pepys** often frequented it: he tells of one occasion when he had been there with Doll Lane and had 'played with her a good while'; he was seen going out by one of his neighbours near his office and two other people that he knew who he 'had no mind to have been seen by…'

Thomas De Quincey was living at 36 Tavistock Square, Covent Garden when he wrote *Confessions of an English Opium-Eater*, published anonymously in 1821. In the book, he explains how he first took opium. It was in the autumn of 1804 when, having gone to bed with wet hair, he awoke with terrible rheumatic pain to his face and this lasted for 20 days. On the 21st day, he went out around Oxford Street, seeking to run away from his torments, and met a college acquaintance who recommended opium.

On his way home via Oxford Street, he sees a druggist's shop where he buys some tincture of opium: this druggist assumes to him, in retrospect, an immortal, beatific aura. The book, however, attempts to see both the good and the terrifying in the drug and is often extremely funny. For example, De Quincey gives a major disadvantage to eating it: '…that if you eat a good deal of it, most probably you must—do what is particularly disagreeable to any man of regular habits, viz., die.'

It is also during this passage of events that he wrote one of his most quoted remarks: 'a duller spectacle this earth of ours has not to show than a rainy Sunday in London'.

Charles Dickens and Covent Garden

Charles Dickens has David buy flowers for Dora from the market in *David Copperfield*, while Tom and Ruth gain some peace after terrible times by wandering around the area early on summer mornings in *Martin Chuzzlewit*:

Many and many a pleasant stroll they had in Covent Garden Market; snuffing up the perfumes of the fruits and flowers, wondering at the magnificence of the pineapples and melons; catching glimpses down side avenue, of rows and rows of old women, seated on inverted baskets, shelling peas; looking unutterable things at the fat bundles of asparagus with which the dainty shops were fortified as with a breastwork; and, at the herbalist's doors, gratefully inhaling scents as

Covent Garden tube is on the Piccadilly (blue) Line.

of veal-stuffing yet uncooked, dreamily mixed up with capsicums, brown paper, seeds, even with hints of lusty snails and fine young curly leeches.

Dickens himself was known to take rooms in the piazza when, for whatever reason, he could not get home of an evening: the offices of his wonderfully successful weekly magazines *Household Words* (1850–59) and *All the Year Round* (1859–70) are just a few yards away on Wellington Street (there is a plaque) and he would frequently work late. Often, he would end his famous night walks in Covent Garden, sometimes accompanied by Charles Frederick Field, a detective and later private investigator, on whom he is said to have based *Inspector Bucket* in *Bleak House*.

Field was, according to Dickens, 'a portly presence with a large, moist knowing eye', and, like *Holmes* a few years later, fond of drama, disguises, and unconventional behaviour but sometimes, his colleagues said, this could be embarrassing.

Dickens' *Night Walks* are probably the most famous walks around the city but he was not the first to write on the subject. In 1716 **John Gay** wrote a poem in heroic couplets, *Trivia, or the Art of Walking the Streets of London*, which runs to about 1,000 lines and advises, amongst other things, on how to dress appropriately, how to avoid chamber pots being emptied over your head, and how to keep hold of your wig in the wind. **Virginia Woolf** published *Street Haunting* in 1927 (see more on this writer in chapter 8 on Bloomsbury) and **E.M. Forster** and **Henry James** also addressed the topic. **James Boswell** in his biography of **Johnson** mentions a memorable walk with some of his friends who, having stayed up drinking until three in the morning, didn't fancy going to bed and took to the London streets for a ramble until dawn.

From this spot, you can wander in all directions and see the great theatres of London and check out what is playing. This walk, though, carries on down Wellington Street in the general direction of the river. Russell Street criss-crosses Bow Street and is home to the famous Theatre Royal, Drury Lane, commonly known as Drury Lane. Dating back originally to 1663 and therefore the oldest theatre in London still in use, it is the fourth on the site. Rebuilt to make it grander and bigger, it burnt down in 1809 when the MP Richard Brinsley Sheridan was the holder of the licence – he is said to have come to watch the conflagration from a café, where he settled himself down with a bottle of wine and remarked that a man was entitled to have a drink by his own fireside.

'Pretty, witty Nell'

Samuel Pepys caught sight of Nell Gwyn near the theatre in this entry of his Diaries on 1 May 1667:

> To Westminster… and saw pretty Nelly standing at her lodgings door in Drury Lane in her smock sleeves and bodice… she seemed a mighty pretty creature.

Nelly or 'pretty, witty Nell' according to Pepys, was a huge star of the period and had two sons by Charles II, the first, Charles Beauclerk (1670–1726), being made Earl of Burford and Duke of St Albans by his father. She was a friend of many literary figures, including **Dryden**, and was herself the lead character of many novels and plays, now largely forgotten. She died, possibly of sexually related illness and a stroke, aged around 37 – her birthdate is not clear – on 14 November 1687. She had amassed a large fortune by the standards of the day. She is buried in St Martin-in-the-Fields.

The noted actor, David Garrick performed at Drury Lane. It is reputed to be haunted by several ghosts including the 'Man in Grey', whose walled-up remains were found in a side hallway in 1848. Another is Charles Macklin who, in 1735, accidentally killed fellow actor, Charles Hallam, by angrily – it was a row over a wig – poking Hallam's left eye out with his cane. Yet another is Joe Grimaldi, the clown, who was to die a reclusive and depressed alcoholic in 1837: he is said to be a helpful ghost, guiding nervous actors about the stage.

Some productions of the present era in this theatre include *Sweeney Todd; Demon Barber of Fleet Street* (see Walk 3), *My Fair Lady*, *The Producers*, *Lord of the Rings*, *Oliver* and *42nd Street*.

The coffee house

The seventeenth and eighteenth centuries saw the rise and continued popularity of the coffee house amongst the literary elite and there were three in Russell Street. At number 10 was Button's which had regulars in **Alexander Pope** and satirist, **Jonathan Swift**. Tom's was at number 17 and had Henry Fielding, the actor, David Garrick and **Tobias Smollett** among its customers. Will's was on the corner of Bow and Russell Streets and here you might sometimes find **Samuel Pepys, John Dryden** or **William Congreve**. Here, Dryden had a special chair reserved for him, near the fire in winter but carried

The Lyceum Theatre.

outside when the weather was fine. Pepys mentions it as 'the great Coffee House' where there is 'very witty and pleasant discourse'.

Just across the road, in the Piazza itself, were two more famous establishments frequented by the great and the good of literary London during the eighteenth century – The Great Piazza Coffee House and the Bedford Coffee House. It was presumably in one of these, although he does not specify as much that, at the end of one of his legendary night walks, **Charles Dickens** came for some breakfast and had an unsettling time when he saw a man, with a head shaped like a horse, a bright red face and nothing more on that he could see than a dirty overcoat, proceeding to order a large pie. He then took a knife from his coat and stabbed the pie several times. Then he ate it all up. Dickens was used to seeing many strange things on his nocturnal wanderings but for some reason, this image stayed with him and he avoided the establishment for a while.

At the bottom of the road to your right, you will see the impressive portico and six large columns of the Lyceum Theatre and it is 'by the third pillar from the left ... tonight at seven o'clock' that *Miss Mary Morstan* is requested to meet a mysterious person in Conan Doyle's *The Sign of Four*. She is told she can bring two friends, so *Holmes* and *Watson* accompany her and they are soon all transported by clattering cab to ***Thaddeus Sholto***'s unusual house. **Bram Stoker**, author of *Dracula*, was business manager of the theatre for 27 years.

The Lyceum was flooded when closed during the pandemic 2020–21 but reopened in July 2021.

This walk ends here: Strand is off to your right, Aldwych, Fleet Street and St Paul's to your left and Waterloo Bridge straight ahead.

WALK 8

Bloomsbury and the British Library

In This Walk: The lives and works of the following people and *fictional characters* are highlighted: William Makepeace Thackeray, Sir James Matthew Barrie, *Peter Pan*, Jane Austen, Virginia Woolf, Duncan Grant, John Maynard Keynes, E.M. Forster, John Leech, Charles Dickens, James Cunningham, Cyril Connelly, Thomas Coram, William Hogarth, William Nutter, Mamie Dickens, 'Plorn' Dickens, Edward Bulwer-Lytton, Ted Hughes, Sylvia Plath, William Morris, Anthony Trollope, Oscar Wilde, Robert Bridges, Anthony Hope, Lady Ottoline Morrell, Henry James, T.S. Eliot, Alberto Moravia, George Orwell, Mary Wollstonecraft, George Eliot, Evelyn Waugh, Dorothy L. Sayers, Christina Rossetti, Abdulrazak Gurnah, T.S. Eliot, W.H. Auden, Sir Stephen Spender, Charles Madge, Lytton Strachey, Catherine Dickens, W.B. Yeats, Ezra Pound, John Masefield, James Joyce, William Blake, Caxton, Chaucer, Shakespeare.

Distance: *See page 126; 3.5 kilometres (about 2.2 miles)*

Time to allow: 2–3 hours for the basic walking, but add on extra time for visits to the Charles Dickens Museum and the British Library.

Walking conditions: Flat, along some very elegant streets. There are locals and tourists about but generally fewer than in other areas of town. Excellent photo opportunities.

Route

Russell Square tube station
Grenville Street
Brunswick Square Gardens
Coram's Fields
Great Ormond Street
Queen Square
Doughty Street
Bloomsbury Way
Museum Street
Bedford Square
Store Street
Keppel Street
Malet Street
Torrington Square

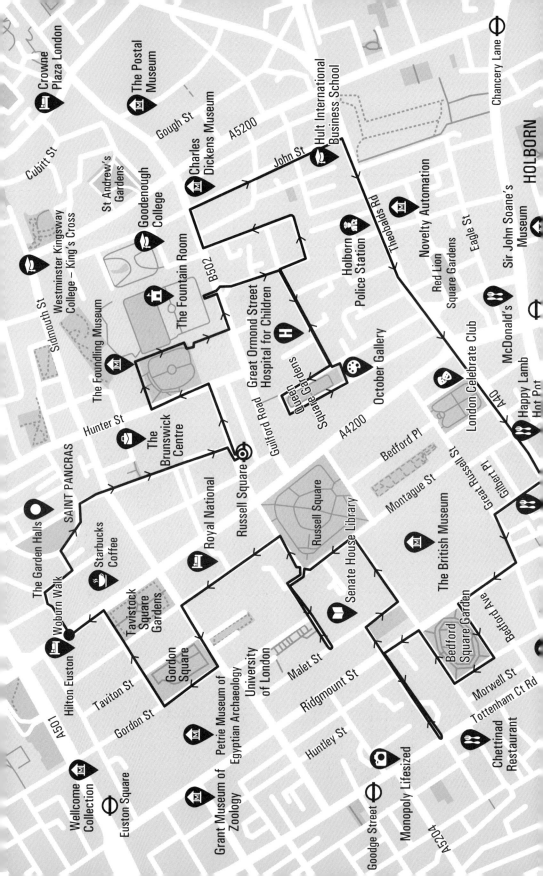

School of Oriental and African Studies, University of London
Russell Square
Gordon Square
Tavistock Square
Woburn Walk
The British Library

This walk can start and end at Russell Square tube station on the Piccadilly Line, or can be extended to include a visit to the British Library as detailed in the text. For international visitors arriving at Heathrow, Russell Square tube is perfect as the underground train

travels directly to all terminals in just over an hour saving much lugging of cases up and down the surprising number of stairs encountered if you have to change lines, which you have to do for nearby stops such as Warren Street. Accommodation in such a central area is very expensive but at certain times great bargains can be had.[56]

Turn right as you leave the station and walk straight ahead. Soon, on your left, you will pass the Brunswick Centre,

a very unusual and striking development featuring tiered residential accommodation, which was taken over by the council as private buyers failed to sufficiently materialise after its completion in 1972, together with shops, restaurants and supermarkets which are owned by private landlords. It is Grade II listed now.

> I hope the reader has much too good an opinion of Captain and Mrs Crawley to suppose that they ever would have dreamed of paying a visit to so remote a district as Bloomsbury…
>
> **William Makepeace Thackeray**, *Vanity Fair*, published in monthly parts 1847–8

The name 'Bloomsbury' probably derives from 'Blemondisberi', which in turn derives from a member of the Blemund family, holders of the manor in early medieval times.

On a house on the corner with Grenville Street, you will see a plaque dedicated to **Sir James Matthew Barrie**, creator of *Peter Pan*, who lived in a house on this site.

Immediately to your left here is Brunswick Square Gardens, a lush and beautiful public space with lots of seats. It is famous for having one of the most magnificent plane trees in England. This is also a most fascinating place for the visitor interested in literature. **Jane Austen** mentions the square in *Emma* and *Isabella* adds 'our part of London is so very superior to most others… we are so very airy.'

Such 'airiness' was very much intentional. The Garden you are in now was once owned by the Foundling Hospital, London's first hospital for babies whose mothers could not look after them, and was designed to be one of two open spaces each side of the medical facilities – the other is Mecklenburgh Square which is not open to the public – which would provide fresh and healthy air to the area. You can visit the Foundling Museum where the old hospital used to be.

The Bloomsbury Group

The rows of houses on three sides of the square have now all gone but, in the nineteenth and twentieth centuries some eminent people, especially authors, lived in them. We have

Plaque in Brunswick Square.

already passed the plaque to **J.M. Barrie** but, on the other side of the square, at number 38, lived (1911–12) **Virginia Woolf**, Leonard Woolf and artist Duncan Grant, members of the so-called Bloomsbury Group, who often referred to themselves as 'Bloomsberries' – there is a plaque. Grant was intimately involved for a time with another member of the Group, the economist, John Maynard Keynes, a man who meticulously tabulated his many gay lovers, much to the annoyance of some of them. Grant was friends as a schoolboy with the 'doomed poet' as many regarded him after his untimely death *en-route* to fight in Gallipoli in the Great War – **Rupert Brooke**. **W.B. Yeats** called Brooke 'the handsomest young man in England'. Brooke was not impressed with the antics of the 'Bloomsberries', however, and watched their lives from the fringes.

> Word, English words, they are full of echoes, memories, associations. They have been out and about, on people's lips, in their houses, in the streets…

> **Virginia Woolf** talking to the BBC in 1937

E.M. Forster, author of *Passage to India, Howard's End* and *A Room with a View*, lived at number 27 and later 26 from 1925–39. **John Leech**, illustrator of some of **Charles Dickens'** novels, lived at number 32 from 1854–62. **John Ruskin**, author, social critic and reformer, was born at 54 Hunter Street at the northwest corner of the square in 1819, and lived there until 1823. Sir Nicholas Conyngham Tindal, Chief Justice of Common Pleas 1829–46 and the lawyer who had previously found international fame when he defended Queen Caroline of Brunswick who was charged with adultery in 1820 (he won), lived at number 9, 1821–5.

Virginia Woolf and walking in London

'For Heaven only knows why one loves it so', writes Virginia Woolf at the beginning of *Mrs Dalloway* (1925); in this novel, the characters connect by walking through the great areas of London. Several years later Woolf published an essay, *Street Haunting: A London Adventure*, where the narrator walks all over London town and imagines the lives of the passing people. A love of London lasted her whole life. She was never calmer than when walking in its parks, gardens and grand thoroughfares such as Strand, Oxford Street, the Royal Parks, Westminster, Tottenham Court Road, Victoria Embankment, the London Docks, Hampton Court and Trafalgar Square, or finding new alleys and courts off Fleet Street.

> To walk alone in London is the greatest rest

> **Virginia Woolf**, 1930

In 1998, American author, **James Cunningham**, wrote *The Hours* which centres on three generations of women affected by *Mrs Dalloway*: it is an imitation and a reworking in important respects; it won the Pulitzer Prize for Fiction in 1999. The title *The Hours* was Woolf's provisional title for the book.

> I prefer men to cauliflowers

> **Virginia Woolf**,
> *Mrs Dalloway*

Opposite Brunswick Square is Lansdowne Terrace and a blue plaque at number 2 commemorates the building from which **Cyril Connelly** and **Sir Stephen Spender** published the *Horizon Magazine* 1940–8. Some questioned the wisdom of founding a literary magazine in the midst of war but it proved very influential. Connelly said that a main aim was to encourage young writers.

One place in England where adults are only allowed if accompanied by a child

Mecklenburgh Square adjoins Coram's Fields, a seven-acre garden established by Thomas Coram in 1739. This enterprise, to benefit children who had been abandoned, still adheres to the rule that a child must accompany any adult into the gardens. Thomas Coram dedicated much of his energy to charitable endeavours which included a scheme for settling English artisans in Nova Scotia and another for educating Native American girls in America, refusing usually to take any monetary reward: he died a poor man, aged 83. **William Hogarth** was a personal friend and painted a famous portrait of him which, reproduced in stipple by William Nutter, is now in the Foundling Museum.

Just south of Coram's Fields is the world-renowned Great Ormond Street Hospital for children. Both of these had a special place in the affections of **Charles Dickens**, whose house in Doughty Street the walk is heading towards now. He supported Coram's Fields by writing of it in his fantastically successful publication *Household Words* and he spoke at the first fund-raising dinner, in St Martin-in-the-Fields, for Great Ormond Street Hospital. He supported the hospital all his life and, following his death in 1870, the chair on which he sat to write at his family home in Rochester, 'Gad's Hill Place', was auctioned and the money given to the hospital.

Mamie Dickens wrote of her father's relationship with children in a small book about 25 years after his death:

> When my father was arranging and rehearsing his readings from 'Dombey,' the death of 'little Paul' caused him such real anguish, the reading being so difficult to him, that he told us he could only master his intense emotion by keeping the picture of Plorn,[57] well, strong and hearty, steadily before his eyes. We can see by the different child characters in his books what a wonderful knowledge he had of children, and what a wonderful and truly womanly sympathy he had with them in all their childish joys and griefs. I can remember with us, his own children, how kind, considerate and patient he always was.

> **Mamie Dickens**, *My Father as I Recall Him* (1896)

Another writer who helped was **Sir J.M. Barrie** who, in 1929, gave the hospital the rights of *Peter Pan*. From only 10 initial beds, by 1880 the hospital had grown to help 1,690 in-patients and 19,000 outpatients, largely drawn from the omnipresent slums.

On one side of Great Ormond Street Hospital is Queen Square, a narrow garden with seats and often a coffee vendor at one end. Faber and Faber, the publishers, set up home here in the 1970s. It was at the Church of St George the Martyr on the edge of the square that, on the very wet day of 16 June 1956, **Ted Hughes** and **Sylvia Plath** were married.

The area around here is largely about children. Left: a sign at the entrance to Coram's Field (see previous page) and right: many of the buildings belong to the world-renowned Great Ormond Street Children's Hospital. Charles Dickens and Sir J.M. Barrie financially supported the hospital.

William Morris (1834–96) established his firm 'Morris, Marshall, Faulkner and Co, Fine Art Workmen in Painting, Carving, Furniture and the Metals', on the ground floor of number 26 from 1865–71. Here he wrote prodigiously and entertained such contemporary luminaries as **Henry James** with his friends, who included **Dante Gabriel Rossetti**.

The Church of St George the Martyr.

At the crossroads in Great Ormond Street, turn right into Lamb's Conduit Street and then left into Rugby Street. Number 18 is the house, owned by Daniel Huwys who went to Cambridge with the groom, where Sylvia Plath and Ted Hughes spent their wedding night.

At the end of Rugby Street, turn left into Millman Street and then right at the top into Guilford Street which leads to Doughty Street, where at numbers 48–9 you will find the **Charles Dickens** Museum. Dickens lived here from March 1837 to December 1839, paying £80 a year for the rental, along with his wife, Catherine (née Hogarth) and the eldest three of their ten children. Dickens was in his mid-twenties and full of his legendary energy when living in the house: whilst here he gained international fame with *The Pickwick Papers* (1836), *Oliver Twist* (1838) and *Nicholas Nickleby* (1838–9). Some of *Barnaby Rudge* (1840–1) was also written here.

Above left, above right and below: *Doughty Street and the Charles Dickens Museum.*

The walk then proceeds down Doughty Street turning right into Theobalds Road, which leads into Bloomsbury Way. Carry on until you come to St George's Church on your right. The church has several claims to fame: not surprisingly, being so close to his home, Dickens mentions it in *Sketches by Boz*; it is featured in **Hogarth**'s 'Gin Lane' and **Anthony Trollope**, a contemporary of Dickens, was baptised here.

Taking a right up Museum Street, a left along Great Russell Street, and then a right at the crossroads will take you into Bloomsbury Street. This leads to Bedford Square, a most elegant Georgian development that was once the centre of the publishing industry: Hodder

133

and Stoughton, Chatto and Windus, Jonathan Cape and Bodley Head – who originally published **Oscar Wilde** – and Hogarth Press, all have a history here. The poet **Robert Bridges** and his mother lived at number 52 and **Anthony Hope**, author of *The Prisoner of Zenda*, at number 41. Lady Ottoline Morrell, who died in 1938, gave famous literary parties at number 44, and later nearby at number 10 Gower Street: her friends and guests included **Virginia Woolf, Henry James, T.S. Eliot** and **Alberto Moravia**. Another famous short-time resident of Gower Street was **Charles Dickens** whose family moved to number 147 in 1823 just before his father was imprisoned for debt – Dickens was 11. University College Hospital in Gower Street is where, on 13 October 1949, **George Orwell** married Sonia Brownell. He died from a burst lung three weeks later, on 21 January 1950.

> A newspaper that wishes to make its fortune should never waste its columns and weary its readers by praising anything

> **Anthony Trollope**, *The Way We Live Now*

Just up the road is Store Street which is where **Mary Wollstonecraft** wrote *A Vindication of the Rights of Women,* and opposite is Keppel Street, birthplace in 1815 of Anthony Trollope.

Anthony Trollope

Anthony Trollope (1815–1882) was an English writer and Post Office employee who first came to notice with *The Warden* (1855), the first of the six *Chronicles of Barsetshire* which he followed up with *The Palliser Novels*. He suffered critically during his lifetime largely due to his prolific output – he published a total of 47 novels and wrote according to a daily schedule. This method of apportioning regular daily time for his writing activities and his large output were not seen as very 'artistic'. However, since his death his reputation has recovered with *The Way We Live Now* (1875) being seen by many as his masterpiece. He was befriended by **George Eliot, Wilkie Collins** and **William Makepeace Thackeray**. More recent admirers include the conservative Prime Minister, John Major, and the actor, John Gielgud, who said he never went anywhere without a Trollope novel.

An unlikely but possible insight into his unusual name is given by a young personal friend and admirer, **T.H.S. Escott** in his 1913 work *Anthony Trollope, His Work, Associates and Literary Originals*. He says that the story given to his fellows at Harrow by Trollope was that the Norman Tallyhosier, who accompanied William the Conqueror to England, when hunting with his royal master in the New Forest, happened to kill three wolves whereupon the King immediately named him him 'Troisloup'. The name became corrupted over the centuries to 'Trollope'. The boys were somewhat sceptical of this and much ragging and worse ensued for the poor Trollope; he had a miserable time at school, writing later about one of his tormentors: 'He must have known me had he seen me as he was wont to see me, for he was in the habit of flogging me constantly. Perhaps he did not recognise me by my face'.

Continue straight ahead, turn right at Malet Street and left into Montague Place where you will come to Russell Square. In Malet Street you pass the Senate House, University of London, upon which it is believed that Orwell's Ministry of Truth was based: certainly, in the Second World War, this great monolith of a building was used by the Ministry of Information and employed, amongst thousands of others, **Evelyn Waugh, Dorothy L. Sayers** and **George Orwell**, whose job it was to raise morale among the general public.

Torrington Square is off Malet Street and it was at number 30 that **Christina Rossetti** (1830–1894) lived from 1877: there is a startling square terracotta plaque here, complete with cherubs. She is best remembered for the lyrics of the popular carol, *In the Bleak Midwinter* and her long poem, *Goblin Market and Other Poems*.

In the bleak midwinter
Frosty wind made moan
Earth stood hard as iron
Water like a stone
Snow had fallen
Snow on snow on snow
In the bleak midwinter
Long, long ago

Christina Rossetti,
In the Bleak Midwinter

Torrington Square borders the campus of The School of Oriental and African Studies (SOAS), University of London. In October 2021 the SOAS issued a statement congratulating **Abdulrazak Gurnah**, who was born in Tanzania but, at the time of the award was recently retired from the post of Emeritus Professor of English and Postcolonial Literatures at the University of Kent, on being awarded the 2021 Nobel Prize in Literature for 'for his uncompromising and compassionate penetration of the effects of colonialism and the fate of the refugee in the gulf between cultures and continents' (Nobel Foundation). SOAS said it marked 'the vital importance of the postcolonial voice in world literature'. Gurnah has been associated with the academic work of the SOAS for many years, collaborating at international conferences and as an external examiner: in 2013 he gave the Centre for African Studies Lecture.[58]

The monetary value of the prize is currently about £840,000 ($1.14 million).

Gurnah is the author of ten novels, including *Paradise* (1994, shortlisted for the Booker and Whitbread Prizes), *Desertion* (2005) and *Afterlives* (2020*)* which was shortlisted for the Orwell Prize for Political Fiction 2021.

Russell Square is best known in literary terms as the headquarters of Faber and Faber at number 24 and their most distinguished author (and publisher), **T.S. Eliot** who had an office and an occasionally-used flat in the building. He worked for the firm for almost 40 years, during which time they published **W.H. Auden, Stephen Spender, Ted Hughes** and **Charles Madge**. In 1944 he rejected **George Orwell**'s *Animal Farm*, remarking that it was 'unconvincing' and he did not think that the anti-Russian tone of the novel suitable for the contemporary delicate world situation. He particularly disliked the pigs. The BBC made a documentary examining this episode as part of its *Arena* series in 2009.

Walking north up Bedford Way will lead you to Gordon Square where number 46 is another address for Virginia Woolf (or **Virginia Stephen** as she then was) who lived here in 1904. **Lytton Strachey** (1880–1932), author of *Eminent Victorians*, lived at number 51, 1919–24.

Nearby Tavistock Square was home to Hogarth Press, run by Leonard and Virginia Woolf, although the building itself was destroyed in the second world war. **Wilfred Owen**, the First World War poet who was killed at the age of 25, had lodgings nearby.

Dickens moved to Tavistock House at the end of 1851 and began work on *Bleak House* (1853) here, followed by *Hard Times* (1854), *Little Dorrit* (1855–7) and *A Tale of Two Cities* (1859). He bought Gads Hill Place in Rochester in 1856 but did not sell the lease to Tavistock House until 1860. Whilst here, in June 1858, he separated from his wife, Catherine, which caused a scandal and, worried that unpopularity would lessen his book sales, Dickens was forced to issue strident press releases in his own defence. Whether or not he was having an affair with the young actress, Ellen Ternan, was a matter of debate, as it remains today. His estranged wife went on to publish a book of her own under the name of **Lady Maria Clutterbuck**, *What Shall we Have for Dinner? Satisfactorily Answered by Numerous Bills of Fare for from Two to Eighteen Persons*. It went through several editions up to 1860 and is still available today.[59]

Turn left at the top of Tavistock Square, walk up Upper Woburn Place and right into Woburn Walk, which is where **W.B. Yeats** lived at number 5, 1895–1919, and where he used to be 'at home' on Monday evenings to guests, including sometimes **Ezra Pound** and **John Masefield**, who would drink wine and smoke cigarettes until the early hours.

The walk then heads back, via Burton Street, Cartwright Gardens and Marchmont Street to Russell Square tube station which is where it began.

The British Library

There is one more essential stop on this walk which can be made either now or separately, as you may want, even on a casual visit, to spend half or a complete day or more there – the British Library. To go on foot, retrace the very beginning of this walk up to Brunswick Square and then follow Hunter Street which in turn becomes Judd Street and cross the Euston Road until you reach the British Library. It is also very easy by tube train from Russell Square – one stop on the Piccadilly line to Kings Cross and then a ten-minute walk along Euston Road.

The British Library has over 150 million items, both here and at other sites, including original manuscripts by **Jane Austen, James Joyce** and others. It is possible to access electronic copies of other material, too, including work by **William Blake, William Caxton**'s two editions of **Chaucer**'s *Canterbury Tales,* referred to earlier, the *Gutenberg Bible* and 107 copies of the 21 plays by **Shakespeare** printed in quarto before the theatre closures in 1642.

The main catalogue is available to see online, as are details of passes, opening times and facilities. You can just 'drop in' to use many of the facilities including cafés, wifi and shops and see the exhibitions but, if you plan to come here to study particular documents or use the reading rooms, best to check out the website as far in advance as possible in order to make all necessary applications.

www.bl.uk

WALK 9

A walk around the City and East End

In This Walk: The lives and works of the following people and *fictional characters* are highlighted: William Blake, John Bunyan, Daniel Defoe, Charlotte Bronte, George Eliot, Thackeray, *Sherlock Holmes, Dr Watson, Mrs Hudson*, William Hogarth, Rahere, Kipling, Rosemary Sutcliffe, Thomas Bodley, Charles Dickens, *Oliver Twist, Mrs Gamp, Arthur Clennam,* Thomas Hood, James Gilray, Kenneth Grahame, *Mole, Rat, Toad, Badger*, P.G. Wodehouse, T.S. Eliot, Thomas Gray, Alexander Pope, Samuel Pepys, John Evelyn, *Mrs Todgers, Scrooge, Mr Dombey, Mr Pickwick, Sir John Falstaff, Mistress Quickly*, William Shakespeare, *Harry Potter*, Wolfgang Amadeus Mozart, Phillis Wheatley.

Distance: *See pages 138–139; about 5.3 kilometres (3.3 miles)*

Time to allow: Half a day for the basic walking but add on time for visits to Bunhill Fields Burial Ground, St Bart's Museum, the churches mentioned, the Bank of England Museum, the Monument and the Tower of London.

Walking conditions: Basically flat with some slight slopes, for example around the Monument area. Cafés and pubs in all areas. There are some food shops and supermarkets, for example, in Eastcheap. Wonderful photo opportunities.

Route

Old Street tube station
Bunhill Fields Burial Ground
Dufferin Street
Charterhouse Street
Smithfield Market
Barts
St Bartholomew the Great and St Bartholomew the Less
St Martin Le Grand
Gresham Street
Cheapside
Church of St Mary-le-Bow
Bank
King William Street
Monument

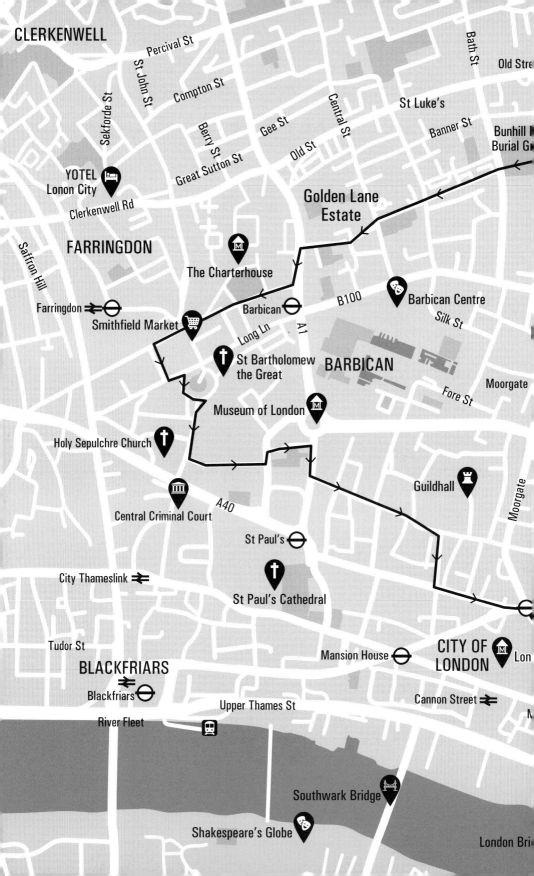

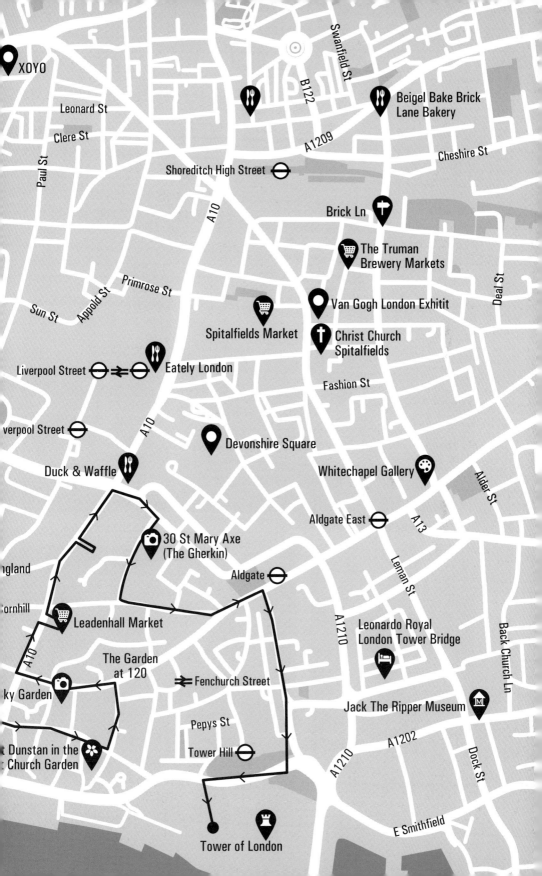

XOYO

Leonard St

Clere St

Paul St

Beigel Bake Brick Lane Bakery

Swanfield St

B122

A1209

Cheshire St

Shoreditch High Street

A10

Brick Ln

The Truman Brewery Markets

Deal St

Primrose St

Appold St

Sun St

Spitalfields Market

Van Gogh London Exhitit

Christ Church Spitalfields

Liverpool Street Eately London

Fashion St

A10

verpool Street

Devonshire Square

Whitechapel Gallery

Alder St

Duck & Waffle

Aldgate East

A13

30 St Mary Axe (The Gherkin)

Aldgate

Leman St

ngland

A1210

Leonardo Royal London Tower Bridge

Cornhill

Leadenhall Market

A10

The Garden at 120

Fenchurch Street

Jack The Ripper Museum

Back Church Ln

ky Garden

Pepys St

Dunstan in the Church Garden

Tower Hill

A1210

A1202

Dock St

Tower of London

E Smithfield

Pudding Lane
Eastcheap
Leadenhall Market
Great St Helens
St Mary Axe
Minories
Tower of London

The walk begins at Old Street tube station (Northern Line – black). Make your way out of the station, following the route shown on the maps located here to Bunhill Fields Burial Ground, which is a short walk away (10 minutes).

Bunhill Fields Burial Ground has five enclosed areas containing over 2,300 memorials, as well as a beautiful garden with magnificent trees which is open to the public and has

Bunhill Fields Burial Ground.

Grave of Daniel Defoe.

Headstone of William Blake.

John Bunyan's grave.

benches. It is a Nonconformist burial ground dating from about 1660 and has witnessed 123,000 burials, including those of **William Blake, John Bunyan, Daniel Defoe** and **Isaac Watts**. There are very clear noticeboards at the entrances so it is easy to find your way around, including to the graves of Blake, Bunyan and Defoe, which are within yards of each other. Many people are especially drawn to Blake's memorial stone which often has fresh flowers and trinkets laid upon it.

John Bunyan (1628–1688) published *Pilgrim's Progress from This World to That Which Is to Come,* a Christian allegory, 10 years before his death. It went through 11 editions within the next decade and became one of the most influential books of all time. He wrote much of it in Bedford jail, convicted for being an itinerant, unauthorised preacher. As a work depicting a character on a journey through spiritual life, it influenced **Charlotte Brontë** in *Jane Eyre*, **Thackeray** in *Vanity Fair* (the title of which comes from the work) and **George Eliot**'s *The Mill on the Floss.*

'Now, now look how the holy pilgrims ride' writes Bunyan. *Pilgrim's Progress* tells the tale of Christian who travels from Earth to Heaven, meeting various characters on the way, such as Pliable and Obstinate. It sold perhaps over 100,000 copies within a few years. The Victorians produced many editions, some lavishly illustrated.

Daniel Defoe (1660–1731) is primarily known as the author of *Robinson Crusoe* (1719), *Moll Flanders* (1722) and *Roxana* (1724), although the British Library estimates that he produced at least 318 publications, many on the state of the nation. He was twice briefly sent to prison for debts, although managed to extricate himself on both occasions with the help of friends.

William Blake

William Blake (1757–1827), famous today as a painter, poet, mystic and inventor of a unique printing process, was largely ignored during his own lifetime and towards the end of his life was considered by many to be insane. After his death, his reputation grew. **Algernon Charles Swinburne** wrote in his *William Blake. A Critical Essay*, published in 1868, that 'In his time he had little enough of recognition or regard from the world.' In the same essay, Blake is described by Swinburne as 'A man perfect in his way, and beautifully unfit for walking in the way of any other man.'

Blake was born in Soho, one of seven children, and as a boy experienced the first of many visions upon seeing angelic wings 'like stars' on every bough of a tree in Peckham. It was the first of his spiritual sightings, the last glorious one of which was on his deathbed when he began singing of the things he saw in heaven.

He was greatly influenced by the teachings of the Swedish mystic, **Emanuel Swedenborg**, and throughout his life experienced wild mental highs and lows.

In 1772 he was apprentice to a printmaker and was often to be found in Westminster Abbey where he made drawings of monuments and medieval artwork. Ten years later he married Catherine Boucher with whom he shared the rest of his life. He was very successful as an engraver and produced some extraordinary works of his own using a printing process he invented in 1789: these include *Songs of Innocence and Experience* (1794 but worked upon in the years following first publication), *The Book of Thel* (1789–93), *Visions of the Daughters of Albion* (1793), and *Jerusalem The Emanation of the Giant Albion* (worked on various aspects from 1804 until his death in 1827).

Cut through Bunhill Fields Burial Ground into Dufferin Street and straight on until you see signs for Barbican tube station and, on reaching this, proceed down Charterhouse Street to Smithfield Market. Meat has been sold here for 800 years. It was also the scene used for major medieval tournaments – the original name may have been 'Smoothfield' which denoted a smooth, flat piece of land suitable for jousting. It was also well-known for public hangings of heretics – between 1400 and 1601, 43 were hanged and six burned here – and others who had fatally fallen foul of the law. There once was a market for unwanted wives.

For *Sherlock Holmes'* fans, there is, on the southern side of Smithfield, St Bartholomew's Hospital, known as St Barts or just Barts, founded in 1123. In probably the most famous introduction in literature, young *Stamford* introduces *Dr Watson* to *Sherlock Holmes* in this building. They shake hands and *Holmes* says 'You have been in Afghanistan, I perceive.' *Watson* replies in astonishment: 'How on earth did you know that?' The stories are well and truly afoot; as a result of the meet-up, they are soon to begin sharing *Mrs Hudson*'s rooms at 221B Baker Street.

Barts also has a very unusual museum, often referred to as 'weird' in an interesting sense, which houses surgical instruments, medieval manuscripts and paintings by William Hogarth. It is situated under the North Wing archway. Entry is free and it is open weekdays from 10 am to 4 pm.

St Bartholomew the Great and St Bartholomew the Less are here, both founded at about the same time. Rahere, a courtier to Henry I, made a pilgrimage to Rome where he became ill. In his delirium, Saint Bartholomew came to him and told him to found a church in his name in Smithfield, London, for the poor of the district. This he did, as well as a priory for Augustinian canons: he lived to see its completion and, indeed, became both prior and master of St Barts Hospital. He died in 1145 and his tomb is in the church. Today St Bartholomew declares itself an inclusive church with no discrimination on the grounds of gender or disability or race or age or sexual orientation or social class.

Rahere is a legendary character whose exact history is unclear – he is reputed to have been a cleric, monk, court jester, herald, a minstrel and canon of St Paul's Cathedral, maybe even all of them at one time or another. He inspired **Kipling** and is the subject of his poem *Rahere*, where the protagonist 'came to reeking Smithfield where the crowded gallows are.' He is also a character in **Rosemary Sutcliff**'s children's book *The Witch's Brat* (1970).

Rahere is said to haunt the church.

The church has appeared in numerous films including *Four Weddings and a Funeral* (1994), *Shakespeare in Love* (1998), *Sherlock Holmes* (2009), and *Testament of Youth* (2014).

St Bartholomew the Less was once the church of Barts Hospital in whose grounds it lay, but since 2015 it has been what is called a 'chapel of ease' which is a church building but one which is not the parish church: it can be used by those who may have difficulty attending the 'official' church. Sir Thomas Bodley (1545–1613), founder of the Bodleian Library at Oxford, the second-largest library in the UK by number of books held (13 million) to the British Library, worshipped here.

The location is an attractive one for writers. **Charles Dickens**, always with a keen eye for the dramatic and humorous, uses the great Smithfield area in *Oliver Twist*, *Great Expectations*, *Barnaby Rudge* and *Nicholas Nickleby*. In *Oliver Twist*, when *Oliver* and *Sikes* pass through here on the way to a robbery, he writes that, as a result of the slaughter of animals, 'the ground was covered, nearly ankle-deep, with filth and mire'. Specifically regarding Barts, he chose the hospital as the place where the immortal *Mrs Gamp* in *Martin Chuzzlewit* has a friend who works as a nurse. In *Little Dorrit*, *Arthur Clennam* helps a wounded man into Barts where they see a surgeon. The injured man has been hit by a coach. The surgeon notes that the man's injuries are serious 'with the thoughtful pleasure of an artist contemplating the work on an easel...'

This walk heads south down St Martin's Le Grand and left into Gresham Street and, after 200–300 metres, left into King Street which will bring you to Cheapside. Here, almost opposite you to the right is the Church of St Mary-le-Bow. **John Keats** had lodgings just before the church when he was working at Guy's Hospital.

The inside of the Church of St Mary-le-Bow is very beautiful, having been restored following bombing during the Blitz in May 1941. It was one of many originally designed by Sir Christopher Wren following the Great Fire of London in 1666. It is probably most famous because of its part in the legend of *Dick Whittington*, who was persuaded to return to London, where he became Mayor, upon hearing the bells of St Mary-le-Bow. It is said that to be a true Cockney today, you must be born within earshot of the 'Bow Bells'.

Turn left on coming out of the church and walk down Cheapside towards Bank: just before the station, it becomes Poultry where, in 1799, the poet **Thomas Hood**, friend of **Thackeray** and writer of *The Bridge of Sighs* and *Song of the Shirt*, was born. He was associated with various magazines all his life, sometimes as a contributor, but also as editor in the cases of *London Magazine* and *New Monthly Magazine*. He was always a sickly man but his output was astonishing before he died, aged 45, on 3 May 1845: the house where he breathed his last, 28 Finchley Road, St John's Wood, has a blue plaque.

> I like you, Mrs. Fry! I like your name!
> It speaks the very warmth you feel in pressing
> In daily act round Charity's great flame—
> I like the crisp Browne way you have of dressing,
> Good Mrs. Fry!
>
> **Thomas Hood**, *A Friendly Address to*
> *Mrs Fry in Newgate*

In 1817 Elizabeth Fry had set up a school for children in the prison and went on to organise sewing classes and bible study for the women inmates.

You will soon come to Bank tube station which has several exits, one of which is to a seated area fronted by the old Royal Exchange – which is now converted to cafés, offices and top-end shops – opposite the imposing edifice that is the Bank of England. This is much frequented by city workers, has seats, and is an excellent place to have a rest or eat your sandwiches while watching the comings and goings in this, the heart of the city's financial district.

Bank of England.

The Bank of England was established in 1694 and was often referred to as 'The Old Lady of Threadneedle Street' after a satirical cartoon by James Gilray. Its main function was to act as the banker to the United Kingdom government, although until 2016 employees could also hold personal accounts with it. The bank alone can issue bank notes in England and Wales and has done so since 1694. Granted independence in setting monetary policy in 1998, the bank also now holds the gold reserves of the United Kingdom and 30 other countries in a vast underground vault. In 2020 the total value of the gold was £194 billion, enough, apparently, to cover the whole of the UK in gold leaf. There is a museum, free to enter, open on weekdays and very much worth a visit, the entrance of which is in Bartholomew Lane, off Threadneedle Street.

One of the most successful books of all time, *The Wind in the Willows,* was written after retirement by a Bank of England employee of 30 years, **Kenneth Grahame**. Publication was in 1908 and during the next 20 years, the Edwardian adventures of *Mole, Rat, Toad* and *Badger* went through 30 printings. It has been adapted for stage and film, the latest being a musical written by **Julian Fellowes** in 2016.

> 'After all, the best part of a holiday is perhaps not so much to be resting yourself, as to see all the other fellows busy working.'
>
> **Kenneth Grahame**, *Wind in the Willows*;

As he worked here for three decades, Grahame probably had this area in mind when writing this

P.G. Wodehouse was another, most reluctant it would appear, a staff member of this and other banks until 1902. **T.S. Eliot** worked for Lloyds Bank in Cornhill, 1919–22. **Thomas Gray**, best known for *Elegy Written in a Country Churchyard,* was born in Cornhill in 1716.

Alexander Pope (1688–1744) was born in Plough Court, between Lombard Street and King William Street.

The walk, when you are ready to leave the area of Bank, drops down King William Street to the Monument. Built between 1671 and 1675 to commemorate the Great Fire of London, you can climb to the top for a great view of this part of London.

Approaching Monument.

The square in which it sits has seats and often international food stalls – there are traditional supermarkets also just around the corner in Eastcheap which sell more traditional fare such as sandwiches and sushi – and so is a good place for a rest or bite. A few yards away is Pudding Lane, where the Great Fire began in 1666 in the king's bakers, and also Fish Street through which it roared, although now, with granite-faced offices and modern paving, both streets bear no similarity at all to the ramshackle timbered structures of the seventeenth century. This is **Pepys**:

> September 2 1666: …By and by and Jane comes and tells me that she hears that above 300 houses have been burned down to-night by the fire we saw, and that it is now burning down all Fish Street, by London Bridge …

So down, with my heart full of trouble, to the Lieutenant of the Tower, who tells me that it begun this morning in the King's baker's house in Pudding-Lane… And among other things, the poor pigeons, I perceive, were loth to leave their houses, but hovered above the windows and balconys till they were …burned …and fell down.[60]

Pepys was living and working in Seething Lane at this time, very close to Tower Hill.

John Evelyn

Another diarist who covered the great fire was John Evelyn. He wrote, on and off, over a longer period than Pepys, from 1640 when he was 20 up to his death in 1706. He says that the 'deplorable fire, near Fish street in London' began at about ten o'clock and after prayers, he and his wife and son took a carriage to Southwark and, like Pepys, watched it 'exceedingly astonished'. He writes that the next day the city bore 'a resemblance of Sodom, or the last day…'

John Evelyn and Samuel Pepys were good friends, as recorded in Evelyn's Diaries, for 40 years. They often went on business trips together and dined frequently. Evelyn's diaries are illuminating on life in the late seventeenth century and about Pepys in the period from when Pepys' diaries ceased in 1669 (he stopped as the writing was affecting his eyesight) up to his death on 23 May 1703. We hear of the trip to Evelyn's brother, Richard, who had undergone an operation which removed a stone 'as big as a tennis ball', in order to encourage Pepys to have his own stone, which was causing him agony, cut out; and of how, when Pepys was imprisoned, Evelyn sent him a side of venison and went to dine with him. He tells us that, upon laying down his office, Pepys went to live in 'a very noble house and sweet place' in Clapham with Mr Hewer, formerly his clerk, and that at this time he was in 'great prosperity'. When he died, Evelyn was given a complete set of mourning clothes and a request 'desiring me to be one to hold up the pall at his magnificent obsequies; but my indisposition hindered me from doing him this last office'.

Evelyn also wrote on other matters, including gardening, and he was regarded as an expert on trees. He encouraged landowners to plant various varieties but not for environmental reasons; rather he was concerned that there should be enough wood to build ships for the navy. He did, however, write *Fumifugium* in 1661, the first book to address the appalling air pollution in London.

This area is also the place where **Dickens** set *Mrs Todgers'* boarding establishment for young gentlemen in *Martin Chuzzlewit*. Today, it is still an area of small streets and alleyways, and it is easy to cast your mind back to 1844 when Dickens wrote that 'you groped your way for an hour through lanes and byways, and courtyards and passages; and you never once emerged upon anything that may be reasonably be called a street'. It was also a very poor, ramshackle area at that time: this is the scene from *Mrs Todgers'* roof:

There were steeples, towers, belfries, shining vanes, and masts of ships: a very forest. Gables, housetops, garret-windows, wilderness upon wilderness. Smoke and noise enough for all the world at once.

It is also in this area – from here, up to Bank, Cornhill and Threadneedle Street – that *Scrooge* in *A Christmas Carol* and *Mr Dombey* in *Dombey and Son* would barter and bargain, and buy and sell debts, ruining many poor souls in the process. *Sam Weller* also saunters about here, planning to save his hapless but good-hearted master, *Mr Pickwick*, in *The Pickwick Papers*.

It is interesting to walk down Eastcheap where, at numbers 33–35 you cannot miss an extraordinary piece of Victorian Gothic architecture, designed by R.L. Roumieu (1814–1877) and finished in 1868. Look at the top of the Central Gothic window to see a stone carving of a wild boar peeping out from long grass. This is to commemorate the famous Boar's Head Inn once near here, where *Sir John Falstaff* and his disreputable cronies – including a young *Prince Hal* – caroused in **Shakespeare's** *Henry IV*. It was run by *Mistress Quickly*. There are many taverns called The Boar's Head Inn[61] that claim a Shakespearean connection, but the one referred to here was most likely the 'real' one as the Bard lived and worked in this area. Walk back again to Monument.

PRINCE 'Now Harry, whence come you?'
FALSTAFF 'My noble lord, from Eastcheap.'
PRINCE 'The complaints I hear of thee are grievous.'
FALSTAFF 'Sblood, my lord, they are false. – Nay, I'll tickle ye for a young prince, i'faith.'

William Shakespeare, *Henry VI Part I*

It is worth a trip from here, along Gracechurch Street, to see Leadenhall Market which you will come to on your right. Some fans think that was used as the setting for Diagon Alley in the *Harry Potter* films (although some say that Cecil Court, once the home of Wolfgang Amadeus Mozart who lived at number 9, and which runs between Charing Cross and St Martin's Lane is more likely, especially as it contains some magic shops). The market is well worth seeing in its own right, anyway, and does have a magical quality. It dates back to the fourteenth century and has been used in several films

If you walk straight on, Gracechurch Street becomes Bishopsgate and off to the right is Great St Helens which has a claim to having been **Shakespeare's** home during the late 1590s when he wrote, among other plays, *A Midsummer Night's Dream* and *The Merchant of Venice*. We know that he likely had lodgings in this area and also in Silver Street near St Giles Cripplegate, which is just north of here, living with a family called the Mountjoys, who made wigs for the great people of the day, and also probably for use in theatrical productions.[62]

Phillis Wheatley

You can then drop down St Mary Axe and turn left along Leadenhall Street which becomes Aldgate High Street. Here, at number 9, you will find the Dorsett City Hotel which has a plaque to Bell's Booksellers, who published Phillis Wheatley (1753–84), the first African American woman to have a book of poetry in print.

Phillis Wheatley was born in West Africa, taken to America and enslaved in the household of prominent Boston businessman, John Wheatley. Showing a literary talent, she was encouraged to read and soon became immersed in **Alexander Pope**, **John Milton** and the classics. John Wheatley was to write, in a subsequent letter to a publisher, that, from the age of seven or eight, it had taken her just 16 months to learn the English language to the extent that she was able to read the 'Most Difficult Parts of the Sacred Writings' to the 'great Astonishment of all who heard her'. He adds that she then had an inclination to learn Latin. She began to compose poems, encouraged by the Wheatleys, and these found a ready and appreciative audience in Boston where she became a local celebrity.

She travelled to London to be greeted by the rich and famous of the day, which included Benjamin Franklin and the **Earl of Dartmouth**, himself a published poet. It was a strange existence – prominent in society and yet still enslaved (she was eventually freed). In 1773, she published her *Poems on various subjects, religious and moral*: this included *On Being Brought from Africa to America*. This made her an international name.

She married John Peters and had three children, all of whom died in infancy. The married couple struggled financially and John Peters spent much time in jail for debt. Eventually, Wheatley was forced to take employment as a maid. She died in Boston on 5 December 1784, aged 31.

From here it is a short walk down Fenchurch Street to Fen Court, which is off to the right. Here you can see 'Gilt of Cain', a sculpture by Michael Visocchi with poetry by Lemn Sissay (see Walk 3 for more details of his life). It consists of 17 granite columns arranged around a viewing podium and commemorates the abolition of the transatlantic slave trade in 1807. Walk back again to the Minories on your right-hand side and follow it to the Tower of London.

The walk ends here. Tower Hill tube is very close – District (green) and Circle (yellow) lines – and the train will take you quickly back into the city centre. Hop on/hop off buses operate from here, too. Alternatively, you could cruise back along the river. Or, of course, stay for a while, see the Crown Jewels and explore the Tower along with the Thames riverside area. If you travel any further east you will be in Whitechapel. which is significant in that it was the area where 'Jack the Ripper' operated.

WALK 10

Elsewhere in London, north of the river

In This Walk: The lives and works of the following people and *fictional characters* are highlighted:

Brentford, London Borough of Hounslow: E.L. James.

Chelsea: Peter Llewelyn Davies, Sir J.M. Barrie, *Peter Pan*, John Osborne, Jez Butterworth, Errol John, Khan Din, Hanif Kureishi, David Bowie, E.R. Braithwaite, Sidney Poitier, Caryl Churchill, Thomas Wolfe, Ian Fleming, *James Bond*, John Le Carré, *George Smiley*, P.G. Wodehouse, P.L. Travers, *Mary Poppins*, Emily Blunt, Dame Emma Thompson, Sir John Betjeman, Mark Twain, Charles Dickens, Catherine Hogarth, Charles Kingsley, Henry Kingsley, Sir John Goss, Dylan Thomas, Sir Osbert Sitwell, Thomas Carlyle, A.A. Milne, *Winnie-the-Pooh*, Christopher Robin, Laurie Lee, Dame Agatha Christie, Nick Drake, Pink Floyd, Elton John, The Who, Fairport Convention, Henry James, Sir Thomas More, John Donne, Izaak Walton, Jonathan Swift, Thomas Shadwell, Katherine Mansfield, Dante Gabriel Rossetti, Algernon Charles Swinburne, Henry James, T.S. Eliot, Ian Fleming, *James Bond*, Tobias Smollett, Laurence Sterne, Thackeray, Bram Stoker, Dylan Thomas, Hilaire Belloc, Elizabeth Gaskell, Pamela Hansford Johnson, Thomas Carlyle, John Stuart Mill, Leigh Hunt, John Keats, Robert Browning, Lord Alfred Tennyson, Shelley, William Hazlitt, Charles Lamb, Lady Jane Wilde ('Speranza'), Oscar Wilde, Anthonia White, Lord Alfred Douglas ('Bosie'), Jerome K. Jerome.

Chiswick: Alexander Pope, Ralph Griffiths, Georgina, Duchess of Devonshire, G.K. Chesterton, W.B. Yeats, E.M. Forster, Harold Pinter, Nancy Mitford, Dame Iris Murdoch, J.G. Ballard, Anthony Burgess, Alun Davies Owen, Robert Bolt, John Osborne, William Makepeace Thackeray, James Berry.

Hampstead, South: H.G. Wells, Sir Walter Besant, George Bernard Shaw, Peter Cook, Sir Paul McCartney, John Lennon, Peter Ustinov, Kenneth Tynan, Dame Joan Collins, Sir Herbert Beerbohm Tree, John Constable, E.V. Knox, Arthur Llewelyn Davies, Sir J.M. Barrie, Gerald Du Maurier, Bram Stoker, *Dracula*, Aldous Huxley, George Orwell, William Shakespeare, Sigmund Freud, T.S. Eliot, John Keats, Fanny Brawne, Beryl Gilroy.

Hampstead, North: Robert Louis Stevenson, Joanna Baillie, Sir Walter Scott, John Galsworthy, Pamela Lyndon Travers, *Mary Poppins*, John Constable, Dame Daphne Du Maurier, Katherine Mansfield, Ibsen, Tolstoy, Lady Ottoline Morrell, D.H. Lawrence,

Virginia Woolf, Julia Donaldson, *The Gruffalo*, Axel Scheffler, Charles Dickens, Lord Byron, Bram Stoker, William Blake, Evelyn Waugh, Alan Hollinghurst, Paul Mendez, Will Self.

Harrow: Michael Rosen, Helen Oxenbury.

Highgate: Gerald Manley Hopkins, Sir John Betjeman, T.S. Eliot, Samuel Taylor Coleridge, Robert Southey, J.B. Priestley, Douglas Adams, Lucy Lane Clifford, George Eliot, Paul Foot, William Foyle, Karl Marx, Anthony Schaffer, Sir Leslie Stephen, Max Wall.

Holland Park and Notting Hill: P.D. James, Sir Kazuo Ishiguro, Malcolm Bradbury, Angela Carter, Sir Anthony Hopkins, Dame Emma Thompson, Samuel Selvon, Zadie Smith.

Islington: Charles Dickens, Peter Ackroyd, Zadie Smith, Joe Orton, Sir Terence Rattigan, Kenneth Halliwell, George Gissing, Andrea Levy, Richard Adams, Oscar Wilde, Dr Samuel Johnson, *Harry Potter*, J.K. Rowling, Vladimir Lenin, Charles Lamb, Ben Okri, George and Weedon Grossmith, *the Pooters*, Francesca Simon, Kenneth Williams, Sir Salman Rushdie, Stephen Fry, Evelyn Waugh.

Kensington; Percy Bysshe Shelley, Harriet Westbrook, Mary Godwin, *Frankenstein*, *Peter Pan*, Sir J.M. Barrie, Henry James, Robert Browning, Arnold Bennett, George Gissing, Max Beerbohm, H.G. Wells, Sir Terence Rattigan, Sir David Suchet, T.S. Eliot, Groucho Marx, Thackeray, Bunyan, Dickens.

To the north of Kensington High Street: G.K. Chesterton, Ezra Pound, Siegfried Sassoon, Harold Pinter, Ford Madox Ford, Violet Hunt, Cecil Day-Lewis, Kenneth Grahame, James Joyce, Ezra Pound, Dorothy Shakespear, Thackeray.

Paddington: Michael Bond, *Paddington Bear*, *Dr John H. Watson*.

Teddington: Sir Noël Coward.

Walthamstow: Solomon T. Plaatje.

BRENTFORD

This was home to **E.L. James** when she wrote *Fifty Shades of Grey* in 2011 and *Fifty Shades Darker* and *Fifty Shades Freed* the following year. The books in the trilogy have sold over 150 million copies and a film version was released to sometimes unfavourable reviews – although it made money – in 2015. In an interview with the *Guardian* published on 31 August 2012, her husband, writer Niall Leonard, says that as the incredible sales mounted, they looked at each other in their tatty old kitchen and uttered a few choice expletives…

CHELSEA

This section forms quite a long walk but it splits readily into two halves – firstly along, and on and off, Kings Road and secondly down to, and along, the Embankment and Cheyne Walk. A map accessed on the internet or a mini *AtoZ Visitors Guide* will be very useful. It is a wonderful walk, packed with interest.

The walk begins at Sloane Square tube station – District (green) and Circle (yellow) lines. It was at Sloane Square station that the publisher Peter Davies threw himself under a train. He had apparently been drinking heavily in a bar at The Royal Court Hotel; he was aged 63. **Peter Llewelyn Davies** was one of the boys that **J.M. Barrie** nurtured and upon whom *Peter Pan* was subsequently based. He regarded his 'outing' by J.M. Barrie as the inspiration for *Peter Pan* as very much a mixed blessing, much of the time a distinct curse.

The Royal Court Theatre

Close to the station is the Royal Court Theatre. Beginning life in September 1888 as the New Court Theatre it now calls itself the writers' theatre, promoting new work and writers 'undiscovered, emerging and established'.[63] It is the home of The English Stage Company.

The Royal Court staged **John Osborne's** eighth play, *Look Back in Anger,* in 1956 which caused few ripples at first but then became a massive hit, many people thinking that it did no less than revive British theatre. Osborne lived up to his angry young man image from a young age when he was expelled at 15 for hitting his Devon headmaster (although this is disputed), to the end when he reputedly enjoyed terrorising the local Shropshire vicar by threatening to withdraw his financial support for the parish church. In between he was married five times, all the while producing plays that were both hits and flops. Some of the former were *The Entertainer*, which opened at the Royal Court in 1957 with Laurence Olivier in the lead, *Inadmissible Evidence* in 1964 and *A Patriot for Me* in 1965.

The English playwright, **Jez Butterworth**, won the Olivier Award for the best new comedy with his debut at the Royal Court, with *Mojo* in 1995. His other plays for the Royal Court include *The Night Heron* (2002) and *The Winterling* (2006). His play *Jerusalem*, with Mark Rylance in the lead, premiered there in 2009 before transferring to the West End and Broadway: in all, it totalled almost one thousand performances. This was followed by *The River* (2012). Possibly his best-known play, *The Ferryman*, opened in April 2017, receiving five-star reviews across the board and becoming the fastest-selling play in the history of the Royal Court Theatre. It transferred to Broadway in 2018.

He has also worked in film. Among very many awards has been The E.M. Forster Award from the American Academy of Arts and Letters (2007).

Errol John premiered his *Moon on a Rainbow Shawl* here in 1958 which gained him the *Observer* Award for Best New Playwright. He had turned to writing largely because of the lack of parts for black actors. The play won a Guggenheim fellowship which enabled him to carry on writing as well as acting. In 1962 he played a much-praised *Othello* at the Old Vic, but he remained frustrated with the lack of equal opportunities for black performers. He died in 1988 in Camden, London at the age of 63.

Ayub Khan Din's *East is East* was produced here to critical acclaim in 1996 and a film followed, winning a 1999 BAFTA (Outstanding British Film). His sequel, *West is West*, was produced in 2011, with both productions seen as landmark plays.

Hanif Kureishi worked at the Royal Court before gaining a commission from Channel Four to write what became *My Beautiful Launderette* (1985), which centred on a gay British Pakistani youth in 1980s London and which won The New York Film Critics Best Screenplay Award and an Oscar nomination for Best Screenplay. His other work has included *The Buddha of Suburbia* (1990) which included music from David Bowie. He was awarded a C.B.E. in 2008. Hanif Kereishi is a great admirer of the writings of **E.R. Braithwaite** and was commissioned by the BBC to write a new film adaptation of his famous novel set in an East End school, *To Sir, with Love*.[64]

Caryl Churchill has regularly opened at the Royal Court and *What If If Only* was produced from September to October 2021. Her 1979 production at the Royal Court, *Cloud 9*, brought her wide recognition and won an Obie Award, a feat repeated in 1982 with *Top Girls*.

Down the Kings Road and off to the left is Wellington Square, where **Thomas Wolfe** (1900–38) lodged in 1926, at number 32, while he wrote *Look Homeward Angel*, which he said 'was a book made out of my life'. The book was published in 1929, greatly trimmed from its original length at the request of the publisher: it had two previous titles, *The Building of a Wall* and *O Lost*. It was published to some rave reviews and some that were not so good. His landlord used to bring him breakfast in bed to set him up for a day of writing, walking and planning. The title comes from **Milton**'s *Lycidas*:

> Look homeward Angel now, and melt with ruth:
> And, O ye Dolphins, waft the hapless youth.

It is also believed by some that **Ian Fleming** – who lived as a teenager and young stockbroker at nearby 119 Cheyne Walk – meant *James Bond* to live in this square as it fits the bill perfectly when, in *Casino Royale*, we are told that he lived in a square off the King's Road, in a flat converted from a Regency House: it undeniably has a suitable elegance.

Interestingly, on the opposite side of King's Road is Bywater Square which features in the tales of another spy – **John Le Carré** placed his protagonist, *George Smiley*, in *Tinker, Taylor, Soldier, Spy* and other best-selling books, at number 9.

Next square along but on the right is Markham Square, where **P.G. Wodehouse** (1881–1975) lived in 1900.

P.L. Travers and *Mary Poppins*

Smith Street leads off to your left shortly afterwards, and number 50 has a blue plaque commemorating **P.L. Travers** (1899–1996), author of the *Mary Poppins* books, the fourth of which was written during her life here 1946–62. It was also here, after many years' resistance, that she finally succumbed to the charms of Walt Disney and agreed to the filming of the tales. Although she was unhappy at the 'sugar-coating' of the character's darker aspects, the film was an immense and enduring success, gaining

Travers worldwide recognition. There has been a sequel, *Mary Poppins Returns* with Emily Blunt in the leading role (2018) and also a film concentrating on Disney's wooing of her when seeking the rights of the book – *Saving Mr Banks*, starring Dame Emma Thompson (2013).

She led a very colourful life, claiming to come from Ireland before living in Australia and then England; some claim that she exaggerated and embellished her life story and it is thus not always possible to tell fact from fiction. She is reputed to have had numerous affairs but refused to discuss her personal life. She adopted an Irish child, Camillus Travers, at the age of 40 and told him that she was his birth mother, but when he was 17, his twin brother appeared at the front door. (see also comments on Admiral's House, Chelsea below).

Leading off on the left is Radnor Walk and here, at number 29, **Sir John Betjeman** spent his final London years. Nearby, 23 Tedworth Square was the London home of **Mark Twain** (1835–1910) during his stay in London on his lecture tour of 1896–7. There is a blue plaque on the first floor of this red-brick building.

Farther along, on your right, is Chelsea Manor Street which leads to Britten Street and ahead of you is St Luke's Church, designed by James Savage in 1819; it is one of the earliest Gothic Revival churches in London. **Charles Dickens** and Catherine Hogarth – who lived in Chelsea at the time – were married here in April 1836. *The Pickwick Papers* had been published just two days previously, a book which was to make Dickens, at the age of 25, a star in the literary heavens. The father of **Charles Kingsley** – author of the 1863 didactic classic *The Water Babies, A Fairy Tale for a Land Baby* – and Henry Kingsley became rector in 1836. Sir John Goss, who wrote the music for *Praise my Soul, the King of Heaven* (1869), became organist here, a most prestigious post with a very substantial salary of £100 a year, in 1824.

Up the street and off to the right of Kings Road is Manresa Road where **Dylan Thomas** (1914–1953) lived during the Second World War and very close by is Carlyle Square; number 2 was the home of **Sir Osbert Sitwell** (1892–1969). The square was originally called Oakley Square but the name was changed to honour **Thomas Carlyle** in 1872.

Carry on to the next junction where Old Church Street leads off to the right. On the left is Mallord Street which is where, at number 13 (formerly number 11), **A.A. Milne** (1882–1956) wrote *Winnie-the-Pooh*. His son, Christopher Robin, was born here.

A short walk brings you to Elm Park Gardens where, at number 49, lived **Laurie Lee** (1914–97): he described it as 'a three-sided square of kipper-coloured houses' where all the boys played cricket in the road. He published the first part of his trilogy and probably best-known work, *Cider With Rosie*, in 1959. There followed *As I Walked Out One Midsummer Morning* (1969) and *A Moment of War* (1991).

A short walk farther north is 22 Cresswell Place where **Dame Agatha Christie**, the best-selling novelist of all time, lived for a period in the 1920s. There is a blue plaque on the top right-hand side of the front door. (see Walk 2 for more details of her life and work).

Returning to Kings Road, cross over and follow Old Church Street to the bottom. At 46a were the recording studios *Sound Techniques* where Nick Drake, Pink Floyd, Elton John, The Who and Fairport Convention were among the musicians who laid down tracks 1964–72.

Near the bottom of the street, you will find Chelsea Old Church where **Henry James** (1843–1916) worshipped and which held his funeral. **Sir Thomas More** (1478–1534) built a large house close by in around 1520 with access to the river for quick travel to London: he also attended services here. He wrote an unfinished biography of Richard III which was published after his death, as well as *Utopia*, a satirical work of fiction published in 1516. He was tried for treason and executed at Tower Hill in 1535 – he famously forgave his executioner before the deed was done, kissing him on the cheek – his body, minus the head, being thrown into the mass grave reserved for those convicted of treason. The whereabouts of the head is not universally agreed, with some saying it was taken to St Dunstan's in Canterbury while others believe it was secretly interred in the tomb erected to him here at Chelsea Old Church.

John Donne preached in the church, and others associated with it in some way include **Izaak Walton** and **Jonathan Swift**. **Thomas Shadwell**, who was Poet Laureate in the seventeenth century and and first came to notice with *The Sullen Lovers* in 1668, is buried somewhere here but his grave is unmarked. He has a memorial in Poets' Corner, Westminster Abbey.

> Nymphs and shepherds, come away
> In ye groves let's sport and play.
>
> **Thomas Shadwell**, *Nymphs*
> *and Shepherds*

Katherine Mansfield (see below in section on Hampstead) lived at 141a Old Church Street.

Cheyne Walk

Turn left by the Church and into Cheyne Walk. **Dante Gabriel Rossetti** (1828–1882) lived at number 16. He lived here with his brother, William, and **Algernon Charles Swinburne**. In his back garden, he reputedly kept various animals, including a raccoon, a white peacock and a wombat, and these so annoyed the neighbours that, to this day, leases on houses in Cheyne Walk reputedly forbid such creatures. There is a blue plaque to the front.

Swinburne published *Poems and Ballads* in 1866 to savage criticism from many – the book was immoral, blasphemous and too sensuous, too dramatic. The British Library considers that the volume caused one of the biggest outrages in literary history. Swinburne had always gone out of his way to cultivate a shocking persona, although most doubted he had done anything like the things he said he had done, particularly sexually. He took to print in his defence.

His very near neighbour, **Oscar Wilde**, admired the drama in his writing and Swinburne is considered to have influenced the style of Wilde's *The Picture of Dorian Gray* (1891). Swinburne also knew Oscar Wilde's mother, **Lady Jane Wilde** or **Speranza** as she was known to the reading public (see below, this Walk).

Henry James lived at number 21, Carlyle Mansions, moving into the flat in 1913. Other residents of the block included **T.S. Eliot** who moved into number 19, below that previously occupied by James, in 1946. **Ian Fleming**, creator of *James Bond*, lived in the block in the early 1950s but feeling claustrophobic with a wife and children, took himself off to Jamaica where he wrote *Casino Royale*, returning to the flat to finish it off. The publishers, Jonathan Cape to whom he presented it, were not at all impressed; they published it reluctantly in 1953.

Before moving into Cheyne Walk, **Henry James** had previously lived very close-by at 10 Lawrence Street: he was born an American but became quite enamoured of Chelsea.

Another resident of Lawrence Street, almost 200 years before, had been **Tobias Smollett** who lived at number 16 for twelve years from 1750 and here he wrote *Peregrene Pickle* (1751), *Ferdinand, Count Fathom* (1753) and *Sir Launcelot Greaves* (1760–62). **Laurence Sterne**, **Thackeray**, **Dickens** and **George Eliot** all reference Smollett in their work. He was prolific, writing fiction, non-fiction, plays, poems and articles for magazines; he was also a surgeon (see Walk 6).

Once, when Mr. Crawley asked what the young people were reading, the governess replied 'Smollett.' 'Oh, Smollett,' said Mr. Crawley, quite satisfied. 'His history is more dull, but by no means so dangerous as that of Mr. Hume.'

William Makepeace Thackeray, *Vanity Fair,* Chapter 10

Bram Stoker lived nearby at 18 St Leonard's Terrace – there is a blue plaque.

Number 50 was the site of The King's Head pub where **Dylan Thomas** (1914–53) used to play shove ha'penny and drink himself under the table.

It was also home to a famous coffee house called Don Saltero's, opened in 1695 by a former servant of Sir Hans Sloane named James Salter. He collected and displayed in his coffee house a collection of curiosities given by his former employer. It became a very fashionable place to linger over coffee and put the world to rights; it lasted until 1860.

Other authors who lived in Cheyne Walk included **Hilaire Belloc** – there is a blue plaque to him at number 104 – in the early 1900s, **Thomas More** (see above) and **Elizabeth Gaskell** was born at number 93 in 1810. George Eliot moved into number 4 with her new husband, John Cross, in 1880 but died shortly afterwards from kidney infections. **Pamela Hansford Johnson**, Baroness Snow, lived for a while in the 1930s at number 6 where she worked on her first novel *This Bed Thy Centre* (1935).

Off Cheyne Walk is Cheyne Row, where **Thomas Carlyle** (1799–1881) lived at number 5, later 24. Here he wrote his monumental history of the French Revolution; he lent the original manuscript of the first volume – there were three eventually – to **John Stuart Mill** who left it lying around his house in Kensington Square. The maid found it and used it to light the fire. It is the stuff of literary legend that he completed volumes two and three and then rewrote the first again from scratch. *The French Revolution: A History* was published in 1837. It was immediately extremely well received. **Charles Dickens** reportedly used the work as research for *A Tale of Two Cities*.

This leads to Upper Cheyne Row where **Leigh Hunt** (1784–1859) lived at number 22, and here there is a blue plaque. He was a friend of **Keats, Robert Browning, Alfred Tennyson** and **Shelley**, the last of whom helped him financially as he was generally short of money. He co-established the radical periodical *The Examiner*. The so-called 'Hunt Circle' in Hampstead included **William Hazlitt** and **Charles Lamb**. He wrote his autobiography in 1850 at the age of 64, a copy of which is held by the British Library.

Upper Cheyne Row comes to a T-junction with Oakley Street where number 87 was the home of **Oscar Wilde**'s mother, **Lady Jane Wilde**, from 1887–96. Oscar would stay with her in the run-up to his trial when hotels refused to put him up. She was herself a poet and writer with the pen name **Speranza**. She contracted bronchitis in 1896 and, dying, asked to see Oscar who was then in Reading gaol. This request was refused: Oscar Wilde claimed to see her 'fetch', i.e. apparition, in his cell as she passed away. She was buried in an anonymous grave in Kensal Green Cemetery and in 1999 a Celtic Cross was erected where she lay by the Oscar Wilde Society. There is now a blue plaque on the white-painted lower portion of number 87.

Cheyne Row also leads to Glebe Place where number 38 was home to **Antonia White** 1921–5. She is best known for *Frost in May* (1933), set in a convent school and largely based on her own life.

Oscar Wilde and Lord Alfred Douglas

Tite Street leads off the Embankment and at number 34 is a blue plaque to 'wit and dramatist' Oscar Wilde. He was at the peak of his career: he took a lease from 1884 and when living here he wrote *The Picture of Dorian Gray* (1891), *Lady Windermere's Fan* (1892), *A Woman of No Importance* (1893), *The Importance of Being Earnest* (1895) and *An Ideal Husband* (1895). He worked at a desk once used by Thomas Carlyle in a room painted primrose, much of the rest of the house being decorated, as he put it, in 'shades of white'. It was from here that he threw out the 8th Marquess of Queensbury, infuriated by Wilde's relationship with his son, Lord Alfred Douglas, in 1894. Wilde sued for libel. Following conviction for 'gross indecency,' the entire contents of the house were sold. On his release from Reading gaol, Wilde travelled to the Continent where he died in ignominy and debt.

Tite Street was laid out in 1877 by the Metropolitan Board of Works as part of the response to The Great Stink of 1858 (see Walk 6) and named after William Tite who was a member of the Board. It immediately became a voguish address for artists and people of letters. Over the years it has maintained its fashionable air and at the beginning of 2022 was named the most expensive street in the UK, with with complete houses – as opposed to those split into flats – costing an average of £28.9 million.

'The love that dare not speak its name', mentioned at Wilde's trial, is widely misattributed to Wilde. It actually comes from the poem, *Two Loves*, published by Lord Alfred Douglas in *The Chameleon* in 1894, when he was 24.

'I am jealous of everything whose beauty does not die. I am jealous of the portrait you have painted of me. Why should it keep what I must lose? Every moment that passes takes something from me, and gives something to it. Oh, if it was only the other way! If the picture could change, and I could be always what I am now!'

Oscar Wilde, *The Picture of Dorian Gray*, 1890

Mark Twain lived at the adjacent Tedworth Square, 1896–7, at number 23.

Slightly to the north, in Chelsea Bridge Road, are Chelsea Gardens where **Jerome K. Jerome** (1859–1927) lived when writing *Three Men in a Boat*. There is a blue plaque to the left of the block's front door.

CHISWICK

Many writers over the years have either lived in or written in Chiswick, now an affluent green suburb of London although considered by many locals to be more of a large village. This section gives some of the most notable in both categories.

Eighteenth Century

Alexander Pope (1688–1774) translated Homer's *Iliad* while living in what is now Chiswick Lane South, 1716–19. The house was on the site of the present Mawson Arms pub which bears a blue plaque. An essayist, poet and satirist, he is a very oft-quoted man. Some of his phrases have entered the English Language – these include 'damning with faint praise' and 'to err is human; to forgive, divine'.

Ralph Griffiths (1720–1803), publisher of *Fanny Hill,* lived in Linden Gardens for several decades.

Georgiana, Duchess of Devonshire (1757–1806) sensationally published *The Sylph* when living in Chiswick House; the novel features a young lady who marries a rake and libertine: he spends his money on high living, women and gambling and is destroyed in the end by his inability to pay his debts. The Duchess herself became addicted to gambling and incurred enormous debts, the extent of which – some estimates say between three and four million pounds in today's money – was only discovered upon her death. The book was published anonymously under the name 'A Young Lady' and was very successful but there remain doubts in some quarters as to the genuine author.

The Duchess is the great-great-great-great aunt of Diana, Princess of Wales and their lives bear startling similarities – unhappy, unloved in marriage but adored by the people, with tangled love lives and both given massive attention by the press and media of their day.

A film, *The Duchess*, starring Keira Knightly and Ralf Fiennes, based on her life was released in 2008 to mostly positive critical acclaim. It was nominated for two Academy Awards, winning in the Best Costume Design category.

Nineteenth Century to present day

Some of the most notable authors associated with Chiswick during this time are the following. **G.K. Chesterton** (1874–1936) set scenes from *The Man Who Was Thursday* here. The winner of the Nobel Prize for Literature, 1923, **W.B. Yeats** (1865–1939) wrote *The Lake Isle of Innisfree* in Chiswick. **E.M. Forster** (1879–1970) has a blue plaque at Arlington Park Mansions, where he lived in the 1940s and 50s.

Harold Pinter (see Walk 1) lived here in the 1950s and wrote *The Caretaker* in a first floor flat on Chiswick High Road. **Nancy Mitford** (1904–73) lived in Strand on the Green in the 1930s. **Dame Iris Murdoch** (1919–92), author of novels including *The Sea, The Sea*, and winner of the Booker Prize 1978, grew up here. **J.G. Ballard**, author of *Empire of the Sun*, lived in the area for a time. **Anthony Burgess** (1917–93), who wrote *A Clockwork Orange*, lived in Chiswick in the 1960s. **Alun Davies Owen** (1925–94), who scripted the Beatles film *A Hard Day's Night* which won him a nomination for an Academy Award, lived in Upham Park Road in the 1980s and 90s. **Robert Bolt** C.B.E. (1924–1995) – *A Man for All Seasons* and screenwriter for *Dr Zhivago* and *Lawrence of Arabia* (see Walk 6) – lived in Hartington Road for some years. He won two Academy Awards for best-adapted screenplay. **John Osborne** (see above, this Walk, under 'Chelsea') reputedly wrote *Look Back in Anger* on a houseboat in Chiswick.

William Makepeace Thackeray's *Vanity Fair* (1847–8, published in parts) begins here. The first sentence reads:

> While the present century was in its teens, and on one sunshiny morning in June, there drove up to the great iron gate of Miss Pinkerton's academy for young ladies, on Chiswick Mall, a large family coach, with two fat horses in blazing harness, driven by a fat coachman in a three-cornered hat and wig, at the rate of four miles an hour.

James Berry O.B.E. (1924–2017) lived in the area for some years: he published seven volumes of poetry including *Windrush Songs* (2007): a recording of Berry was made at the launch of the volume and can be accessed through the British Library. Among his awards was the Smarties Prize, 1987.

HAMPSTEAD
South Hampstead
This section can form a walk that begins and ends at Hampstead tube station – Northern (black) line – and is circular in a roughly anti-clockwise direction. A map accessed on the internet or a mini *AtoZ Visitors Guide* will be very useful.

H.G. Wells bought the house at 17 Church Row in 1909 and lived in it with his wife, Jane, and two sons, George and Frank Richard, until 1912. He wrote prolifically while in the house, novels including *The History of Mr Polly, Tono Bungay* and *The New Machiavelli*. A frequent visitor was **George Bernard Shaw**.

In 1965, the house was bought at auction by **Peter Cook** for £24,000 – some of his friends were horrified at the price he paid, saying that he would never get his money back – and he reputedly worked on his comedy sketches with **Dudley Moore** in the attic. Peter Cook's first wife, Wendy, a superb cook, held dinner parties which included as guests at various times Paul McCartney, John Lennon, Peter Ustinov, **Kenneth Tynan** and **Joan Collins**.

26 Church Row was the home, from 1907, of 'Bosie' or **Lord Alfred Douglas**, lover of Oscar Wilde.

Frognal Gardens leads off Church Row and at Frognal End is a blue plaque to **Sir Walter Besant** (1836–1901, see Walk 3).

In the churchyard of The Parish Church of St John-at-Hampstead, Church Row, lie **Sir Herbert Beerbohm Tree**; **Sir Walter Besant**; John Constable; **Peter Cook**; **E.V. Knox**; **Arthur Llewelyn Davies**, his wife Sylvia and their children Jack and Peter and, in a separate grave, their brother Michael – who befriended **J.M. Barrie** and helped inspire *Peter Pan*; **Gerald Du Maurier**, father of novelist **Daphne**; and Alec Waugh, brother of Evelyn. Additionally, the churchyard may have inspired Bram Stoker when writing *Dracula*.[65]

16 Bracknell Gardens was briefly home to **Aldous Huxley** 1919–20. Aldous Huxley (1894–1963) is probably best known for *Brave New World* (1932) which is often compared to Orwell's *1984*: indeed, the two were friends and corresponded about this. Huxley said that the utopian novels of **H.G. Wells** were an influence. The title comes from *The Tempest* by **William Shakespeare** Act V. Miranda is speaking:

> O, wonder!
> How many goodly creatures are there here!
> How beauteous mankind is! O brave new world,
> That has such people in't!

Similarly, *Mortal Coils* (1921), a collection of five fictional pieces, is taken from *Hamlet* while the American title of his essay *Tomorrow and Tomorrow and Tomorrow* (1956) comes from *Macbeth*.

Sigmund Freud (1856–1939) lived at 20 Maresfield Gardens for the last year of his life. His daughter, Anna, lived in the house until 1982. It was opened as a museum in 1986.

T.S. Eliot lived at Fairhurst, Compayne Gardens following his first marriage in 1915, although he regarded the house as 'gloomy'.

George Orwell (Eric Arthur Blair) lived at 77 Parliament Hill briefly in 1934–5 (he changed his name partly because he thought 'Eric' sounded like a Victorian prig).

John Keats moved into Keats House, 10 Keats Grove, which was owned by his friend, Charles Armitage Brown, in December 1818 and stayed until his departure for Rome in August 1820. Fanny Brawne, who he found hopelessly distracting when trying to work, lived next door. Here he finished *Eve of St Agnes* and wrote *Ode to a Nightingale*. Threatened by demolition in 1920, the house was saved following a fundraising drive in the UK and America and now operates partly as a museum under the auspices of the City of London Corporation.

> A thing of beauty is a joy for ever:
> Its loveliness increases; it will never
> Pass into nothingness; but still will keep
> A bower quiet for us, and a sleep
> Full of sweet dreams, and health, and quiet breathing.

John Keats, *Endymion* (1818)

In West Hampstead, at Beckford Primary School, **Beryl Gilroy** (1924–2001) became the first black headteacher in the borough of Camden and she published her autobiographical account of the experience in *Black Teacher* in 1976. She became one of the most published Caribbean writers in Britain, with poetry and novels such as *Frangipani House* (1986), *Boy-Sandwich* (1989) and *Sunlight on Sweet Water* (1994). Her final novel, *The Green Grass Tango*, was published posthumously in 2001.

North Hampstead

This section can form a walk that begins at Hampstead tube station – Northern (black) line – you can either go 'up the hill and down again' or you can trek straight from Hampstead tube station to Golders Green tube station (Northern line again). It is quite hilly at the beginning. A map accessed on the internet or a mini *AtoZ Visitors Guide* will be very useful.

You will see a plaque to **Robert Louis Stevenson** who stayed in a house at Mount Vernon, June – July 1874. He was in London many times, including in Hampstead, for short periods often on the way to somewhere else. He was fascinated by what he referred to as 'the climate of Hampstead', so healthy and beautiful, and yet you could find yourself in the centre of the city in almost no time at all.

Joanna Baillie (1762–1851), poet, playwright and friend of **Sir Walter Scott**, who lived at Windmill Hill, was celebrated in her lifetime and the Victorian age, even being referred to as 'a female Shakespeare'.[66] Her adult life was largely spent in Hampstead. Her poems often meditated on nature, life and youth, first gaining contemporary attention with *Poems: Wherein it is Attempted to Describe Certain Views of Nature and of Rustic Manners* (1790). She wrote 27 plays, including *A Series of Plays: in which it is attempted to delineate the stronger passions of the mind, each passion being the subject of a tragedy and a comedy* (1798). Much to her satisfaction, all of her writings apart from her religious works were gathered together in one single volume just before she died. Her sister, Agnes, lived to be 100 and both are buried alongside their mother in Hampstead Parish churchyard.

> Nor, O, despise my last adieu!
> I've lov'd thee long, and lov'd thee true.
>
> **Joanna Baillie**, *A Melancholy Lover's*
> *Farewell to His Mistress*, Poems (1790)

Admiral's Walk was where **John Galsworthy** (1867–1933), best known to many for *The Forsyte Saga*, lived at Grove Lodge. He was educated at Harrow and Oxford and

> It was such a spring day as breathes into a man an ineffable yearning, a painful sweetness, a longing that makes him stand motionless, looking at the leaves or grass and fling out his arms to embrace he knows not what.
>
> John Galsworthy, *The Forsyte Saga*, 1922

began writing at the age of 28 under the pseudonym **John Sinjohn**. He published a book of short stories in 1930, *On Forsyte Change*. Also a playwright, he championed social injustices in his work, *The Silver Box* (1906) highlighting inequalities in the treatment of the upper and lower classes; *Strife* (1909) focused on the confrontation of capital and labour; and his most famous play, *Justice*, in 1910 led to prison reform. He was awarded the Nobel Prize in Literature, 1932. He refused a knighthood.

Next door is the Admiral's House, with the roof shaped into a quarter-deck. An occupant of the house, Admiral Barton, who liked to fire canons just like *Admiral Boom* in the books, is said to have inspired **Pamela Lyndon Travers** when writing the *Mary Poppins* series, subsequently turned into one of the most successful films of all time by the Disney Corporation (see also comments on 50 Smith Street, Chelsea, above).

Admiral's House itself was frequently depicted by John Constable in his paintings.

On the edge of the Heath, Cannon Hall was the childhood home of **Dame Daphne Du Maurier, Lady Browning**, (1907–1989). Her first novel *The Loving Spirit* was published in 1931 and she was described as the most highly paid woman writer in the world when at the height of her success with *My Cousin Rachel* in the 1950s. Some of her most famous novels and short stories such as *Rebecca* – probably the most noted version is that directed by Alfred Hitchcock in 1940 – *Jamaica Inn*, *The Birds* and *Don't Look Now* have been turned into films.

Katherine Mansfield

Katherine Mansfield (1888–1923), and her husband, literary critic, **J.M. Murry** (1889–1957) lived at 17 East Heath Road. Katherine Mansfield is one of the most celebrated short story writers of the twentieth century. Her output was prolific – she wrote reviews and letters also – and was instrumental in shaping modernism before her untimely death from tuberculosis in 1923.

An extraordinary life began in New Zealand in a prosperous household, and in 1903 she came over to study in London at Queens College where she thrived, studying writers and writing, especially **Ibsen, Tolstoy, Wilde** and **Shaw**, and also met Ida Baker who became a lifelong friend (Mansfield later referred to her as a 'wife', so great was the caring given when she was becoming very ill). She briefly went back to New Zealand for the last time in her life, returning to England in 1908. She married a singing teacher but immediately left him and for the rest of her days had what is often referred to as a turbulent love life. She spent some time at the spa in Bad Worishoven which inspired her first collection of short stories *In a German Pension* in 1911: at this time also she was disinherited by her mother and met **John Middleton Murry**, editor of *Rhythm*. In 1916 she formed a friendship with Lady Ottoline Morrell (see Walk 8) who introduced her to the literati of the day. She became very close to several people, especially **D.H. Lawrence**. In 1918 **Virginia Woolf**'s Hogarth Press published *Prelude*. She married Murry and published two other highly-praised story collections in 1920 and 1922. On the evening of 9 January 1923, she became ill and is reported as saying 'I think I am going to die' which she did minutes later. Murry subsequently published almost all of her works.

Mansfield inspired an immense amount of newsprint in her day in many types of publications from the *Daily Mirror* to the *Spectator* to *International Woman*

Suffrage News. Lady Morrell considered her, in part, a very talented actress, while the *Westminster Gazette*, the year before her death, wrote that she 'made and perfected the short story'[67] as she wrote it. Such a combination, and an extraordinary output, even when she was becoming ill, produced one of the media stars of her age.

Well Walk leads off East Heath Road and where it forms a junction with New End Square, you will find Burgh House, a Queen Anne period mansion that hosts musical and literary events. **Julia Donaldson** told the *Ham and High*[68] newspaper that her mother sang alto in the Hampstead Choral Society there and that her father researched the history of the house and put on wonderful concerts of songs and music. Julia Donaldson was born and raised locally, near Hampstead Heath, in a three-story house containing relatives and a cat called Geoffrey. In 1995 she came across a Chinese story that intrigued her; she experimented with various changes and finally produced *The Gruffalo*, which she asked Axel Scheffler to illustrate. It was an immediate and very considerable success winning many awards, including the *Smarties Prize* (1999). It has since sold over 10 million copies. Many books have followed, including *The Smeds and the Smoos* (2020) where the Smeds (who are red) refuse to mix with the Smoos (who are blue). So what will happen when one of the Smeds falls in love with one of the Smoos? The lovestruck pair, Janet and Bill, have to face their parents' strong disapproval as the fun begins. Julian Donaldson was also Children's Laureate 2011–13.

The Spaniards Inn, Spaniards Road, was probably built in its original form about 1585, one of the seventeenth century landlords having reputedly been Dick Turpin's father, and legend has it that the infamous highwayman was born in the building – certainly, in the eighteenth century it was a drinking haunt for the criminal classes who robbed those travelling over the Heath or through Hampstead. It is claimed that patrons have included **Dickens, Keats** and **Byron.** Dickens mentions it in *The Pickwick Papers* when *Mr Raddle* and *Tommy* escort *Mrs Bardell* and accompanying ladies to the pub for refreshments which, consisting of 'sundry plates of oranges and biscuits and a bottle of old crusted port… afforded unlimited satisfaction to everybody.' **Bram Stoker** also mentions the pub in *Dracula.*

There is a blue plaque on 'Old Wyldes', North End, commemorating the fact that **William Blake** stayed here as a guest of John Linnell, the painter (1792–1882).[69]

Evelyn Waugh

Evelyn Waugh (1903–66) was born in a house in Hillfield Road, West Hampstead, near the cricket ground and moved to 145 North End Road when he was three. He famously referred to Hampstead as 'a pleasure garden' for Londoners. He attended Oxford University, from which he emerged without a degree.[70] In 1928, *Decline and Fall*, which was partly infused with his own feelings of being a teacher, and, in 1930, *Vile Bodies*, made him famous.

Following the dissolution of his marriage to Evelyn Gardener he converted to the Roman Catholic faith, an act which for him was the most important of his life. He was a prolific writer and the next few years produced, among other works, *A Handful of Dust* (1934) and *Scoop* (1938). When war broke out he enlisted in the Royal Marines, becoming Captain Waugh. He continued to write and in 1945 came a work with which he is sometimes defined – *Brideshead Revisited* in which, perhaps more than in any other work, his Catholic faith is on display: it became an enormous success in literary and financial terms.

His output did not slow down after the war and in the 1950s came his war trilogy – *Men at Arms* (1952), *Officers and Gentlemen* (1955) and *Unconditional Surrender* (1961). The critics were never quiet right up to his death on Easter Sunday 1966 but he remains one of literature's great stylists, often provocative and, at times, absurdly funny. After his death, he gained a new and passionate audience upon the filming in 1981 of *Brideshead Revisited*.

Alan Hollinghurst lives in Hampstead with his partner, **Paul Mendez**. His first novel was *The Swimming Pool Library* (1988). He won the 2004 Man Booker Prize for his novel *The Line of Beauty*. In 2011 his novel *The Stranger's Child* was longlisted for the Man Booker Prize. Paul Mendez is a black British writer who has written the semi-autobiographical *Rainbow Milk* (2020): it is the story of a black gay man who, outed by his community, leaves home.

Will Self, author of novels including *Shark* (2014) and *Phone* (2017) as well as short story collections and non-fiction work, was brought up in north London between East Finchley and Hampstead Garden Suburb.

HARROW
Michael Rosen, children's author, poet, performer, scriptwriter and political columnist was born in Roxborough Park, Harrow in 1946. He has written or been involved in other ways with over 140 books. On his comprehensive and interesting website[71] he says that he began writing poetry at the age of 12, about people he knew. His *We're Going on a Bear Hunt* (1989), illustrated by Helen Oxenbury, won numerous awards including the Nestle Smarties Book Prize. He served as Children's Laureate 2007–2009.

HIGHGATE
Gerard Manley Hopkins (1844–1889) and **Sir John Betjeman** (1906–1984) attended Highgate School. **T.S. Eliot** taught there in 1916. Number 31, Highgate West Hill, was the childhood home of **Sir John Betjeman**.

Highgate's most visited resident in his day was undoubtedly **Samuel Taylor Coleridge** (1772–1834), who lived with the Gillman family at number 3, The Grove, from 1823 – although their association had begun in another house in 1816 – until his death. Faced with his opium addiction, the Gillmans did their level best to give Coleridge a peaceful and affectionate home. He was already a celebrated writer, companion and talker, following the publication of *The Rime of the Ancient Mariner* (1798), *Kubla Khan* (1816) and *Christabel* (1816), *Sybilline Leaves* and *Biographia Literaria* – a critical autobiography – in 1817. The great and the good vied for his company. His opium addiction continued and he managed to regularly obtain a secret supply of drugs from a sympathetic chemist in the village where he would wait by a special door at a pre-arranged time. He is buried in the local cemetery.

He was a great friend of **Robert Southey** (1774–1843), Poet Laureate for the last 30 years of his life. They had previously discussed establishing a perfect society to be based, first in America and then in Wales, but nothing was to come of it. They collaborated on a three-act play, *The Fall of Robespierre*, in 1894. Southey himself is credited with the original story which became *Goldilocks and the Three Bears*. In 1837 he published Th*e Story of the Three Bears* in his collection *The Doctor*, and over the next few decades this was modified until it became the story we know today.

Coleridge's Highgate home was bought by **J.B. Priestley** (1894–1984) and he lived here from 1933–1939, luxuriating in the atmosphere as he sat and typed in **Coleridge**'s old room.

Highgate Cemetery

Many people come to see Highgate Cemetery which is in two parts on either side of Swain's Lane.

In the 1800s London had a rapidly-expanding population of over one million people and no provision of any real kind for burials. Often, almost any piece of land – between houses, shops and inns or beside a road – was used for a shallow burial: many times quicklime was added to facilitate fast decomposition so that the 'grave' could be used again. Parliament decided that seven new private cemeteries should be provided in London and one of them was Highgate.

The West Cemetery was opened in 1839 and the East Cemetery followed in 1855. It was designed and run by the London Cemetery Company under the direction of Stephen Geary, an architect and civil engineer, and included chapels, a Colonnade on the west side of the entrance, the Lebanon Circle preceded by an Egyptian Avenue and the Terrace Catacombs. The whole was landscaped with wide gravel pathways, chestnut trees, flowers and evergreens and was seen as a wonderful place to promenade and enjoy the views over London. By the 1850s land for plots was becoming scarce and the eastern section, which doubled the cemetery's size, was added. By 1888 there were 25,000 graves with up to four bodies in each. With cremations becoming ever more popular, finances became a problem until in the 1960s the cemetery ran out of money and was left neglected. In 1975 'The Friends of Highgate Cemetery' took up the mantle and they still run things today. There continue to be burials – there are now over 53,000 graves – but the site is of especial interest to many of the visitors who come for the architecture and natural history. In July 2021 a new 25-year masterplan was announced to ensure that the cemetery remains historic and sustainable for both grave owners and visitors. Entry is between 10 am and 5 pm by timed ticket for either a tour or self-guided visit.[72]

Those buried here include **Douglas Adams,** author of *The Hitchhiker's Guide to the Galaxy*; Lucy Lane Clifford, better known as **Mrs W.K. Clifford**, novelist; **George Eliot**, poet and novelist whose most famous work is probably *Middlemarch* (published in eight instalments 1871–2); **Paul Foot**, journalist; William Foyle, co-founder of bookseller's Foyles; John Lobb, society bootmaker; **Karl Marx**, co-author with Friedrich Engels, of *The Manifesto of the Communist Party*; **Anthony Shaffer**, playwright and novelist, whose works include *Sleuth* (1970); **Sir Leslie Stephen**, author and father of **Virginia Woolf**; and entertainer, Max Wall.

Holland Park and Notting Hill

To the north of this area is Holland Park and Notting Hill. **P.D. James** (1920–2014) lived in Holland Park Avenue. Nearby, off Ladbroke Grove, is 31 Kensington Park Gardens which was the home of the Llewelyn Davies children, the inspiration behind *Peter Pan*, from 1897 to 1904.

Sir Kazuo Ishiguro

In the spring of 1979, Nobel Laureate, Sir Kazuo Ishiguro (born 1954 in Nagasaki, Japan), worked in the Notting Hill area for the charity, West London Cyrenians. He had just graduated from the University of Kent. Here he met his wife, Lorna MacDougall. It was here as well, while still working for the Cyrenians that he decided to apply for an MA in the pioneering Creative Writing course at the University of East Anglia (UEA) – at the time the only such course in the UK. A small course of just a few participants each year, it was run by novelist, **Malcolm Bradbury**. **Angela Carter**, whose best-known work, *The Bloody Chamber*, was published in 1979, became his personal tutor and they remained friends until her untimely death at the age of 51 in 1992. There is now a blue plaque at her home for the last sixteen years of her life, 107 The Chase, Clapham.

Following his MA at UEA, Ishiguro returned to work for the Cyrenians but became a full-time writer following the publication of his novel, *A Pale View of Hills* in 1983.

The University of East Anglia, designed by Sir Denys Lasdun, where Sir Kazuo Ishiguro signed up for the famed Creative Writing course.

He received the Booker Prize in 1989 for *The Remains of the Day* which was turned into a famous film starring Sir Anthony Hopkins and Dame Emma Thompson and directed by James Ivory: it was nominated for eight Academy Awards. There followed, among other novels, *Never Let Me Go* (2015) and *Klara and the Sun* (2021). He received the Nobel Prize in Literature in 2017. He has received many other awards including the Order of the Rising Sun, Gold and Silver Star, from Japan. Sir Kazuo Ishiguro still lives in London.[73]

The Notting Hill, Bayswater and North Kensington areas are today mainly affluent but it was not always so – in **Samuel Selvon**'s *The Lonely Londoners* (1956) many people of Caribbean descent and newly arrived in Britain struggle to find a job and a purpose on the streets here while living in tiny rooms cut out from large, decrepit houses. The book is narrated in creolised English and is in some ways the precursor of novels such as **Zadie Smith**'s *White Teeth* (see below).

ISLINGTON

Here you will find Sadler Wells Theatre, in Roseberry Avenue. This magical theatre traces its story back to an equally magical spring in 1683. As the official website puts it, people came to see the spring and stayed on for the music. The Royal Ballet, Birmingham Royal Ballet and English National Opera all began here. **Dickens** came here as a boy to watch the clown Joe Grimaldi and as an adult saw his own *Oliver Twist* put on here. **Peter Ackroyd**, one of Dickens' biographers, a famous literary resident, writes of the area in books such as *The House of Dr Dee* (1993) and the *Clerkenwell Tales* (2003).

Another contemporary writer is **Zadie Smith** whose *NW* (2012) features Willesden, Kilburn and Hampstead Heath. *White Teeth* (2000) is also rooted in Willesden and has won multiple awards. Her fifth novel, *Swing Time*, was long-listed for the Man Booker Prize 2017. Tahmima Anam lives in Kilburn.

Joe Orton

Number 25, Noel Road was home to the cramped flat of Joe Orton who wrote *Entertaining Mr Sloane, Loot,* and *What the Butler Saw*. A most unlikely fan was **Sir Terence Rattigan** (see above, this Walk), who came from a completely different era in terms of sexual mores, but his investment of £3,000 enabled 'Sloane' to transfer to the West End.

He lived his extraordinarily successful (following a spell in prison for defacing library books) but short life here with his lover, Kenneth Halliwell from 1959–67. Some critics at the time and since have compared his acerbic wit to that of **Oscar Wilde**. Tormented by sexual jealousy and probably lack of success in his own right, Halliwell battered 34–year-old Orton to death with a hammer in the early morning of 9 August 1967. He then killed himself with a drug overdose. He left a note saying that all will be explained if the finder looks at Orton's diaries, which is usually taken to mean the descriptions of his multiple sexual encounters.

The library book incidents which sent them to jail involved Orton and Halliwell going to their local library where they would add comedy collages to the book jackets, as well as cutting out whole pages with which they decorated the walls of their flat, and this so infuriated the librarian, Sidney Porrett, who had a very good idea of who was responsible, that he devised a 'sting' operation to catch them. He wrote to Halliwell about an illegally parked car and received a sarcastic, typed reply saying that Halliwell did not own a car. This was exactly what he wanted and he was able to match the typeface of the letter to that on the defaced books. Old Street magistrates came down hard on them – Orton said this was 'because we're queers' – and whereas a fine might have reasonably been expected, they were sent to separate prisons where Orton used the time to gather information that he would use in his subsequent work.

Joe Orton rarely appeared on TV, but in 1967 he said this to Eamon Andrews – the big 'chat' host at the time – when questioned about the library books:

> Oh, it was really just a joke. I didn't like libraries anyway… I thought they spent far too much money on rubbish.

On the same programme he also said: 'I had a marvellous time in prison'. Kenneth Halliwell was broken by it.

George Gissing (1857–1903) lived just up the road at number 60. In a tumultuously tortured existence, he married a prostitute who had infatuated him but in the end, he was forced to pay her to stay away. Critical and financial success largely eluded him. He died in 1903 at the age of 46. His reputation improved in the decades following his death, and the most famous of his works now are *The Nether World* (1889), *New Grub Street* (1891), *Born in Exile* (1892) and *The Odd Women* (1893). He also wrote *Charles Dickens: A Critical Study* (1898).

Andrea Levy (1959–2019) was born in the Archway area of the borough. She began writing in her mid-thirties and produced five novels and two short story collections. Her father came over to the UK in 1948 on the *Empire Windrush* and her novels explore the experience of Black Britons and the relationship between Britain and the Caribbean. Her work includes *Every Light in the House Burnin'* (1994), *Small Island* (2004), *The Long Song* (2010), *Uriah's War* (2014) and *Six Stories and an Essay* (2014). She has won many awards including the Orange Prize for *Small Island* and the Commonwealth Writer's Prize: she was also elected a fellow of the Royal Society of Literature.

Some more notable people and locations in brief

The area is teeming with writers, fictional characters and places of note in a literary sense, past and present. The following are some of the most notable people and addresses for a variety of reasons.

Holloway Prison: **Oscar Wilde** was held here while awaiting trial for gross indecency in 1895.

Dr Samuel Johnson (1709–84) worked in St John's Gate in the south of the Borough on the *Gentleman's Magazine* in the 1730s and '40s. It was hugely popular and one of the first general-interest magazines carrying pieces on literature, history, art, natural sciences, politics, medical matters and medicine.[74]

Kings Cross Station: this is the station from which *Harry Potter* takes the train to Hogwarts from Platform 9¾ in **J.K. Rowling**'s books. The exterior shots of the location in the films are actually the adjacent St Pancras Station which is much more striking. The headquarters of the mysterious Order in Harry Potter and the *Order of the Phoenix* (2003) is probably just up Pentonville Road, leading out of the city and just after Calshot Street.

Vladimir Lenin edited *Iskra* (The Spark) from rooms in Clerkenwell Green, 1902–3. *Iskra* declared in 1900 that the Social-Democratic working-class movement was destined to grow and grow and would, in the end, surmount all obstacles that confront it.

Number 64 Colebroke Cottage, Colebroke Row, was the home of essayist, **Charles Lamb** (1775–1834), from 1823–1827. The road is now Duncan Terrace.

Ben Okri, author of *The Famished Road* (1991) and Booker prize-winner, knew the area well.

Pemberton Gardens: This is often thought to be home of the *Pooters* in George and Weedon Grossmith's *Diary of a Nobody* – in the book their address is given as The Laurels, Brickfield Terrace, Holloway.

Francesca Simon, writer of the *Horrid Henry* series (1994–) lives here.

Kenneth Williams (1926–1988), comedian, actor and diarist was born off the Caledonian Road, where Bingfield Street is now. In *The Kenneth William's Diaries* (1993) he hilariously details, amongst many, many other things, his relationship with **Joe Orton** and **Kenneth Halliwell** which included going on holiday with them to Tangier where Orton went off on homosexual adventures, with Williams and Halliwell too timid to follow his lead.[75]

Winsome Pinnock, a British playwright of Jamaican heritage, was born here in 1961. Her plays include *Mules*, *Talking in Tongues* and *Leave Taking*.

Other literary residents of the area include, or have included, Salman Rushdie, George Orwell, Stephen Fry, Evelyn Waugh and Diran Adebayo.

KENSINGTON
Percy Bysshe Shelley, Harriet Westbrook and Mary Godwin

Kensington Gardens is where, in Long Water, Harriet Shelley, first wife of **Percy Bysshe Shelley** (1792–1822) drowned herself. Percy Bysshe Shelley and Harriet Westbrook had eloped to Scotland when Shelley was 19 and she 16.

In 1814 Shelley met and fell in love with **Mary Godwin**. The couple travelled to Lake Geneva where Shelley spent a great deal of time with **Lord Byron** and it was during this period that Mary devised her great novel, *Frankenstein, or The Modern Prometheus*. In 1816, Harriet, having first retreated to her father's house which she found restricting, and then into lodgings at Hans Place, Knightsbridge, wrote a sombre suicide note, walked to Long Water, and drowned herself: she was 20 years old and pregnant, although by whom is unknown while speculation abounds to this day.

Shortly afterwards, Shelley and Mary Godwin were married and left England for the last time to settle in Italy. This was the period that Shelley produced all his major works, including *Prometheus Unbound*. Shelley himself was drowned, just before his 30th birthday, on 8 July 1822 while sailing his ship, *Don Juan*, towards La Spezia. The ship had been specially built for him but may have been unstable. His body was washed up ten days later and a copy of **Keats'** *Lamia* was found in his pocket.

And the sunlight clasps the earth
And the moonbeams kiss the sea:
What is all this sweet work worth
If thou kiss not me?

Percy Bysshe Shelley, from
Love's Philosophy (1819)

Shelley wrote on many subjects, including to promote atheism (after he died, some in the press wrote that he would *now* know if there was a God or nay) and radical politics. He was an early advocate of vegetarianism, maintaining a vegetable diet, with some lapses, from 1812: he wrote two essays on the subject, including *A Vindication of Natural Diet* (1813).

In Kensington Gardens, also, is the statue of *Peter Pan*, commissioned and paid for by **J.M. Barrie** himself. It was erected at night on 30 April 1912, the idea being that the following morning it would appear to walkers that *Peter Pan* had arrived by magic. It was here that Barrie met the upper-class Llewellyn Davies boys, grew increasingly fond of them and became the guardian of all five when their mother died. They became the

Knightsbridge. Harriet Shelley was staying in lodgings in Hans Place, just south of this grand thoroughfare, in her final days. Harrods itself was where, in 1921, A.A. Milne reputedly bought a bear for his son, Christopher Robin; the bear 'became' Winnie-the-Pooh. The honey-loving bear is regularly voted one of the best-loved literary characters in the United Kingdom and he has a star on the Hollywood Walk of Fame.

models for *Peter Pan* but lived far from magical lives, in that Michael drowned when he was 20, George perished in the First World War at the age of 21 and Peter committed suicide in 1960 (see above).

South of Kensington Road

De Vere Gardens, to the south of the gardens and off Kensington Road, housed **Henry James** in 1886, at number 34 on the fourth floor and, opposite, the following year, **Robert Browning** at number 29. Whilst here, James agreed to contribute to a new radical publication, *The Yellow Book*, which had an illustrious contributor list that included **Arnold Bennett** – who submitted, and had accepted, an early piece after it had been turned down by *Tit-Bits*, **George Gissing**, **Max Beerbohm** and **H.G. Wells**. Its yellow cover reminded people of the racier French novels and it became associated in part with decadence: Lord Henry gives a book with a yellow, slightly frayed edges, to *Dorian Gray* as he descends into depravity in **Wilde**'s novel.

Nearby, at 29 Hyde Park Gate, lived **Enid Bagnold** (1889–1981), best known for *National Velvet*, published in 1935. There is a round blue plaque here.

South of De Vere Gardens is Cornwall Gardens and it was at number 3 (now 100) that **Sir Terence Rattigan** (1911–77) was born. A blue plaque was unveiled here in 2005 by the actor famous for portraying **Agatha Christie**'s detective, *Poirot*, David Suchet. Widely seen as one of the greatest playwrights of the twentieth century, Rattigan's plays include *The Winslow Boy* (1946*), The Browning Version* (1948) and *The Deep Blue Sea* (1952). Unrequited love, repression and unequal relationships form themes in much of his best work – at Oxford University he had suffered unrequited love for a fellow male student, and this motivated him to write his first published work, co-written with that same student, *First Episode*, in 1933, although the homosexual tone was considerably toned down for fear of the censors. He spent the last ten years of his life in the Bahamas.

T.S. Eliot lived in number 3 Kensington Court Gardens and liked to exercise in the park. Whilst here, he formed a great friendship with Groucho Marx, having discovered that Marx was a fan of his poetry; they dined together a number of times. He died here on 4 January 1965.

Thackeray Street was named after the novelist whose house at number 16 Young Street is nearby. In this handsome double-fronted property he wrote his masterpiece, *Vanity Fair* (published in eagerly awaited instalments 1847–8), and *Pendennis* (1848–50). The title of the former is taken from **Bunyan**'s *Pilgrim's Progress* where it is the centre of human corruption, a place which, according to the author, 'is a very vain, wicked, foolish place, full of all sorts of humbugs and falseness and pretensions'. It was intended to be not just entertaining but moral and instructive also. **Thackeray** was seen thereafter as the equal of **Dickens** in literary terms. There is a plaque above the front door.

To the north of Kensington High Street

St Mary Abbots Church, Kensington Church Walk, is where both **G.K. Chesterton** (to Frances Blogg) and **Ezra Pound** (to Dorothy Shakespear) arranged their weddings.

In 1931 **James Joyce** moved for a short while into 28b Campden Grove but found it far too quiet. He called it 'Campden Grave'.

Campden Hill Square has several blue plaques, including one to **Siegfried Sassoon** (1886–1967) who lived at number 23 from1925 to 1932. This had also been the home, in the 1890s, of the Llewelyn Davies family, the sons of whom **J.M. Barrie** used as models in *Peter Pan*. Number 52 was the home of **Harold Pinter** in the early 1980s.

Campden Hill Road – number 80 – was the home, 1913–9, of **Ford Madox Ford**, who produced *The English Review*. The house was also owned by **Violet Hunt**, who founded the *Women Writers' Suffrage League*. **Cecil Day-Lewis** lived at number 96 in the mid-1950s.

Kenneth Grahame (1859–1932), author of *Wind in the Willows* (see Walk 9) lived nearby at number 16 Phillimore Place, 1901–8.

G.K. Chesterton

Sheffield Terrace leads off Campden Hill Road and number 32 was the birthplace and home for a few years of G.K. Chesterton (1874–1936), 'the prince of paradox' who created *Father Brown*. At the time of writing, the *Father Brown* television series, based on Chesterton's 53 tales, has become the second longest-running drama show on BBC daytime television and has been sold to 232 countries and territories.

G.K. Chesterton was a prolific writer of novels, poetry and also in newspapers and magazines on a huge range of subjects and often in different styles: his *The Man Who Was Thursday* (1908) has been described as a place where Edward Lear meets Kafka.

> Poets have been mysteriously silent on the subject of cheese

> **G.K. Chesterton**, *Alarms and Discursions* (1910)

He is one of the most quoted people in history and promoter of *clerihews*, named after his friend, Edmund Clerihew Bentley. These are four-line poems with the subject's name being the first line followed by three more lines of irregular length. Edmund Bentley had the first one come to him at school during a science lesson when he was 16 – there are several versions of it, but this is probably the original:

> Sir Humphry Davy
> Was not fond of gravy.
> He lived in the odium
> Of having discovered sodium

One of his most famous is:

> Sir Christopher Wren
> Said, 'I am going to dine with some men.
> If anyone calls
> Say I am designing St. Paul's.'

Towards the end of his life Pope Pius XI invested him as Knight Commander with Star of the Papal Order of St. Gregory the Great. Following his death, a Requiem Mass was held for him in Westminster Cathedral.

There is a very active Chesterton Society: www.chesterton.org

Follow Campden Grove into Holland Place where number 5 Holland Place Chambers is where **Ezra Pound** and Dorothy Shakespear lived following their marriage in 1914; he wrote *Hell Cantos* (1919) here. He left England for Paris in 1920, not to return for over 40 years.

Nearby, at number 2 Palace Green, is the house that **Thackeray** had built and in which he lived for the last year of his life, 1862–3.

To the south of where you are now, **Pound** had lived 1909–14 in nearby number 10 Kensington Church Walk.

Paddington

One famous fictional resident of Paddington is the marmalade-loving *Paddington Bear* who arrived at Paddington Station from darkest Peru with a sign around his neck saying 'Please look after this bear. Thank you' (*Paddington* had been brought up to always be polite: his most extreme action to those who were rude to him was a 'hard stare' which would show them the error of their ways). He was, apparently, originally to have been from Africa but **Michael Bond**'s agent pointed out that there were no bears there. *Paddington* was adopted by *the Brown family* and went to live in Notting Hill, where he had many adventures.

> In London, everyone is different, and that means anyone can fit in.
>
> **Michael Bond**, *Paddington Bear*

He came into being when the BBC employee and part-time author, Michael Bond (1926–2017), noticed a lonely bear sitting by himself on a shelf in a shop near Paddington Station on Christmas Eve, 1956. He bought the bear as a present for his wife.

The books have sold over 35 million copies worldwide and been filmed many times: the 2017 film *Paddington 2,* directed by Paul King with the character of *Paddington* voiced by Ben Whishaw, received particularly enthusiastic acclaim.

Paddington's status as a national treasure was reinforced during Queen Elizabeth II's Platinum Jubilee in 2022 when he was 'filmed having tea' with the Monarch. He produced a marmalade sandwich from his hat which he offered to the Queen, only to have her open her handbag to reveal one of her own which she told him she was keeping 'for later'. (The Queen had previously been celebrated in literary and film terms by 'parachuting out of a plane' with *James Bond* into the Olympic Stadium in 2012).

Another famous fictional resident is *Dr John Watson*. He tells us in *The Adventure of the Engineer's Thumb* that, when he left his Baker Street rooms which he shared with *Sherlock Holmes*, he bought a medical practice which was 'no very great distance from Paddington Station'. Indeed, he was friendly with many of the station staff and received some of his patients as a result of their recommendations.

Peter Cushing, who played *Sherlock Holmes* many times, as well as **Sir Arthur Conan Doyle** himself, regarded the consulting detective as arrogant, even unpleasant, and once remarked that he would rather take a job sweeping Paddington Station than ever play the man again.

TEDDINGTON

Just north of the river, a blue plaque at 131 Waldegrave Road, Teddington, marks the house where **Sir Noël Coward** (see Walk 2 for more details) was born in 1899: he died in 1973. He survived two world wars and prospered, particularly in the second, as well as the swinging sixties, and on film, he masterminded *The Italian Job* (1969), in which he starred with Sir Michael Caine.

Wouldn't it be dreadful to live in a country where they didn't have tea?

Sir Noël Coward

WALTHAMSTOW

Solomon T. Plaatje (1876–1932) has a blue plaque at 25 Carnarvon Road, Walthamstow. He was a campaigner for African rights and author of *Native Life in South Africa* (1916) and the historical novel, *Mhudi* (1930).

WALK 11

Elsewhere in London, south of the river

In This Walk: The lives and works of the following people and *fictional characters* are highlighted:

Blackheath: Nathaniel Hawthorne, Dava Sobel, Charles Dickens, Cecil Day-Lewis (Nicholas Blake).

Brixton: Paula Hawkins, C.L.R. James, Monica Ali.

Bromley: H.G. Wells.

Camberwell: Dame Muriel Spark.

Clapham: J.K. Rowling, *Harry Potter,* Roald Dahl, Grahame Greene, G.A. Henty, Malorie Blackman.

Peckham: Una Marson.

Richmond: Virginia and Leonard Woolf, Charles Dickens, Tennyson, William Thackeray, Walter De La Mare.

Stockwell: Joan Littlewood, Shelagh Delaney.

Upper Norwood: Raymond Chandler.

Wandsworth: Oscar Wilde, Thomas Hardy.

Wapping, Shadwell and Limehouse: Joseph Conrad, Sir Arthur Conan Doyle, Oscar Wilde, Charles Dickens.

Wimbledon Common: Algernon Charles Swinburne, Robert Graves, Georgette Heyer.

Woolwich: Bernardine Evaristo.

BLACKHEATH

Blackheath has several literary connections. **Nathaniel Hawthorne** (1804–64), who wrote *Twice Told Tales* (1842), *The Scarlet Lette*r (1850) and *The House of the Seven Gables* (1851), lived at number 4 Pond Road in 1856.

Happiness is like a butterfly which, when pursued, is always beyond our grasp but, if you will sit down quietly, may alight upon you

Nathaniel Hawthorne

His ancestor, John Hathorne, was a judge at the Salem witch trials and Nathaniel added a 'w' to the family name in an effort to distance himself from the tragic events of 1692–3 when 19 people were sentenced to death by hanging. Although he spent time in Europe, he was born and died in America.

Another American writer, who used the area in her 1995 best seller *Longitude* was **Dava Sobel**. It is the tale of a Yorkshireman, John Harrison, who invented the first chronometer accurate enough to determine longitude at sea, a giant leap in navigation.

It has several connections to **Charles Dickens**. It is mentioned in *David Copperfield, A Tale of Two Cities* and *Our Mutual Friend*. Dickens was also known to have enjoyed the famous Whitebait Suppers at the Trafalgar Tavern.

'And so we live on Blackheath, in the charm – ingest of dolls' houses, de-lightfully furnished, and we have a clever little servant who is de-cidedly pretty…'

Charles Dickens, *Our Mutual Friend*

The Poet Laureate, **Cecil Day-Lewis** (1904–72) lived at 6 Crooms Hill from 1954 until his death. To increase his income, he also published 20 very successful detective novels under the pseudonym 'Nicholas Blake'.

BRIXTON

Paula Hawkins wrote *The Girl on the Train* (2015) while living in Brixton. The book has sold over 23 million copies and both it and *Into the Water* (2017) topped the *New York Times* bestseller list. *The Girl on The Train* is also a film starring Emily Blunt, released in 2016. The idea occurred when the author was commuting by train from different places in London, passing the backs of houses and wondering about the lives of the people in them. *A Slow Fire Burning* was released in 2021.

165 Railton Road has a blue plaque to the memory of **C.L.R. James** (1901–89) who wrote, among many other things, probably the finest-ever book about cricket, *Beyond a Boundary*, in 1963. He was also a prominent political activist, author of *The Black Jacobins*, a history of the Haitian revolutions 1791–1804, and published in 1938. In addition, he wrote the novel *Minty Alley* (1936): in 2021 Penguin Books published the book again in the *Black Britain: Writing Back* series curated by **Bernardine Evaristo** (see below, this chapter). **Monica Ali** depicts this area in her writing.

BROMLEY

H.G. Wells was born in Bromley on 21 September 1866. As referred to above, his father played cricket – for which payment was, unfortunately for the family, on a voluntary basis – while his mother, Sarah, did her best to run the largely unprofitable china shop into which the family had sunk all of its savings. The shop was in the high street where a large clothing company operates now, and there is a plaque. Wells wrote later that his mother was obsessed with maintaining the illusion of upward mobility and charged her children with lying about the extent of the domestic help which she was able to maintain. Wells was never fond of the area: he wrote quite a short and sharp letter to a wealthy civic dignitary in 1934 who had offered him the Freedom of Bromley saying that he didn't want it. Bromley became Bromstead in the *New Machiavelli* (1911), where his lack of enthusiasm for the place could hardly be plainer:

> Let me try and give something of the quality of Bromstead and something of its history. It is the quality and history of a thousand places round and about London, and round and about the other great centres of population in the world.

CAMBERWELL

It was in a bedsit in Baldwin Crescent, Camberwell that **Dame Muriel Spark** (1918–2006) wrote *The Comforters* (1957) and *The Prime of Miss Jean Brodie* (1961). She soon had the financial success to enable travel and in the 1960s moved to New York and subsequently to Rome. She received many honorary Doctorates and was twice nominated for the Booker Prize.

CLAPHAM

In 2020, **J.K. Rowling** took to Twitter to divulge that she wrote the first words of the *Harry Potter* books while living above a sports shop in Clapham and she added a picture of a row of shops in Northcote Road. She says that she walked past Severus Road every day and thought later that this must have subconsciously put the name of one of her main characters into her head. The actual *idea* came about, she confirmed, on a train from Manchester to London.

Harry Potter

Harry Potter is a series of seven novels by J.K. Rowling featuring *Harry* and his friends, including *Hermione Granger* and *Ron Weasley*, who attend Hogwarts School of Witchcraft and Wizardry. They leave for school from platform 9¾ at Kings Cross Station in London. Non-magical people are known as '*Muggles*'. The main story centres around the fight between Harry and his friends against the evil *Lord Voldemort*.

The books have sold in their millions and there have been eight films following the books, made by Warner Bros. which have become amongst the most lucrative films in history. J.K. Rowling also co-authored a play, *Harry Potter and the Cursed Child*, which premiered in 2016. The author has written some works deriving from and illustrating aspects of, the books, such as *Fantastic Beasts and Where to Find Them* (2016).

The books have had a significant cultural impact, from fan fiction and artwork to fan events. They have even been responsible for a new sport – Quidditch (the Quidditch World Cup has been held every four years since 1473 but, of course, *Muggles* would not be aware of that). You can go on a Warner Bros. Studio Tour and there are always

Above: *King's Cross Station.*

Right: *St Pancras Station: it adjoins Kings Cross and was used while filming some exterior shots for the* Harry Potter *films. For example,* Harry *and* Ron *fly their blue Ford Anglia around the building in* Harry Potter and the Chamber of Secrets.

The Hogwarts-like minarets and spires of the St Pancras Renaissance London Hotel, adjoining St Pancras Station, seen from the courtyard of the British Library.

tours for *Muggles* operating in central London (any Tourist Information Bureau can give the latest details).

The series has won a host of awards, but literary criticism has sometimes been mixed. Much of the filming for the Warner Bros. movies was done in central London and unsurprisingly *Harry Potter* and his friends crop up in several parts of this book.

Roald Dahl

Roald Dahl (1916–90), writer of many immensely popular children's stories, including *Charlie and the Chocolate Factory*, *The BFG* and *James and the Giant Peach* bought a home in Turnchapel Mews, Clapham in 1982 where he lived for the rest of his life. He called it 'my little piece of London'.

Apart from his work as a writer for children, Dahl also had parallel careers – as a writer of macabre adult short stories which were very successful; and he also wrote the screenplays for *Chitty Chitty Bang Bang* and the Bond film, *You Only Live Twice.*

Stephen Spielberg's 1984 smash hit film *The Gremlins* was based loosely on the characters in his book of that name published in 1943 – Dahl flew Hawker Hurricanes during the war and pilots used to blame gremlins when the planes played up.

Grahame Greene (1904–91) lived at 14 Clapham Common North Side 1935–40. It was while living here that he wrote *Brighton Rock*, a murder thriller set in the town – Greene separated his 'entertainments' as he saw them from his other, more 'literary' works – and it has been filmed at least twice. He was shortlisted for the Nobel Prize in Literature in both 1966 and 1967.

G.A. Henty, (1832–1902), prolific and immensely popular author of exciting historical fiction in the nineteenth century although not as widely read today, lived at 33 Lavender Gardens, Clapham.

Malorie Blackman O.B.E. was born in Clapham in 1962. She was Children's Laureate from 2013–15 and wrote the *Noughts and Crosses* series.

PECKHAM

Peckham was where anti-colonialist and playwright and poet, **Una Marson** (1905–65), initially lodged upon coming to London from Jamaica in 1932. After working for various newspapers, including the *Daily Gleaner*, she self-financed her initial publications. Her best-known work, *Heights and Depths,* came out in 1931. She constantly emphasised the role of black women in the fight for social change. Her work was largely forgotten in the years following her death and an autobiography which she wrote in 1937 has never been located. She is now seen as an important figure in the complex history of Britain's relationship with the Caribbean.

RICHMOND

Richmond is particularly associated with **Virginia** and **Leonard Woolf** who moved to rented rooms at 17 The Green in October 1914, and then in March 1915 moved to Hogarth House in Paradise Road. Virginia Woolf's first novel, *The Voyage Out*, was published at this time and received favourable reviews but the writer herself was having suicidal thoughts. As was to reoccur in future years, the completion of a major work left her in a state of mental exhaustion. Her husband was keen to find a peaceful distraction and in March 1917 he purchased a small hand press. They began modestly in printing terms, publishing *Two Stories* written by themselves, which was just 32 pages long. Soon, however, the business expanded and became famous worldwide. Most notably, they published, in September 1923, *The Waste Land* by **T.S. Eliot** which is noted for misprints (apparently T.S. Eliot was a poor proofreader), any copies of which are now worth a fortune. They moved to 52 Tavistock Square in London in 1924.

It is not easy to find any area of greater London that is not associated in one way or another with **Charles Dickens** and Richmond is no exception. In 1850 he held a dinner, attended by **Tennyson** and **Thackeray**, at the Star and Garter Inn in Richmond Hill (now gone) to celebrate the publication of *David Copperfield*.[76] Dickens also holidayed in the area and liked to burn up some of his legendary energy by taking long swims in the river.

South End House, Montpelier Row, Twickenham was the home of **Walter De La Mare** (1873–1956) from 1940 until he died.

STOCKWELL

Stockwell was the birthplace of playwright and director, **Joan Littlewood** (1914–2002). She initially wrote for the *Guardian* in Manchester and founded the *Theatre of Action* in

1934. She is seen as a radical and visionary, passionately believing in theatre as a part of the community. Her final production *So You Want to Be in Pictures*, was at Stratford in 1973.

Littlewood's theatre company was responsible for the initial staging of A *Taste of Honey* by **Shelagh Delaney** in 1958, three years later being turned into a famous film starring Rita Tushingham.

UPPER NORWOOD

Raymond Chandler (1888–1959) has a blue plaque at 110 Auckland Road, Upper Norwood SE19 2BY. He moved to England from America with his mother in 1900 and was educated at Dulwich College. He became famous for his novels featuring the detective, *Philip Marlowe*: these included *Farewell My Lovely* and *The Long Goodbye*. He was nominated for an Oscar for co-writing the screenplay of *Double Indemnity* in 1943 and wrote the original screenplay for *The Blue Dahlia* in 1945.

WANDSWORTH

Wandsworth has a well-known prison and it was here that **Oscar Wilde** spent the first four months of his prison sentence where he underwent a terrible physical deterioration.[77]

Following the success of *Far From the Madding Crowd*, **Thomas Hardy** (1840–1928) moved here in 1878 from Dorset – to number 172 Trinity Road – to be nearer influential publishers and agents in London. It was all too much for him, though and, following an internal haemorrhage which necessitated several weeks in bed, he moved back to Dorset in 1881.

WAPPING, SHADWELL AND LIMEHOUSE

Wapping, Shadwell and Limehouse are areas of south London that have been used by writers throughout the centuries, especially when, as with **Conrad**, **Conan Doyle**, **Oscar Wilde** and **Dickens**, they wished to set scenes amid poverty, sailors, prostitution, hangings and opium addiction. Dickens' great unfinished last novel, *The Mystery of Edwin Drood*, for example, starts in an opium den in Limehouse. The Bar of Gold opium den, in the *Sherlock Holmes* story *The Man with the Twisted Lip*, could be in this area – although some believe it was up-river, nearer St Paul's – and is described as 'the vilest murder-trap on the whole riverside'. Victorian and early twentieth-century writers were much given to contrasting the domestic bliss and love of a respectable middle-class home with the degradation and terrors that were, for many, just a short addictive habit away.

There were opium dens where one could buy oblivion, dens of horror where the memory of old sins could be destroyed by the madness of sins that were new.

Oscar Wilde, *The Picture of Dorian Gray* (1890)

WIMBLEDON COMMON

Wimbledon Common was beloved of several poets and writers including **Algernon Charles Swinburne** (1837–1909), who retreated here from Chelsea for health reasons and loved walking on the common. Other enthusiasts included **Thackeray** and **Leigh Hunt**.

D.H Lawrence describes 'a day of almost perfect happiness' here watching 'girls trot, and fathers gallop'.

Robert Graves (1895–1985) was born at 1 Lauriston Road, Wimbledon.

Georgette Heyer (1902–74), was born at 103 Woodside, Wimbledon. Inspired by **Jane Austen**, her Regency romance novels sold in their hundreds of thousands in her lifetime, and she is still selling today.

WOOLWICH

Bernardine Evaristo O.B.E., Professor of Creative Writing at Brunel University, was the first black female novelist to win the Booker Prize, in 2019 for *Girl, Woman, Other*, one of eight books of fiction and verse fiction that have won numerous other awards also. Barack Obama has named her as one of his favourite authors. She is the fourth of eight children to an English mother and Nigerian father and grew up in Eglinton Road, Woolwich. She writes that Woolwich Library saved her from boredom at weekends and long summer holidays.

Bernardine Evaristo on Woolwich: 'We weren't allowed to play outside'.[78] She was awarded the Freedom of the Royal Borough of Greenwich in October 2021.[79]

Edgar Wallace, prolific writer of books and articles who dictated many of his books onto the latest technology (wax cylinders) to be typed up later by his secretaries, and probably linked in the public mind for ever with his work on *King Kong*, was born in Greenwich in April 1875.

ENDNOTES

1. *A Study in Scarlet*
2. If you are using buses and underground trains (the 'tube') in London, you can buy tickets as you go; you can buy a daily pass (no travel before 09.30); or, probably most convenient and cheapest, you can buy an 'Oyster card' (travel anytime). This may require some simple planning in advance in order to receive one – https://oyster.tfl.gov.uk/ As regards accommodation, London is very expensive and an excellent and cost-effective alternative to hotels are university rooms, available when students are on vacation – www.universityrooms.com
3. Conan Doyle was to write late in his life that all the drawings in various publications and impersonations of *Holmes* 'were very unlike my own original idea of the man'.
4. Anthony Horowitz has written several *Sherlock Holmes* novels including *The House of Silk* (2011), *The Three Monarchs* (2014) and *Moriarty* (2014).
5. www.madametussauds.co.uk
6. This is how Sir Arthur Conan Doyle introduces *Holmes* in his autobiography *Memories and Adventures*. He says that, as he is basically a calculating machine he lacks shade, and he was prone to tire of him sometimes for this reason.
7. The full interview is available on the *New Statesman* website.
8. The James Tait Black Awards, from the University of Edinburgh, began in 1919.
9. The restaurant is currently called *The Savoy Grill, Gordon Ramsey* and the 'Omelette Arnold Bennett' is priced at £12. There are quite a few versions of it as it is a favourite dish to which celebrity chefs like to 'add a twist'.
10. Taken from *Memories and Adventures*, the autobiography of Sir Arthur Conan Doyle.
11. Speaking at the Hay Festival and reported in the *Independent* 4 March 2014.
12. Quoted in the Memoir to *The Poems of Elizabeth Barrett Browning*, the 'Albion Edition', Frederick Warne and Co, London, New York. David Ogilvy also writes of Elizabeth's hankering after spiritualism and seances. Robert would pace up and down impatiently when she talked of such things. 'And where does it all end?' he said.
13. Alas, since the pandemic struck in 2020/21 some of the biggest names have been forced to shut up shop and, at the time of writing, it is proposed to convert much selling space into offices.
14. Taken from *On the Trail of Sherlock Holmes* by the author.
15. See English Heritage website www.englishheritage.org.uk
16. Article written by de Waal, *Guardian*, 22 February 2020.
17. Kathleen Jamie, *Guardian*, 1 October 2015.

18. www.crownestate.co.uk
19. www.stgeorgeshanoversquare.org
20. https://www.bl.uk/works/the-birthday-party
21. This is taken from the venue's website www.frenchhousesoho.com
22. The material about Dickens in this section is based on that in *On the Trail of Sherlock Holmes*, Pen and Sword (2022) and *The World of Charles Dickens*, Halsgrove (2012) by this author.
23. Public hangings were seen as a source of public entertainment with much drinking, sales of souvenirs, singing and general rowdiness. Two hundred years later, Charles Dickens was one who campaigned against the 'party' atmosphere of these gruesome spectacles. Other well-known places of execution were Tyburn and Smithfield (see text).
24. Pen and Sword has published an excellent account of his life: *The Author Who Outsold Dickens* by Stephen Carver (2020).
25. From *On the Trail of Sherlock Holmes* by the author and published by Pen and Sword (2022).
26. See also Arnold Bennett's omelette, Walk 1.
27. See section on Chelsea for more details of the life of Dante Rossetti.
28. Taken from *The World of Charles Dickens*, by the author, Halsgrove (2012).
29. According to research by the National Archives at Kew, some 13,000 homes as well as 87 churches were lost.
30. A sign on the side wall of the pub claims that some of the people who came, either in search of Dr Johnson or the pub itself, include Voltaire, Congreve, Pope, Tennyson, Boswell, Macaulay, Thackeray, Wilkie Collins, Theodore Roosevelt, Mark Twain, Chesterton and Yeats.
31. He decided against buying Shakespeare on this occasion. Pepys went to the theatre frequently and the diaries give a vivid account of his reaction to the many other playwrights who were famous in his time although some are largely forgotten today. It is interesting that going to see Shakespeare was a relative rarity. He liked all sorts of plays from light comedy to tragedies. Here are a few mentioned in the famous *Diaries*: *The Mayor of Quinborough* by Thomas Middleton (simple); *The English Monsieur* by the Hon. James Howard (pretty and witty); *The Surprizall* by Sir Ronald Howard (did not please); *She Would if She Could* by Sir George Etheredge (dull); *The Sullen Lovers or the Impertinents* by Thomas Shadwell (good in some aspects); *The Island Princesse* by Beaumont and Fletcher (many good things in it); *Knight of the Burning Pestle* by Beaumont and Fletcher (did not like it at all); *The Scornfull Lady* by Beaumont and Fletcher (no opinion given, but as can be seen these playwrights were prolific and Pepys regularly went to their productions); *The Tamer Tamed* by John Fletcher (actors very good); *The Merry Wives of Windsor* by William Shakespeare (very poor actors); *Macbeth* by William Shakespeare (pretty good); *The Lost Lady* by Sir William Barclay (did not like it much and was displeased to see four of his office clerks in a half-crown box while he was in a shilling seat); *Dr Faustus* by Christopher Marlowe (appallingly done); *Parson's Wedding* by Thomas Killigrew which he says was acted entirely

by women (no opinion given); *The Duchess of Malfy* by John Webster (liked it very much especially as it was led by Betterton whom Pepys regarded as the best actor in the world: see also note 38 below); and *The Rival Ladys* by John Dryden (very pleased with it). His wife also went to the theatre sometimes without him and accompanied by a lady friend: on one such occasion, in August 1664, she went to see *The Court Secret* by James Shirley which she reported was the worst play she had even seen, although Pepys does not elaborate.

32. *Little Dorrit* by Charles Dickens, chapter 34.

33. Preface to the 1857 edition of *Little Dorrit.*

34. For more information see www.shakespearsglobe.com and www.bl.uk/shakespeare

35. The population of Stratford-Upon-Avon was about 1,500–2,000.

36. Other suggestions are that 'W.H.' may be a printer's error, and that it should read 'W.S.' i.e., Shakespeare's own initials; it may refer to William Hall, a printer; to Sir William Harvey, stepfather to Southampton; to William Haughton, a dramatist and poet; to William Hart, Shakespeare's nephew; and to Willie Hughes, an ingenious suggestion made by eighteenth century scholar, Thomas Tyrwhitt based on 'clues' and puns contained in the poems themselves.

37. The term 'bard' originally meant one who enjoyed writing poetry and may have done so on a paid basis, maybe to praise an event or a high lord or lady. It is unusual now to hear it used for anyone other than Shakespeare.

38. The actors in the leads were the celebrity couple, Thomas and Mary Betterton. Mary Betterton was the first female to play leads that, until that time had customarily been given to teenage boys. She was to play Lady Macbeth also.

39. Pepys was also much taken with Nell Gwyn – see Walk 7.

40. It is also available for members of the public who wish to find clean, simple accommodation during the student vacations at rates far cheaper than hotels in the area www.universityrooms.co.uk

41. Further details of this area as regards *Holmes* and *Watson*: *On the Trail of Sherlock Holmes* by the author, Pen and Sword (2022).

42. www.charleslambsociety.com

43. From *The World of Charles Dickens* by the author, published by Halsgrove (2012).

44. Book timed tickets online www.soane.org

45. Charles Dickens, *The Old Curiosity Shop*, Chapter 41.

46. The matter of his death is explored in Peter Ackroyd's book, *Chatterton* (Abacus 1987).

47. The British Library holds some manuscripts passed off by Chatterton as the work of Thomas Rowley, as well as correspondence between the boy poet and Horace Walpole whom Chatterton had approached for patronage, and which proved ultimately unsuccessful as Walpole had doubts about the origins of the work. These can be viewed in the Reading Rooms by members without charge and by appointment.

48. Further details: *On the Trail of Sherlock Holmes* by this author, Pen and Sword (2022).

49. At the time of writing, full membership is £510 a year with a special rate of £255 for young people aged between 16 and 29: it can be paid monthly. Details www.londonlibrary.co.uk

50. See www.londonlibrary.co.uk/dracula

51. Wren was commissioned to rebuild 51 churches and St Paul's Cathedral following the Great Fire of London in 1666.

52. www.westminster-abbey.org

53. A famous wood engraving exists, held in the Royal Academy: *The Devil's Acre, Westminster, 1872* by Gustave Dore.

54. www.britishmuseum.org

55. From *On The Trail of Sherlock Holmes* by the author, Pen and Sword (2022).

56. There are several university halls of residence in the area, for example, International House, which is a few minutes flat walk from Russell Square tube station and good, clean rooms, with wi-fi and excellent breakfasts, are available during the times that students are on vacation. The prices are a fraction of the cost of the hotels around here.

57. Edward Bulwer Lytton Dickens, nicknamed 'Plorn', was named after the hugely successful Victorian novelist, Edward Bulwer-Lytton, although his work has not stood the test of time. Plorn was Charles Dickens' youngest son.

58. www.soas.ac.uk and www.nobelprize.org/prizes/literature/2021/gurnah/facts/

59. It features very rich, traditional and, in the main, highly calorific meals and the preparation is not for the faint-hearted. For example, to make Italian cream it is necessary, as a beginning, to mix scalded and fresh cream with sugar and rind of lemons for 'nearly an hour.'

60. Despite the terrible conflagration, the number of recorded deaths was very small; however, this may in part be because the death of the poor was not always recorded and many people in London were not on any official records anyway.

61. There is a Boar's Head Inn in Charlottesville, Virginia, USA and also in Stratford, Ontario, both of which were named after this one.

62. A novel, *The Lodger: Shakespeare on Silver Street*, written by Charles Nicholl, was published in 2008 by Penguin.

63. From the website www.royalcourttheatre.com

64. E.R. Braithwaite, after serving in the RAF in the war, found that his skin colour prevented him gaining work in his chosen profession of engineering and he only accepted the job in the school as a last resort. He came, however, to love the children and this novel brought him to national attention upon publication in 1959. It became a successful film starring Sidney Poitier in 1967: Sidney Poitier died in early 2022.

65. Bram Stoker's great grand-nephew, Dacre Stoker, published a prequel, *Dracul*, in 2018. He wrote this with J.D. Barker, best-selling author of novels including *Forsaken*.

66. American critic, John Neal, *Atlantic Monthly*, 1866.

67. *Westminster Gazette*, 8 March 1922.

68. 11 December 2014

69. See Walk 9 for a description of Bunhill Fields, where Blake is buried, and a section on his work.

70. There is some controversy here as he took the examinations and passed with a 'Third' and, in order to collect it, he was required to stay in residence an extra term but his father refused to pay the fees.

71. www.michaelrosen.co.uk

72. www. highgatecemetery.org.uk

73. For more information www.nobelprize.org

74. Some of the magazines are available to view online and the British Library has some fascinating historical information and articles on them: bl.uk

75. In the diary entry for 17 June 1966 he recounts how a woman appeared on their sun terrace and Kenneth Halliwell and Joe Orton were aghast, Orton declaring it 'a bloody disgrace'. Two years later, in the diary entry of Wednesday 28 August, whilst on another holiday to Tangier, Williams says that he must remember how much he 'loathes' the place – the heat, tedium, flies, bores and the noise – and declares that he has had enough of it.

76. The building was replaced by The Royal Star and Garter Home, built between 1921 and 1924 to a design primarily made by Sir Gilbert Scott in 1915. It is now apartments.

77. See chapter 9 above for more details. There is now a Wilde Place nearby.

78. *Guardian*, Saturday 7 September 2019.

79. The Freedom of a Borough is the highest honour a council can bestow and dates back to ancient times when it was usually accompanied by special gifts and powers but today it is purely honorary.

BIBLIOGRAPHY

Ackroyd, Peter (1997) *Blake* (Minerva)

Ackroyd, Peter (1991) *Dickens* (Minerva)

Ackroyd, Peter (2001) *London The Biography* (Vintage)

Austen, Jane (1994) *Sense and Sensibility* (Penguin Books)

Bailey, Paul (1995) *Oxford Book of London,* (Oxford University Press)

Briggs, Asa (1968) *Victorian Cities* (Penguin Books)

Browning, Elizabeth Barrett (1850), *The Poems of Elizabeth Barrett Browning* (Frederick Warne and co, London, New York)

Browning, Robert, Roberts, Adam et al (2009) *The Major Works* (Oxford World's Classics)

Browning, Stephen (2022) *On the Trail of Sherlock Holmes (*Pen and Sword)

Browning, Stephen (2012) *The World of Charles Dickens* (Halsgrove)

Browning, Stephen (2010) *When Schooldays Were Fun* (Halsgrove)

Chaucer, Geoffrey (2000) *The Canterbury Tales* (The Folio Society)

Conan Doyle, Sir Arthur (1930) *The Penguin Complete Sherlock Holmes* (Penguin Books)

Dickens, Charles (1999) *David Copperfield* (Penguin Books, BBC Books)

Dickens, Charles (1998) *Little Dorrit* (1998)

Dickens, Charles (2000) *Oliver Twist* (Wordsworth Classics)

Dickens, Charles (2002) *Our Mutual Friend* (The Modern Library New York)

Dickens, Charles (1985) *The Christmas Books, Volume 1* (Penguin Books)

Dickens, Charles (2000) *The Old Curiosity Shop* (Penguin Books)

Dryden, John *The Poetical Works of*

Foxe, John (1563) *Foxe's Book of Martyrs (The Acts and Monuments)* (John Day, British Library)

Glinert, Ed (2000) *Literary London* (Penguin Books)

Lahr, John (1980) *Prick up your Ears* (Penguin Books)

Orgel, Stephen (Ed) (2004) *The Portable Shakespeare* (Penguin Classics)

Pepys, Samuel, *Diary of Samuel Pepys* (1924) deciphered by Revd J. Smith, M.A. Volumes 1 and 2 (J.M. Dent and Sons)

Priestley, J.B. (1970) *The Edwardians* (Sphere Books Ltd)

Rogers, Pat (Ed) (1987) *The Oxford Illustrated History of English Literature* (Oxford University Press)

Schlicke, Paul (Ed) (1999) *Oxford Reader's Companion to Dickens* (Oxford University Press)

Shaw, Bernard (1931) *The Complete Plays of Bernard Shaw* (Constable and Co Ltd)

Smith, Stephen, (2004) *Underground London* (Abacus)

Thackeray, William Makepeace (1985) *Vanity Fair* (Penguin Books)

Various (1893) *Temple Bar,98th Volume* (Richard Bentley and Sons)

Wilde, Oscar (1980) *Complete Works of Oscar Wilde* (Book Club Associates, London)

Wilson, A.N. (2003) *The Victorians* (Arrow Books)

INDEX